W9-BKK-786

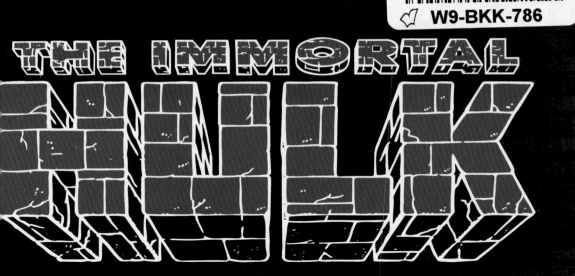

THE IMMORTAL HULK

ABOMINATION

AL EWING
WRITER

JOE BENNETT
PENCILER

RUY JOSÉ (#16-20) WITH
BELARDINO BRABO (#19-20) & **MARC DEERING** (#20)
INKERS

PAUL MOUNTS (#16-20) WITH
RACHELLE ROSENBERG (#19)
COLOR ARTISTS

VC's CORY PETIT
LETTERER

ALEX ROSS
COVER ARTIST

SARAH BRUNSTAD
ASSOCIATE EDITOR

WIL MOSS
EDITOR

TOM BREVOORT
EXECUTIVE EDITOR

COLLECTION EDITOR: **MARK D. BEAZLEY**
ASSISTANT EDITOR: **CAITLIN O'CONNELL**
ASSOCIATE MANAGING EDITOR: **KATERI WOODY**
SENIOR EDITOR, SPECIAL PROJECTS: **JENNIFER GRÜNWALD**
VP PRODUCTION & SPECIAL PROJECTS: **JEFF YOUNGQUIST**
BOOK DESIGNERS: **STACIE ZUCKER** with **ADAM DEL RE**

SVP PRINT, SALES & MARKETING: **DAVID GABRIEL**
DIRECTOR, LICENSED PUBLISHING: **SVEN LARSEN**

EDITOR IN CHIEF: **C.B. CEBULSKI**
CHIEF CREATIVE OFFICER: **JOE QUESADA**
PRESIDENT: **DAN BUCKLEY**
EXECUTIVE PRODUCER: **ALAN FINE**

HULK
CREATED BY
STAN LEE &
JACK KIRBY

IMMORTAL HULK VOL. 4: ABOMINATION. Contains material originally published in magazine form as IMMORTAL HULK #16-20. First printing 2019. ISBN 978-1-302-91667-1. Published by MARVEL WORLDWIDE, INC., a subsidiary of MARVEL ENTERTAINMENT, LLC. OFFICE OF PUBLICATION: 135 West 50th Street, New York, NY 10020. © 2019 MARVEL No similarity between any of the names, characters, persons, and/or institutions in this magazine with those of any living or dead person or institution is intended, and any such similarity which may exist is purely coincidental. **Printed in Canada.** DAN BUCKLEY, President, Marvel Entertainment; JOHN NEE, Publisher; JOE QUESADA, Chief Creative Officer; TOM BREVOORT, SVP of Publishing; DAVID BOGART, Associate Publisher & SVP of Talent Affairs; DAVID GABRIEL, SVP of Sales & Marketing, Publishing; JEFF YOUNGQUIST, VP of Production & Special Projects; DAN CARR, Executive Director of Publishing Technology; ALEX MORALES, Director of Publishing Operations; DAN EDINGTON, Managing Editor; SUSAN CRESPI, Production Manager; STAN LEE, Chairman Emeritus. For information regarding advertising in Marvel Comics or on Marvel.com, please contact Vit DeBellis, Custom Solutions & Integrated Advertising Manager, at vdebellis@marvel.com. For Marvel subscription inquiries, please call 888-511-5480. **Manufactured between 7/12/2019 and 8/13/2019 by SOLISCO PRINTERS, SCOTT, QC, CANADA.**

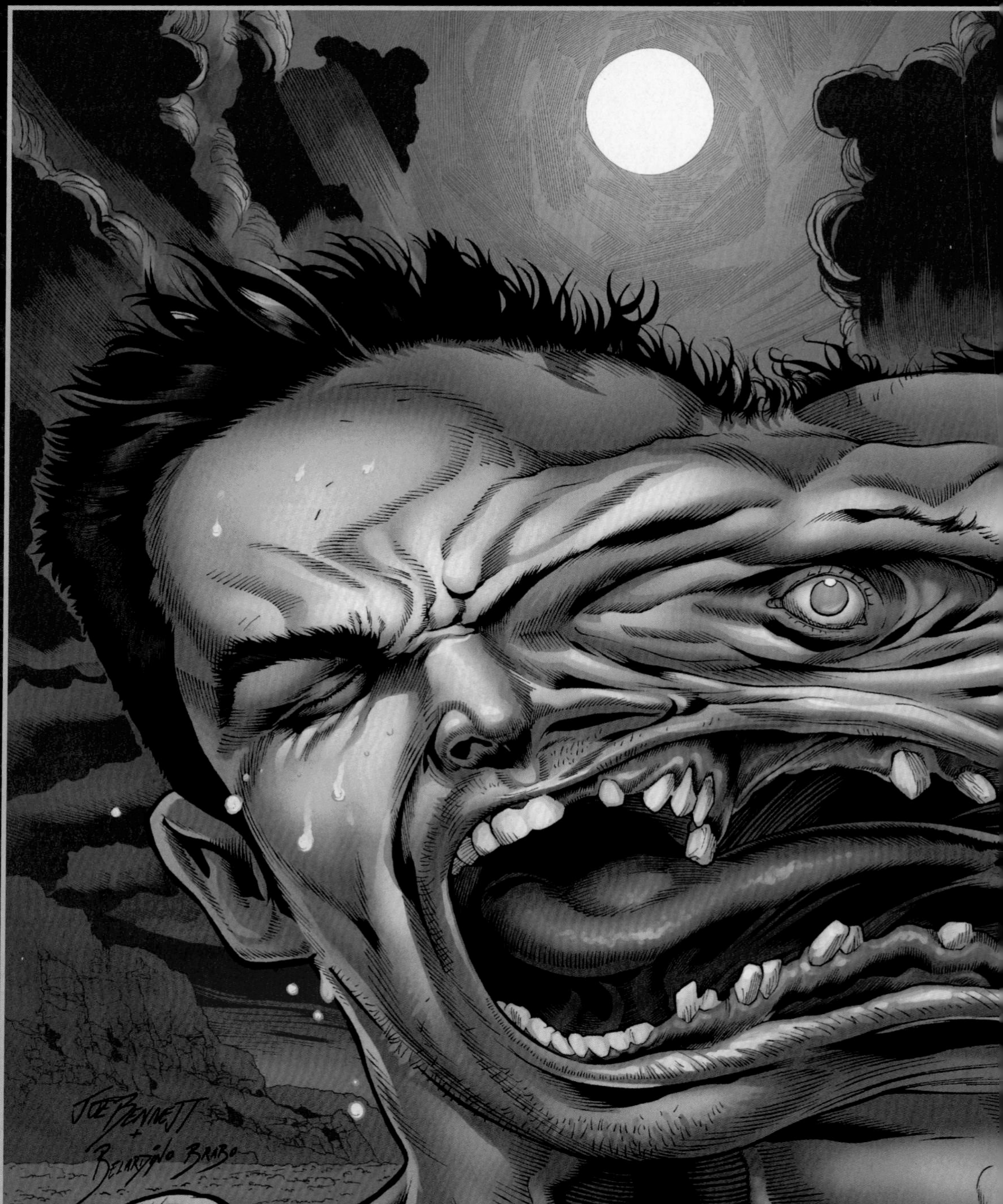
JOE BENNETT
+
BELARDINO BRABO

IN

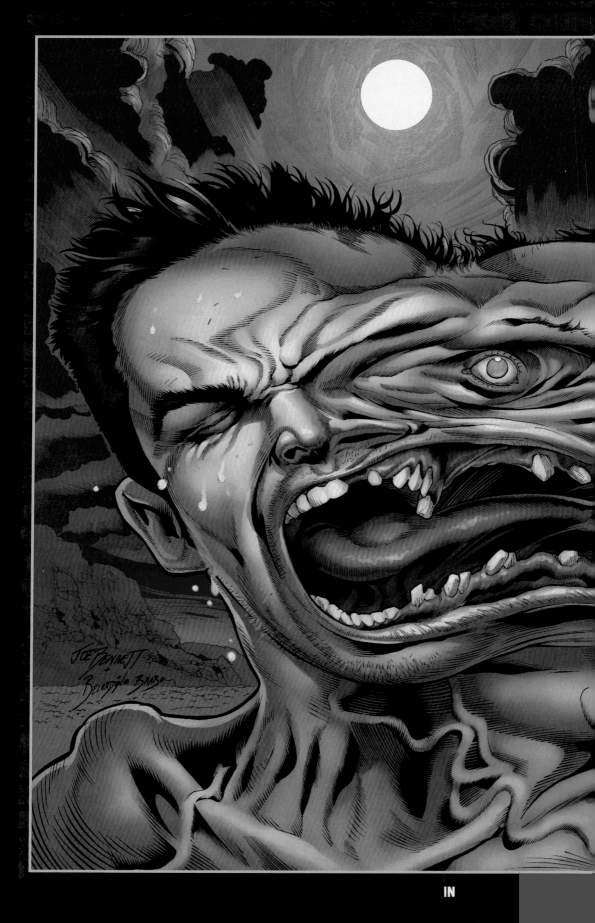

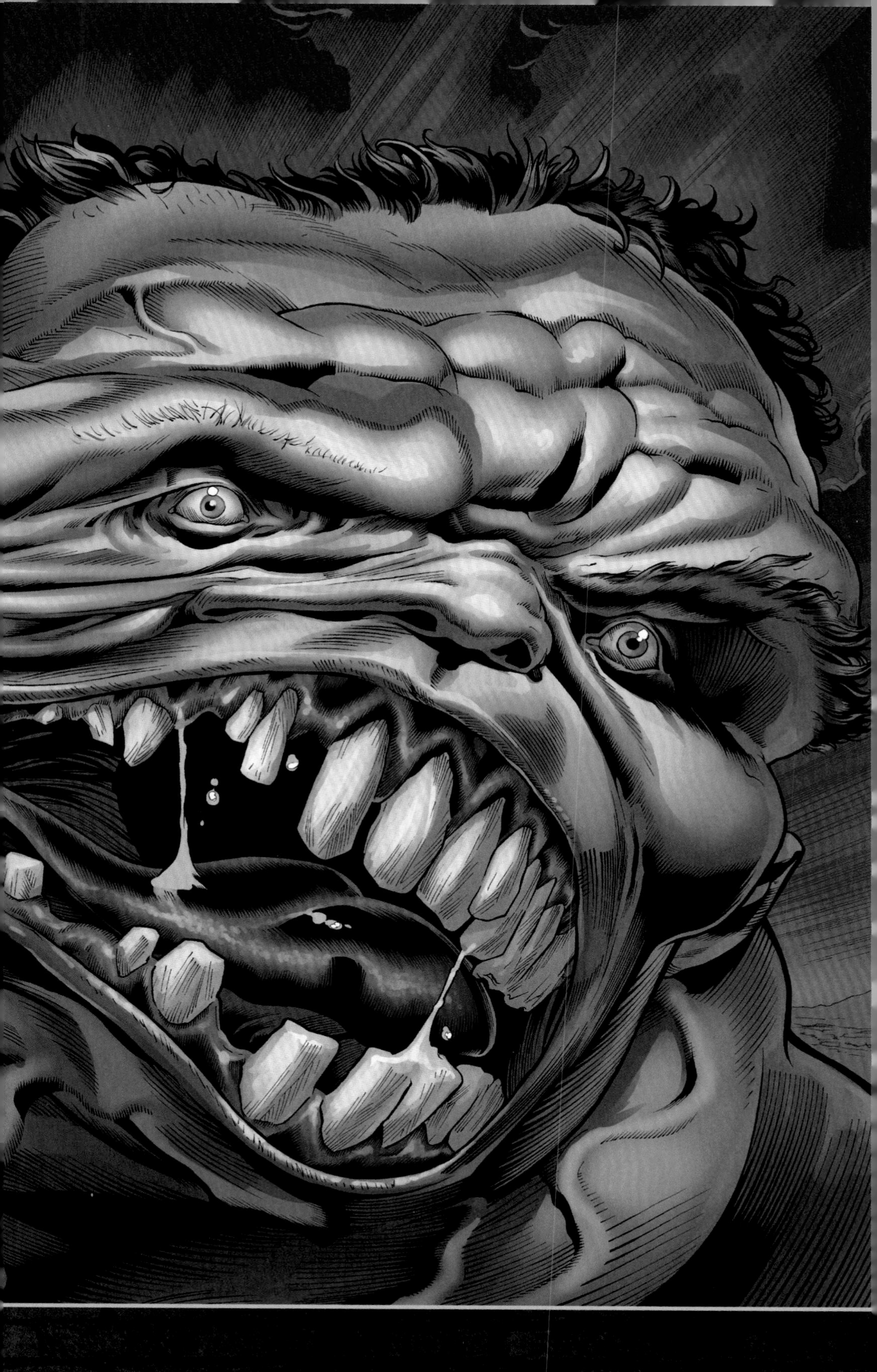

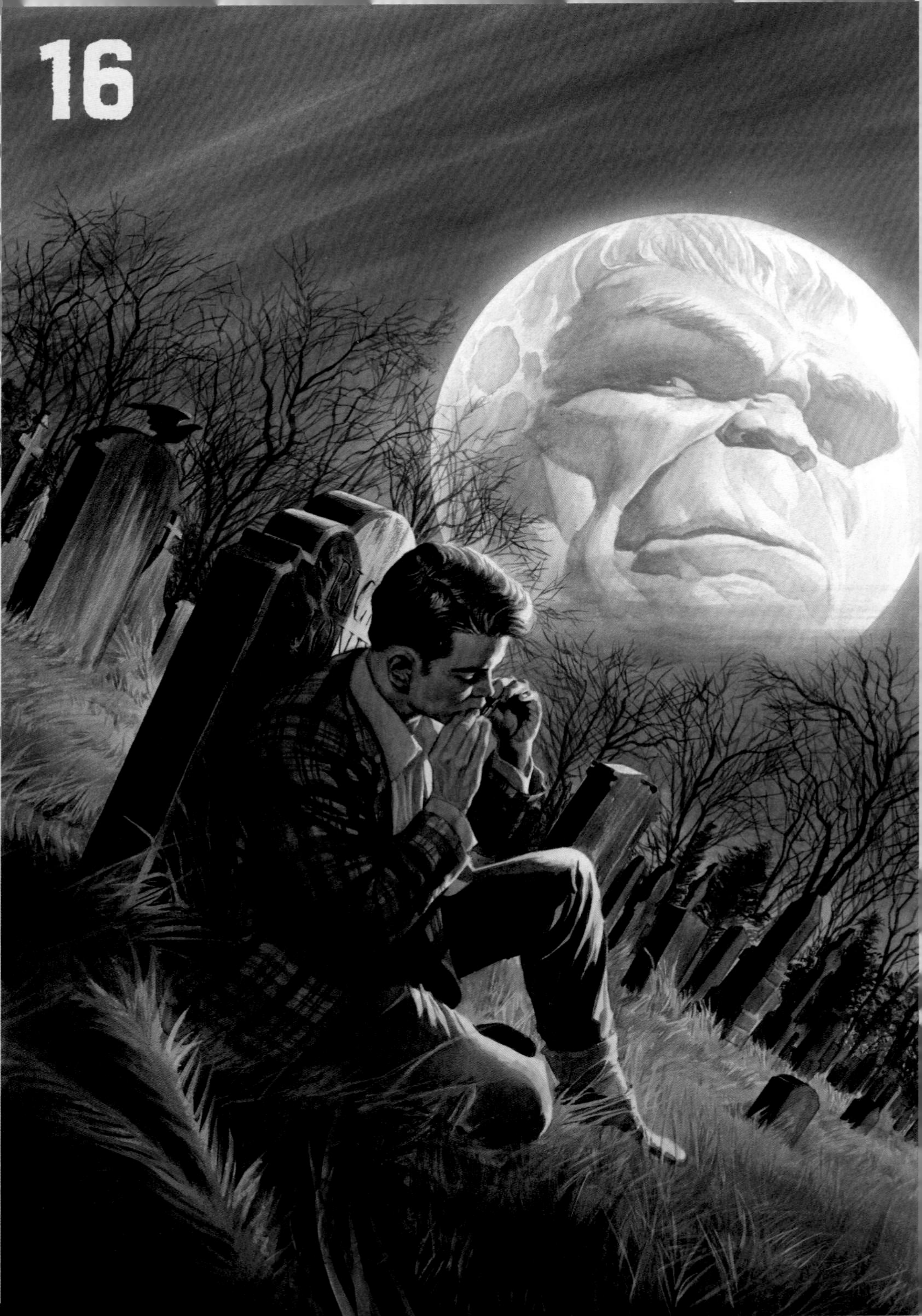
16

"THIS PLACE IS NOT A PLACE OF HONOR. NO HIGHLY ESTEEMED DEED IS COMMEMORATED HERE. NOTHING VALUED IS HERE. WHAT IS HERE IS DANGEROUS AND REPULSIVE TO US. THIS MESSAGE IS A WARNING ABOUT DANGER."

- U.S. DEPARTMENT OF ENERGY

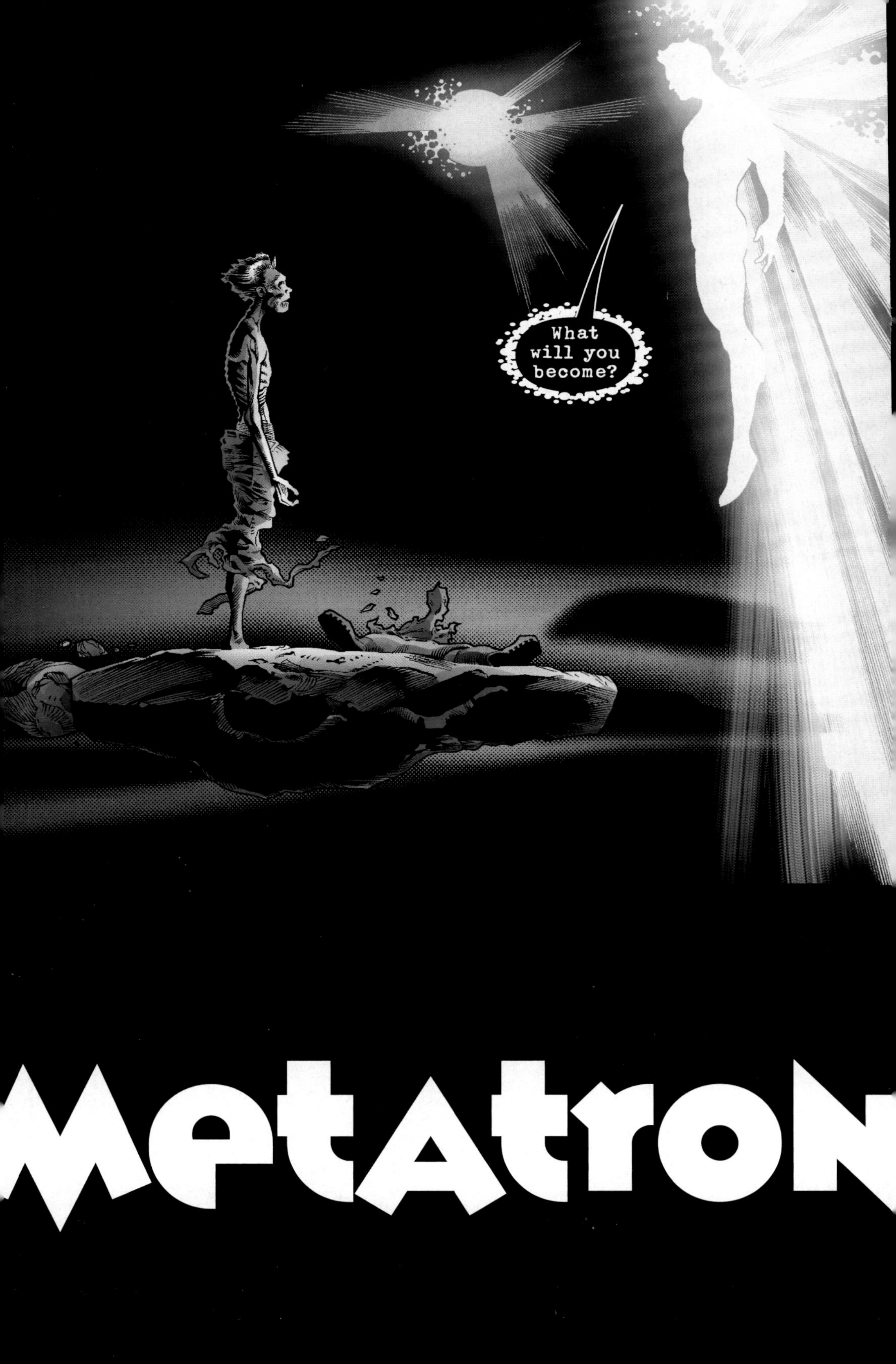
What will you become?
METATRON

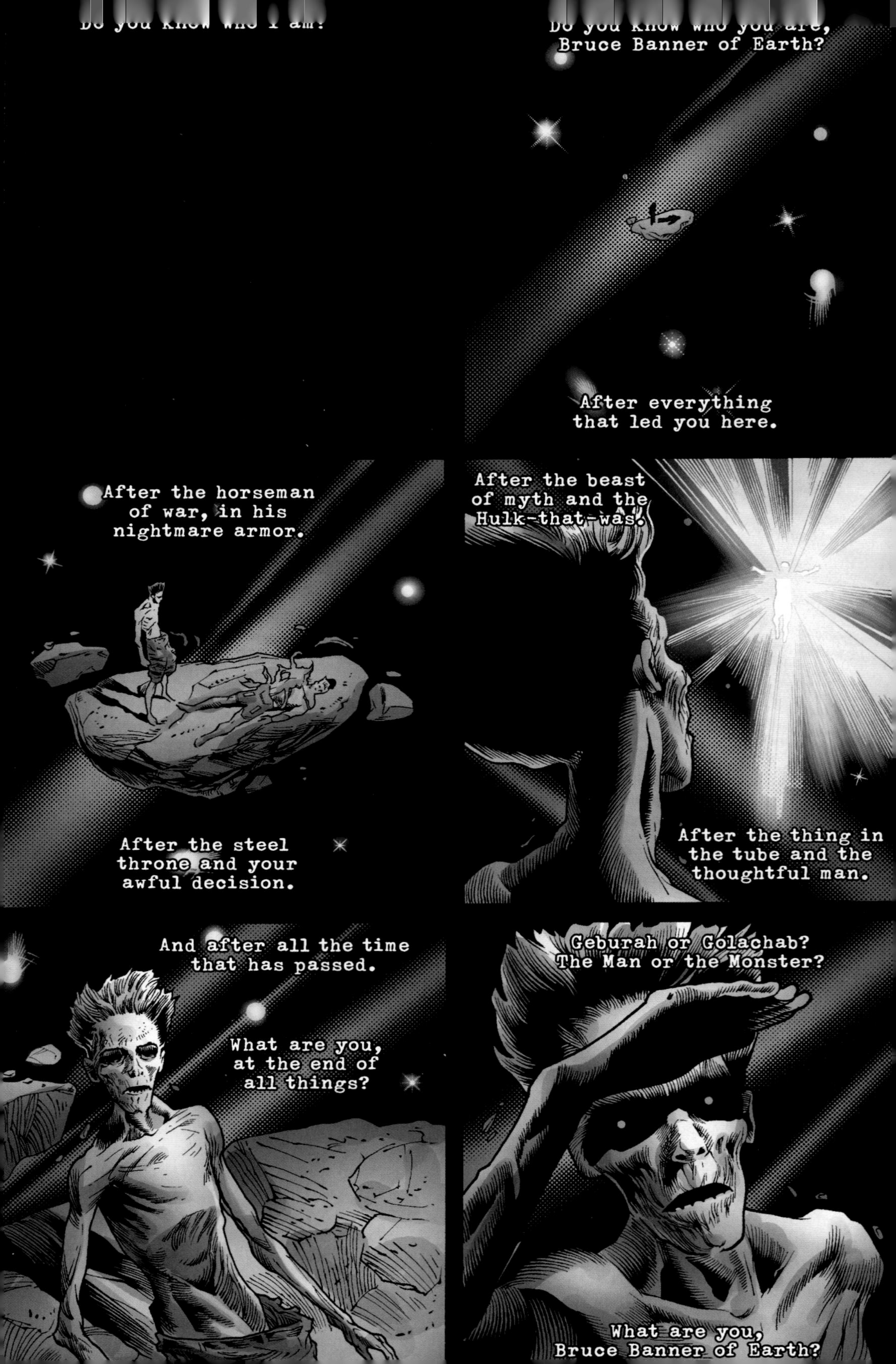
Do you know who I am?
Do you know who you are, Bruce Banner of Earth?
After everything that led you here.
After the horseman of war, in his nightmare armor.
After the steel throne and your awful decision.
After the beast of myth and the Hulk-that-was.
After the thing in the tube and the thoughtful man.
And after all the time that has passed.
What are you, at the end of all things?
Geburah or Golachab? The Man or the Monster?
What are you, Bruce Banner of Earth?

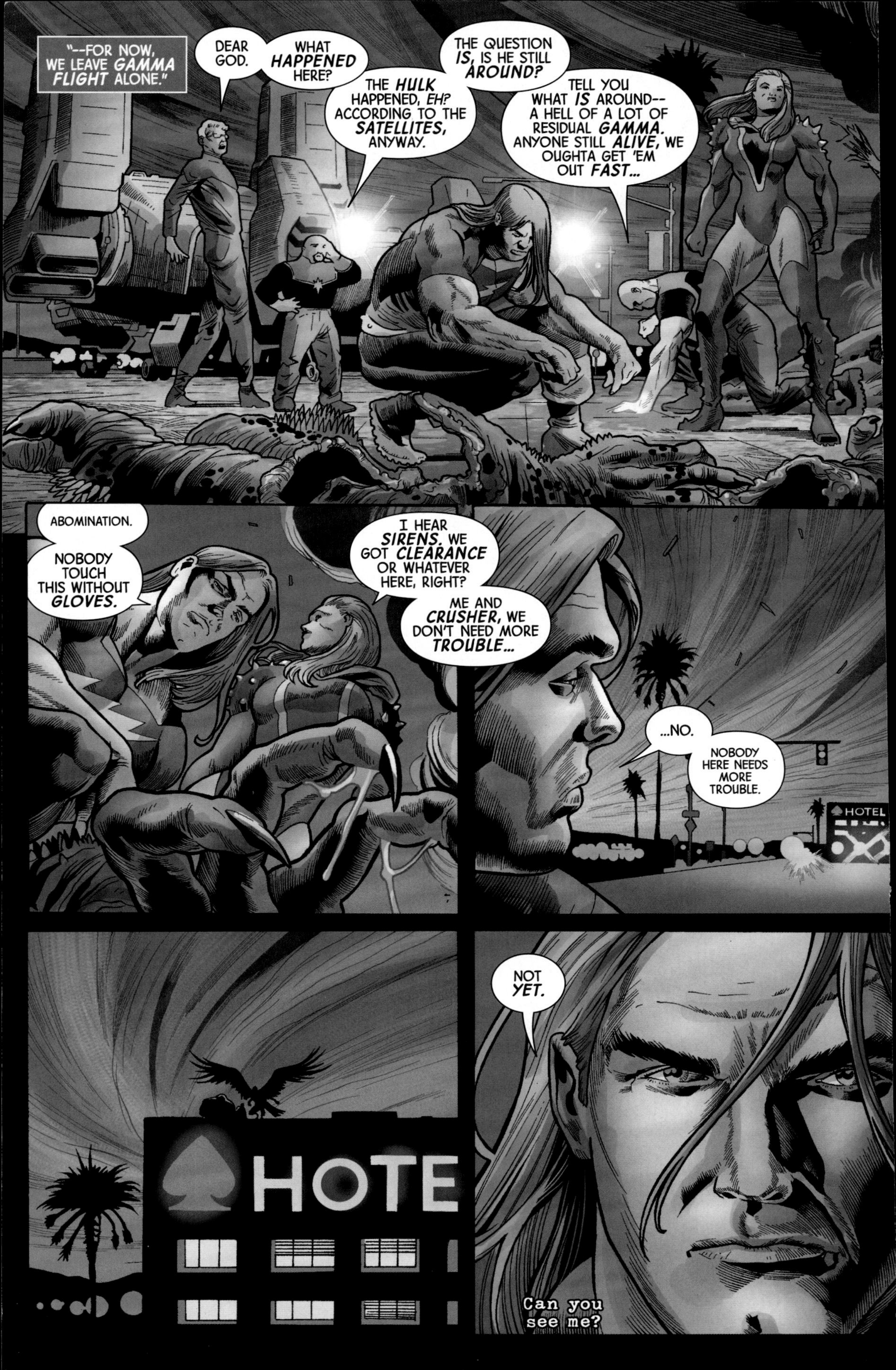
"--FOR NOW, WE LEAVE GAMMA FLIGHT ALONE."
DEAR GOD.
WHAT HAPPENED HERE?
THE HULK HAPPENED, EH? ACCORDING TO THE SATELLITES, ANYWAY.
THE QUESTION IS, IS HE STILL AROUND?
TELL YOU WHAT IS AROUND-- A HELL OF A LOT OF RESIDUAL GAMMA. ANYONE STILL ALIVE, WE OUGHTA GET 'EM OUT FAST...
ABOMINATION.
NOBODY TOUCH THIS WITHOUT GLOVES.
I HEAR SIRENS. WE GOT CLEARANCE OR WHATEVER HERE, RIGHT?
ME AND CRUSHER, WE DON'T NEED MORE TROUBLE...
...NO.
NOBODY HERE NEEDS MORE TROUBLE.
HOTEL
HOTE
NOT YET.
Can you see me?

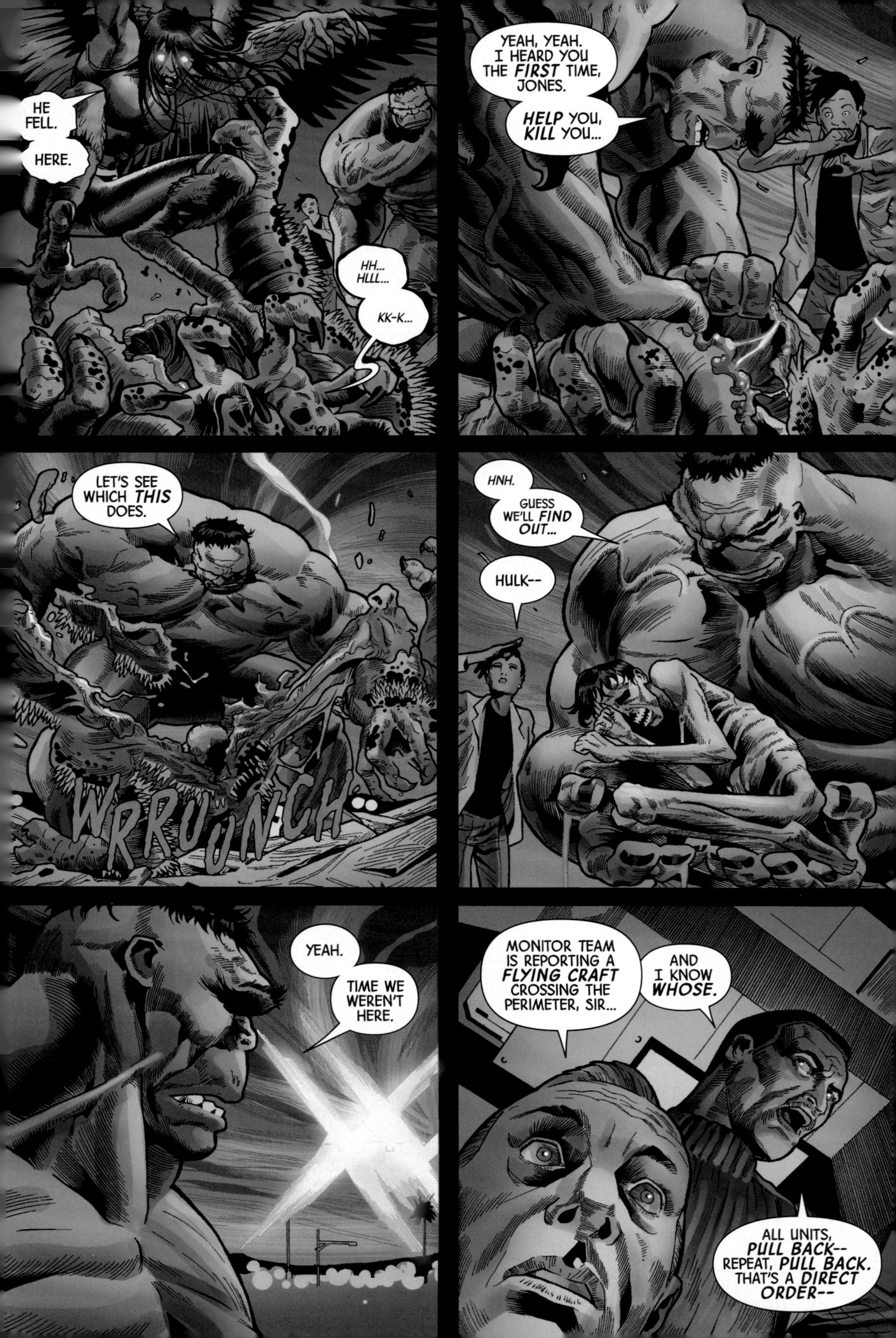
HE FELL.
HERE.
HH... HLLL...
KK-K...
YEAH, YEAH. I HEARD YOU THE FIRST TIME, JONES.
HELP YOU, KILL YOU...
LET'S SEE WHICH THIS DOES.
WRRUUNCH
HNH.
GUESS WE'LL FIND OUT...
HULK--
YEAH.
TIME WE WEREN'T HERE.
MONITOR TEAM IS REPORTING A FLYING CRAFT CROSSING THE PERIMETER, SIR...
AND I KNOW WHOSE.
ALL UNITS, PULL BACK-- REPEAT, PULL BACK. THAT'S A DIRECT ORDER--

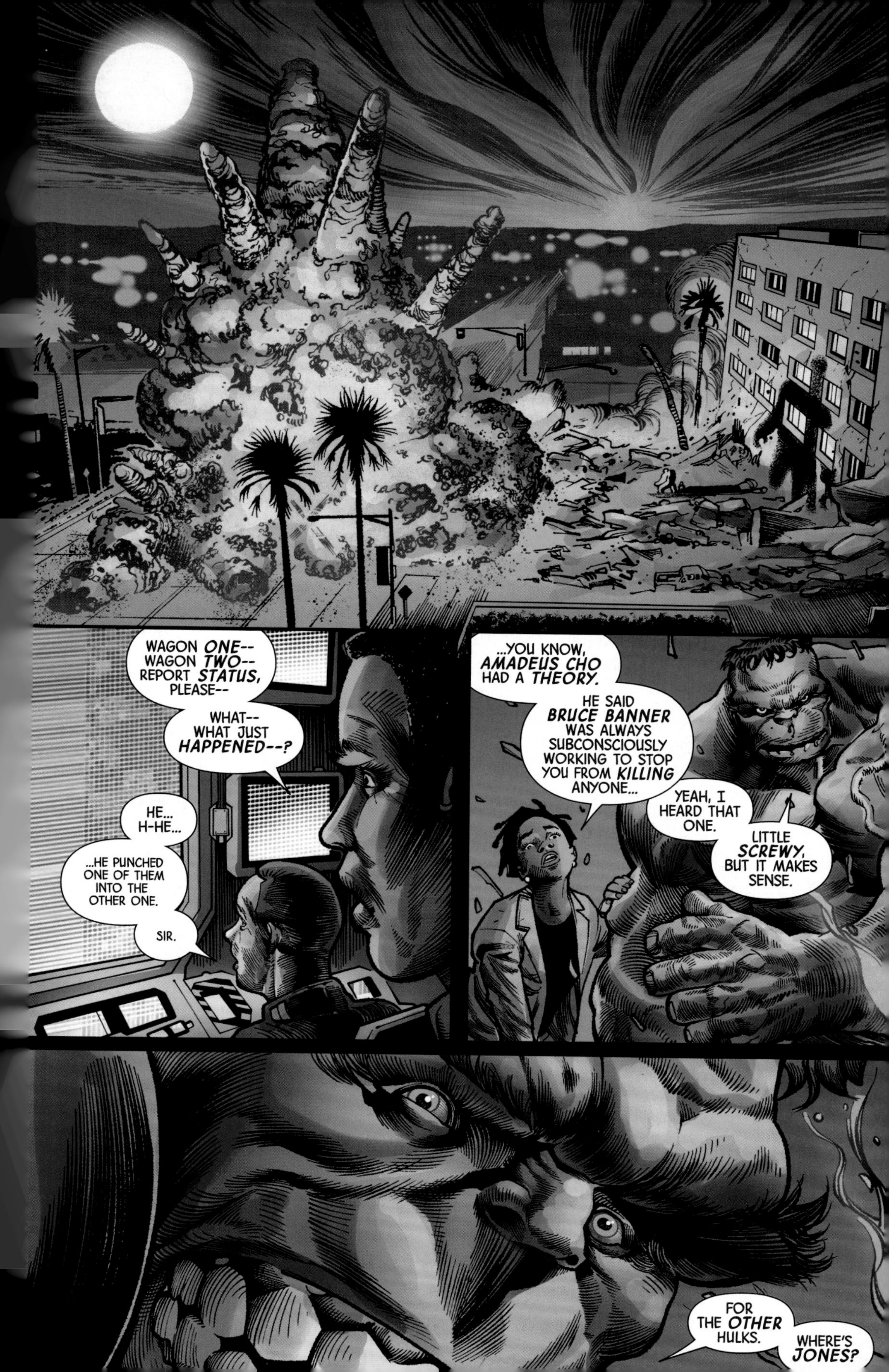
WAGON ONE-- WAGON TWO-- REPORT STATUS, PLEASE--
WHAT-- WHAT JUST HAPPENED--?
HE... H-HE...
...HE PUNCHED ONE OF THEM INTO THE OTHER ONE.
SIR.
...YOU KNOW, AMADEUS CHO HAD A THEORY.
HE SAID BRUCE BANNER WAS ALWAYS SUBCONSCIOUSLY WORKING TO STOP YOU FROM KILLING ANYONE...
YEAH, I HEARD THAT ONE.
LITTLE SCREWY, BUT IT MAKES SENSE.
FOR THE OTHER HULKS.
WHERE'S JONES?

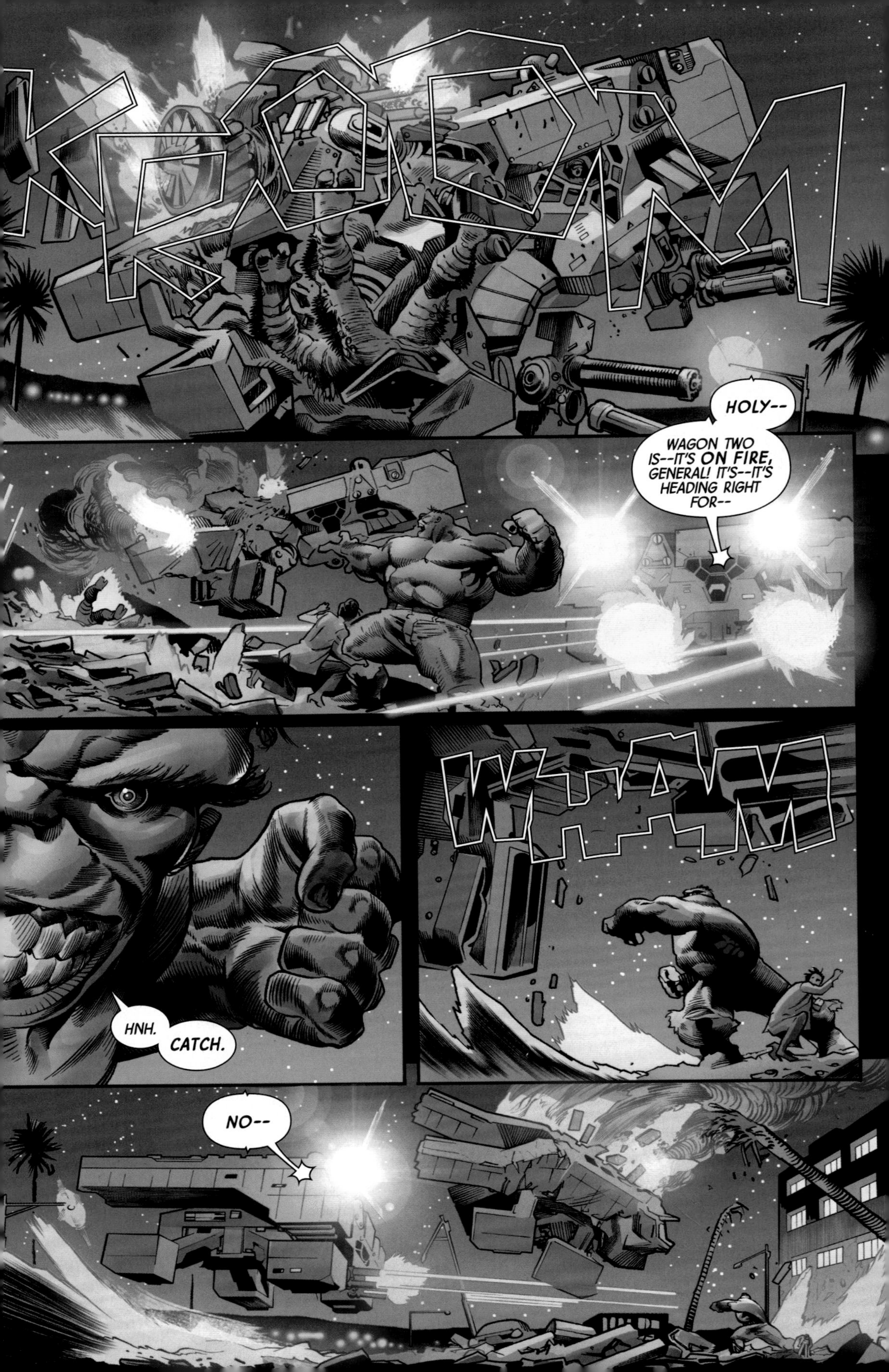
KRooOM
HOLY--
WAGON TWO IS--IT'S ON FIRE, GENERAL! IT'S--IT'S HEADING RIGHT FOR--
HNH.
CATCH.
WHAM
NO--

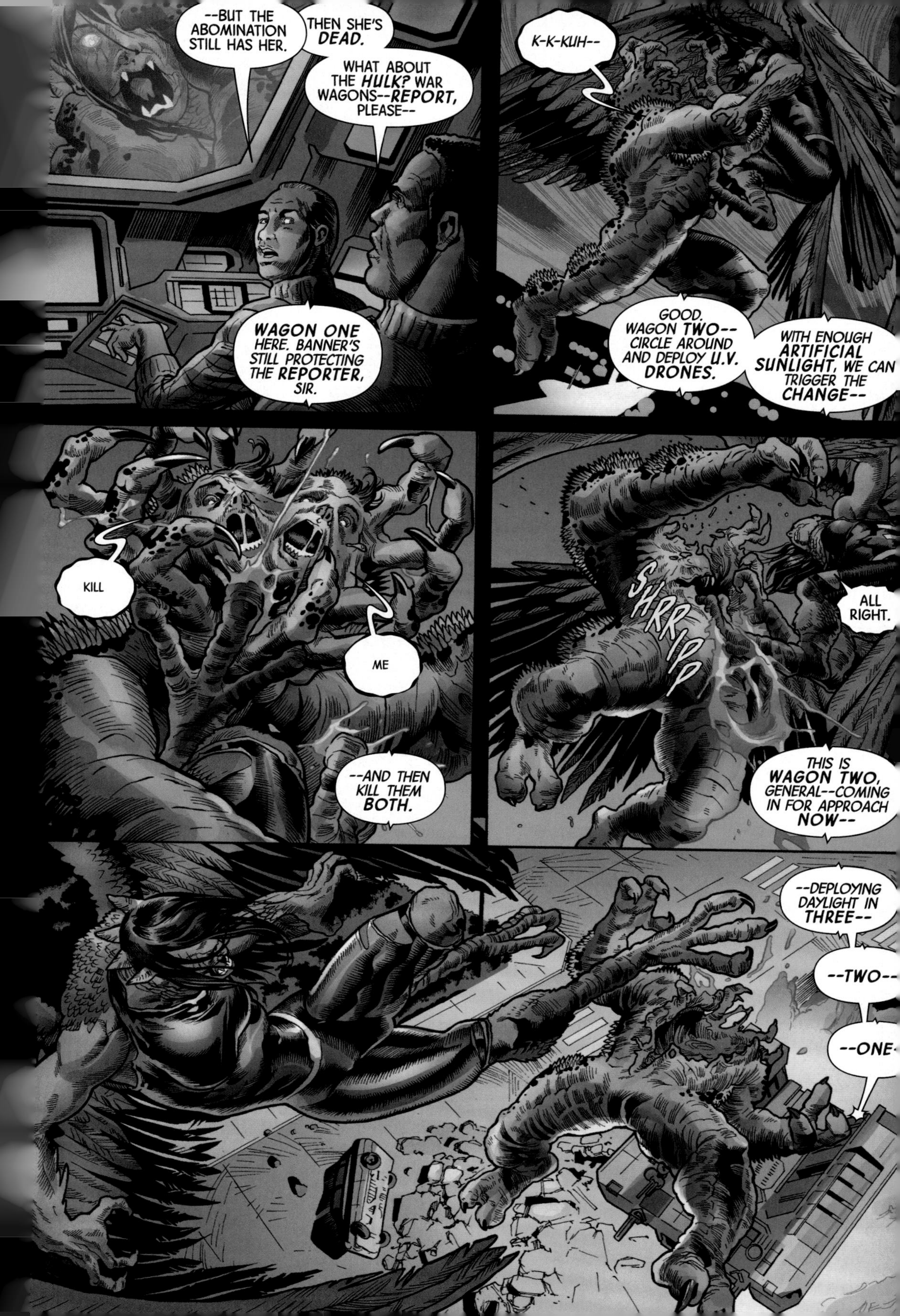

--BUT THE ABOMINATION STILL HAS HER.
THEN SHE'S DEAD.
WHAT ABOUT THE HULK? WAR WAGONS--REPORT, PLEASE--
WAGON ONE HERE. BANNER'S STILL PROTECTING THE REPORTER, SIR.
K-K-KUH--
GOOD. WAGON TWO--CIRCLE AROUND AND DEPLOY U.V. DRONES.
WITH ENOUGH ARTIFICIAL SUNLIGHT, WE CAN TRIGGER THE CHANGE--
KILL
ME
--AND THEN KILL THEM BOTH.
SHRRIPP
ALL RIGHT.
THIS IS WAGON TWO, GENERAL--COMING IN FOR APPROACH NOW--
--DEPLOYING DAYLIGHT IN THREE--
--TWO--
--ONE--

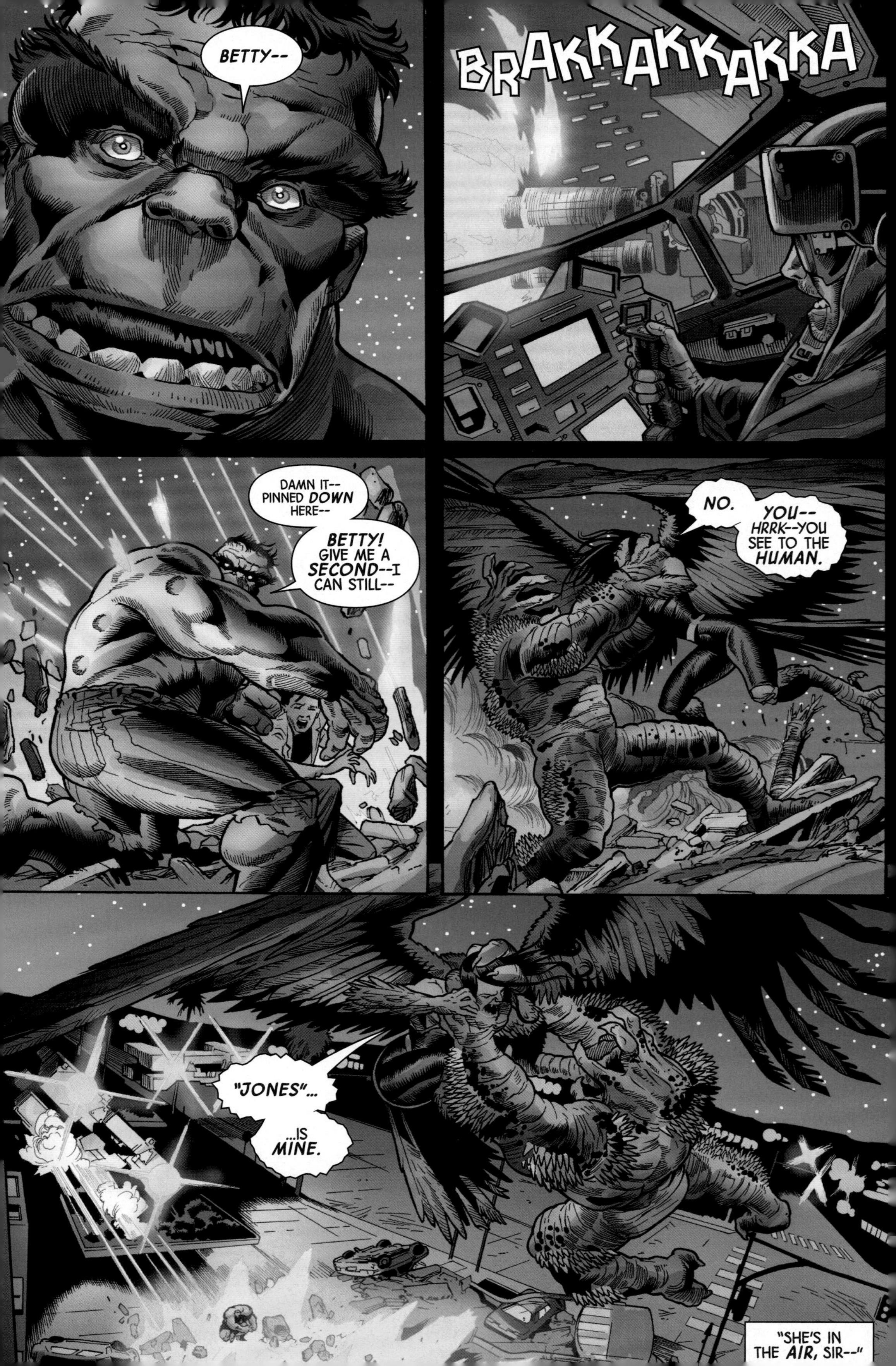
BETTY--
BRAKKAKKAKKA
DAMN IT-- PINNED DOWN HERE--
BETTY! GIVE ME A SECOND--I CAN STILL--
NO.
YOU-- HRRK--YOU SEE TO THE HUMAN.
"JONES"...
...IS MINE.
"SHE'S IN THE AIR, SIR--"

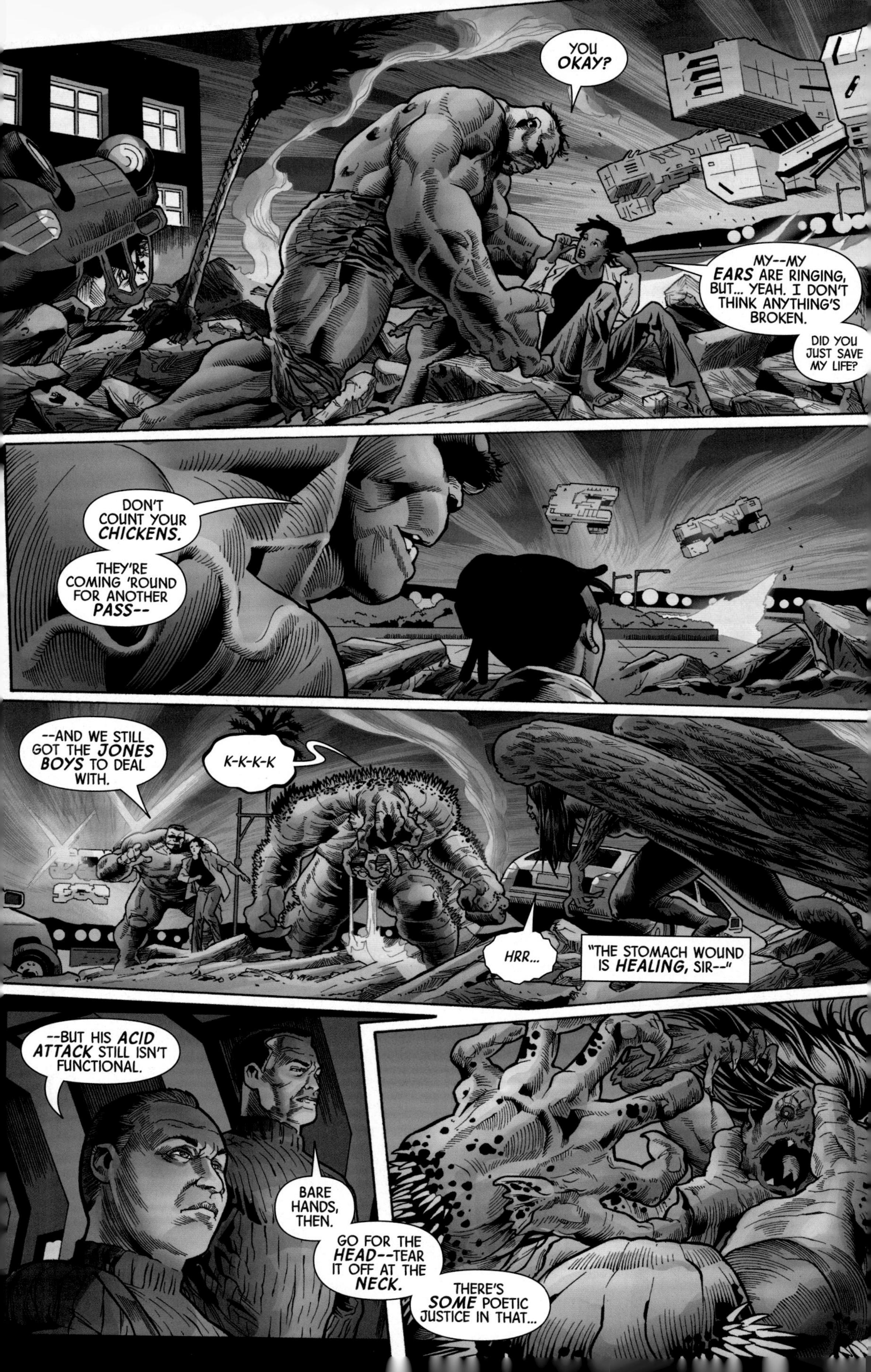
YOU OKAY?
MY--MY EARS ARE RINGING, BUT... YEAH. I DON'T THINK ANYTHING'S BROKEN.
DID YOU JUST SAVE MY LIFE?
DON'T COUNT YOUR CHICKENS.
THEY'RE COMING 'ROUND FOR ANOTHER PASS--
--AND WE STILL GOT THE JONES BOYS TO DEAL WITH.
K-K-K-K
HRR...
"THE STOMACH WOUND IS HEALING, SIR--"
--BUT HIS ACID ATTACK STILL ISN'T FUNCTIONAL.
BARE HANDS, THEN.
GO FOR THE HEAD--TEAR IT OFF AT THE NECK.
THERE'S SOME POETIC JUSTICE IN THAT...

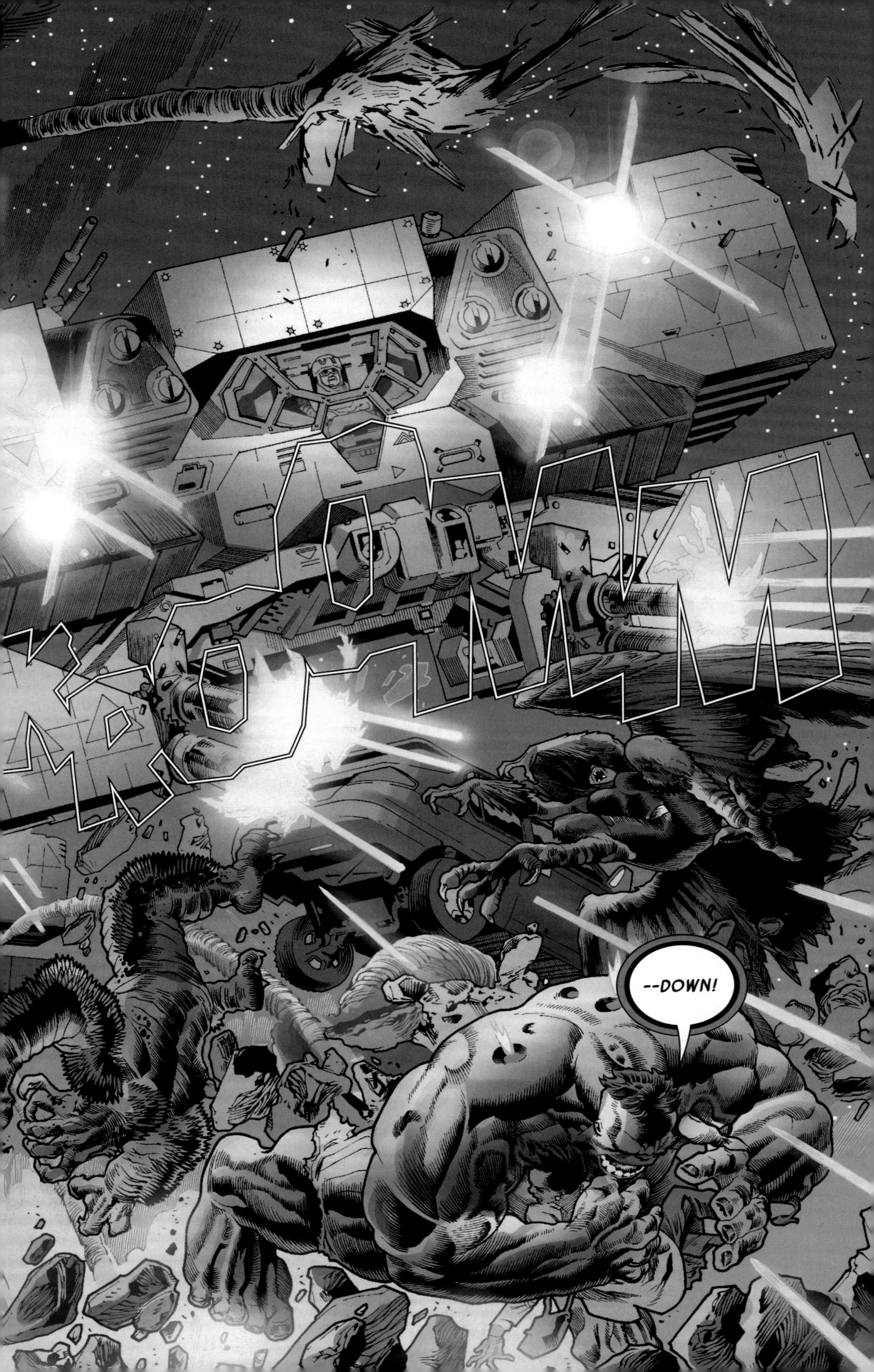
KROOMM
--DOWN!

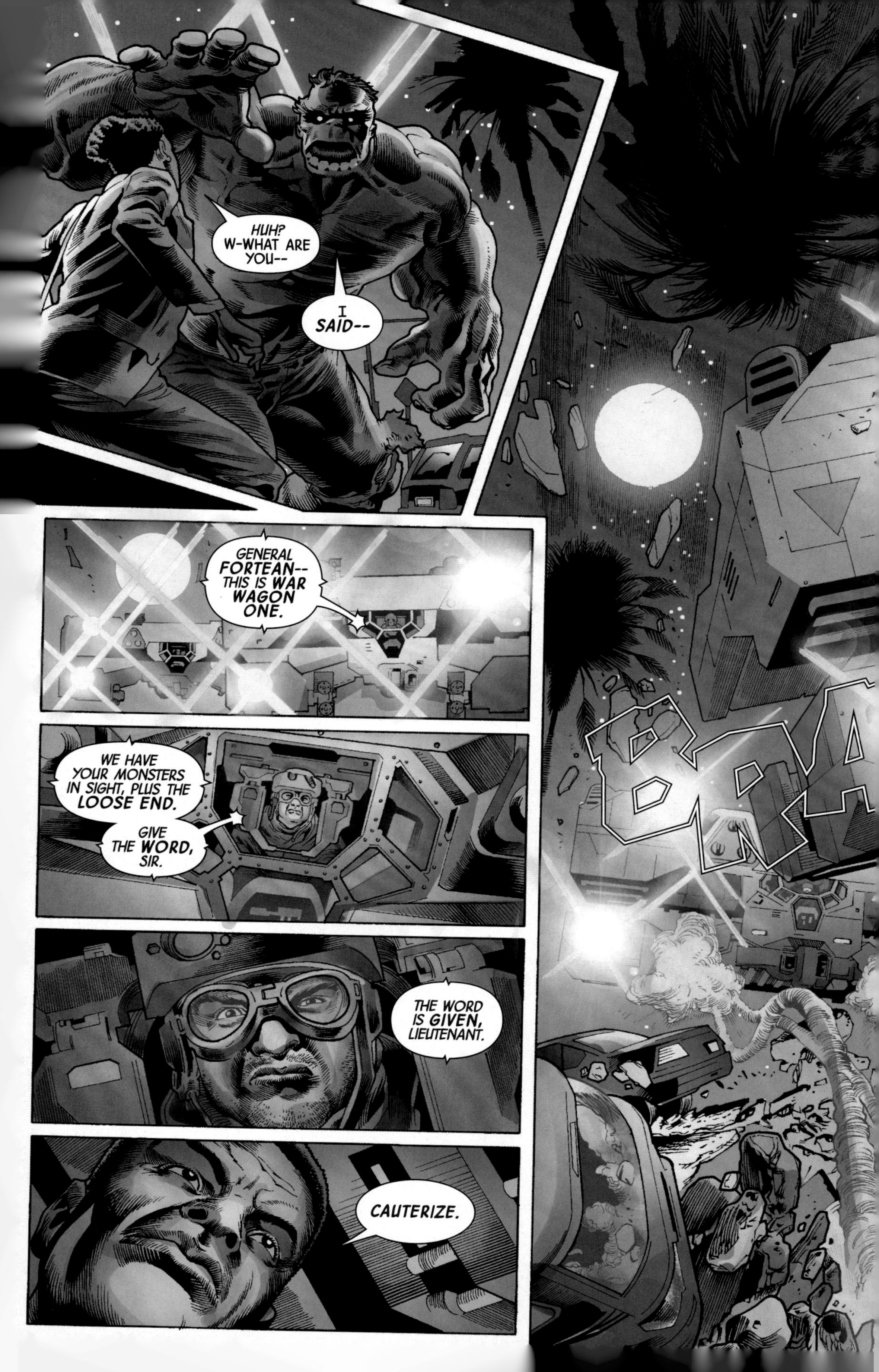
HUH? W-WHAT ARE YOU--
I SAID--
GENERAL FORTEAN-- THIS IS WAR WAGON ONE.
WE HAVE YOUR MONSTERS IN SIGHT, PLUS THE LOOSE END.
GIVE THE WORD, SIR.
THE WORD IS GIVEN, LIEUTENANT.
CAUTERIZE.

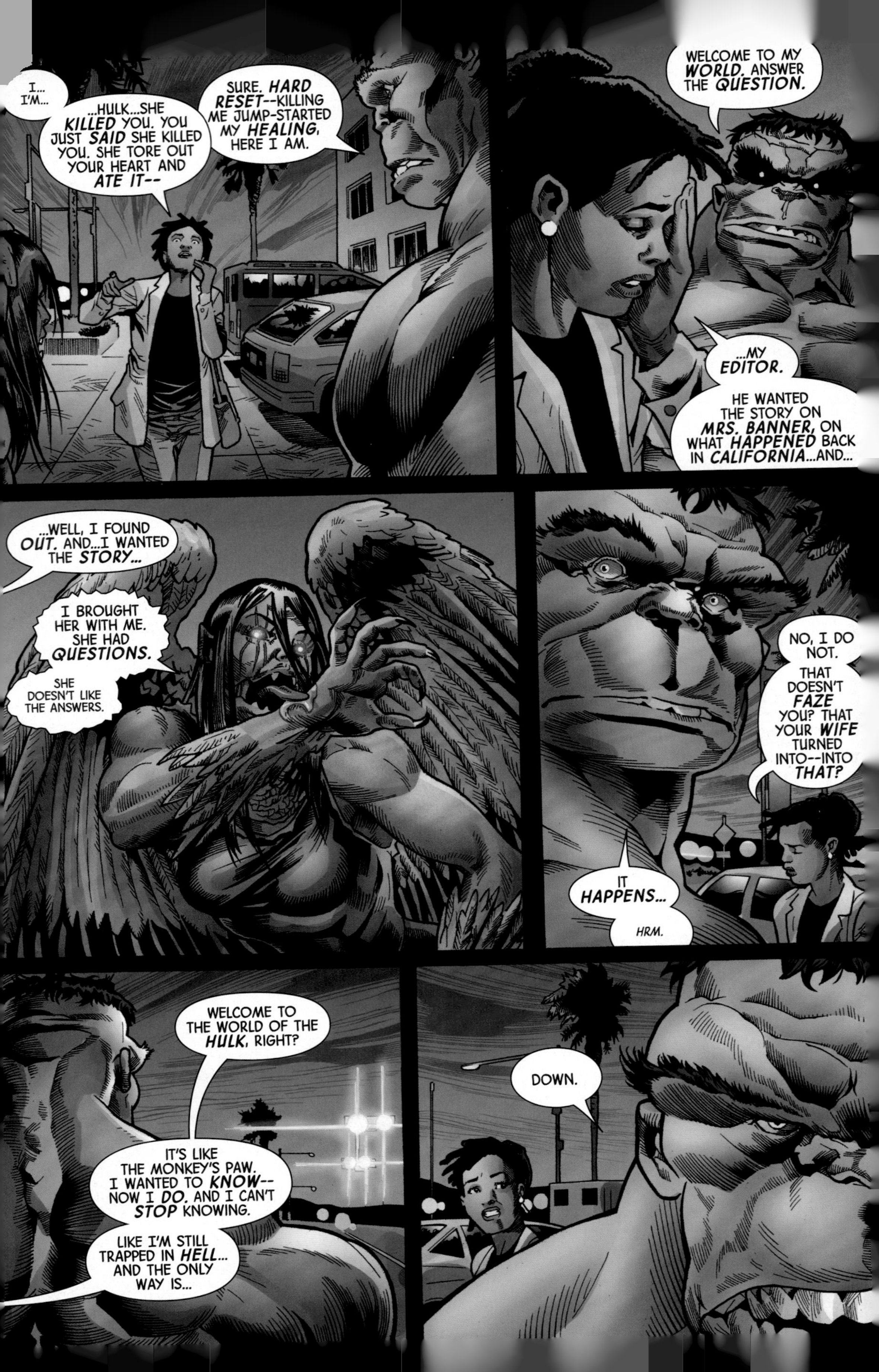

I... I'M...
...HULK...SHE KILLED YOU. YOU JUST SAID SHE KILLED YOU. SHE TORE OUT YOUR HEART AND ATE IT--
SURE. HARD RESET--KILLING ME JUMP-STARTED MY HEALING, HERE I AM.
WELCOME TO MY WORLD. ANSWER THE QUESTION.
...MY EDITOR.
HE WANTED THE STORY ON MRS. BANNER, ON WHAT HAPPENED BACK IN CALIFORNIA...AND...
...WELL, I FOUND OUT. AND...I WANTED THE STORY...
I BROUGHT HER WITH ME. SHE HAD QUESTIONS.
SHE DOESN'T LIKE THE ANSWERS.
NO, I DO NOT.
THAT DOESN'T FAZE YOU? THAT YOUR WIFE TURNED INTO--INTO THAT?
IT HAPPENS...
HRM.
WELCOME TO THE WORLD OF THE HULK, RIGHT?
IT'S LIKE THE MONKEY'S PAW. I WANTED TO KNOW--NOW I DO. AND I CAN'T STOP KNOWING.
LIKE I'M STILL TRAPPED IN HELL... AND THE ONLY WAY IS...
DOWN.

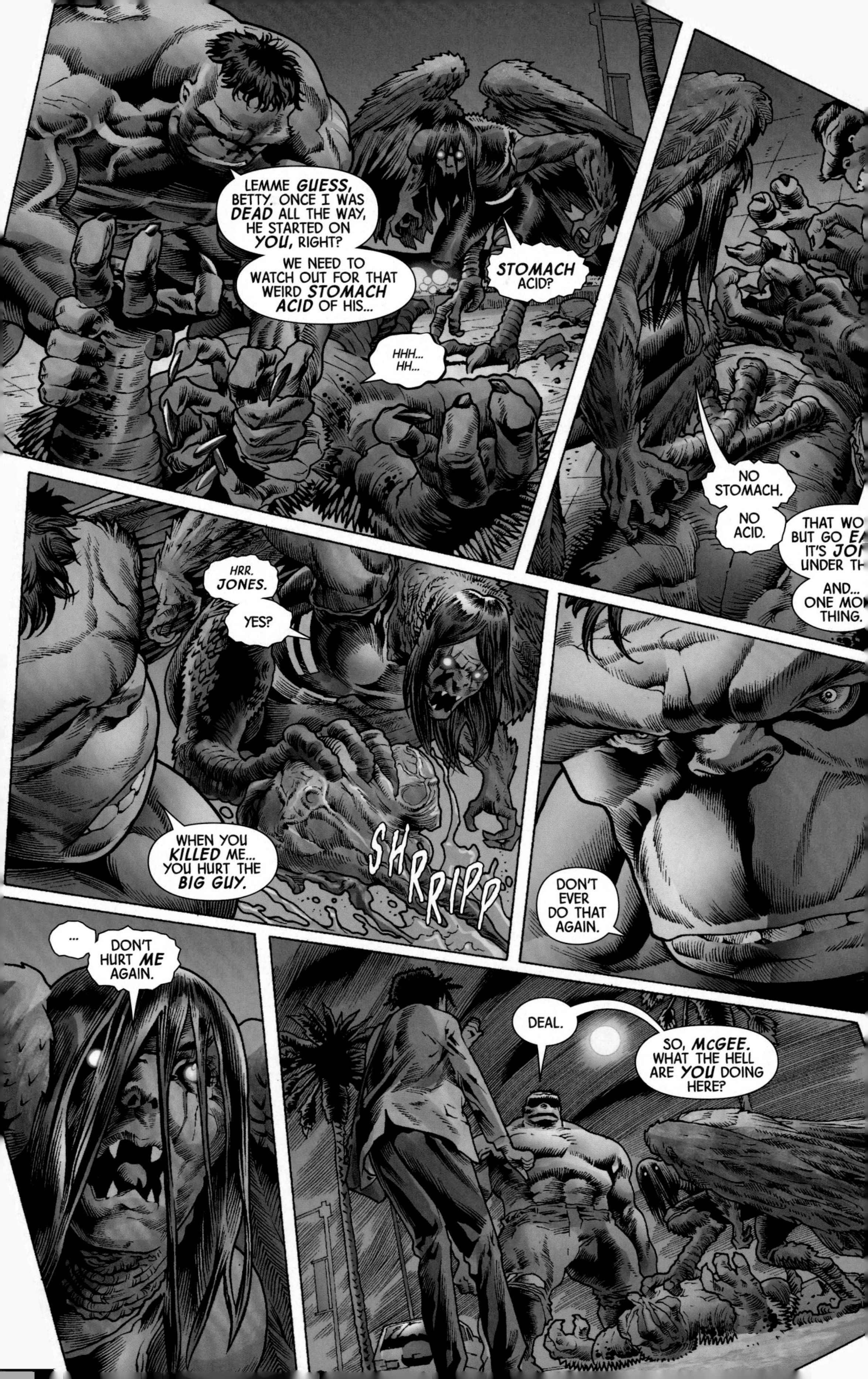
LEMME GUESS, BETTY. ONCE I WAS DEAD ALL THE WAY, HE STARTED ON YOU, RIGHT?
WE NEED TO WATCH OUT FOR THAT WEIRD STOMACH ACID OF HIS...
STOMACH ACID?
HHH... HH...
NO STOMACH.
NO ACID.
HRR. JONES.
YES?
WHEN YOU KILLED ME... YOU HURT THE BIG GUY.
SHRRIPP
DON'T EVER DO THAT AGAIN.
...
DON'T HURT ME AGAIN.
DEAL.
SO, McGEE. WHAT THE HELL ARE YOU DOING HERE?

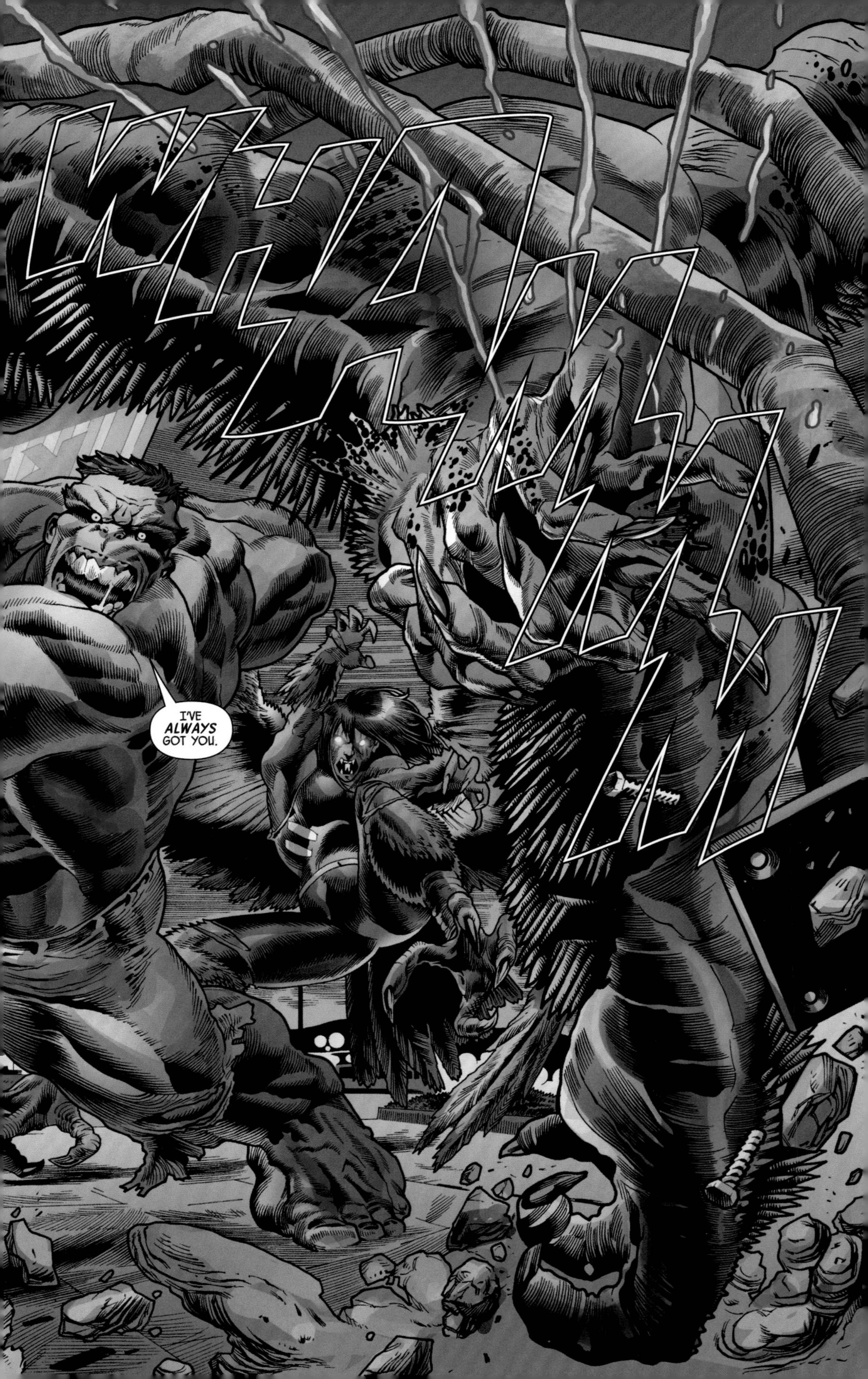
I'VE ALWAYS GOT YOU.

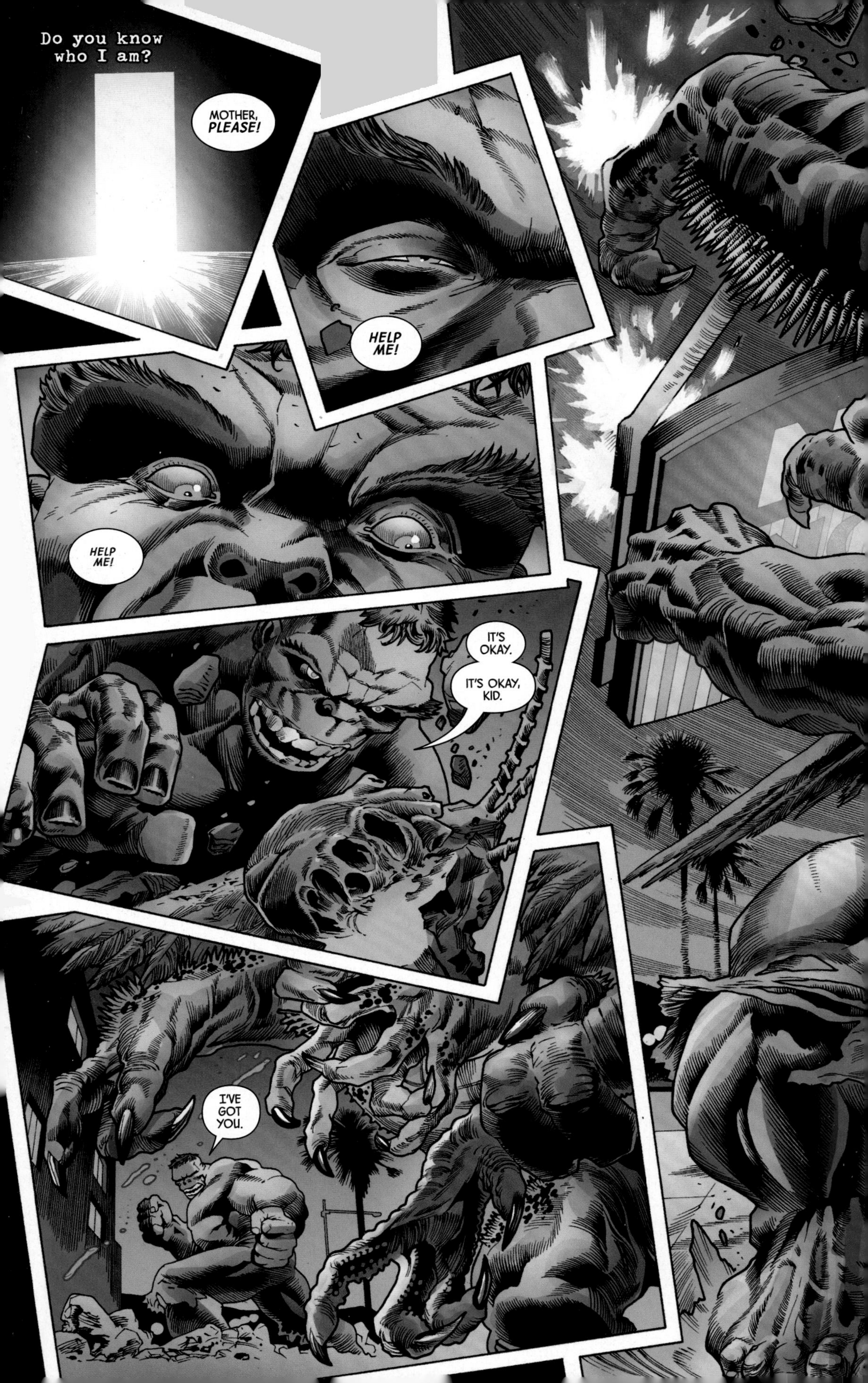
Do you know who I am?
MOTHER, PLEASE!
HELP ME!
HELP ME!
IT'S OKAY.
IT'S OKAY, KID.
I'VE GOT YOU.

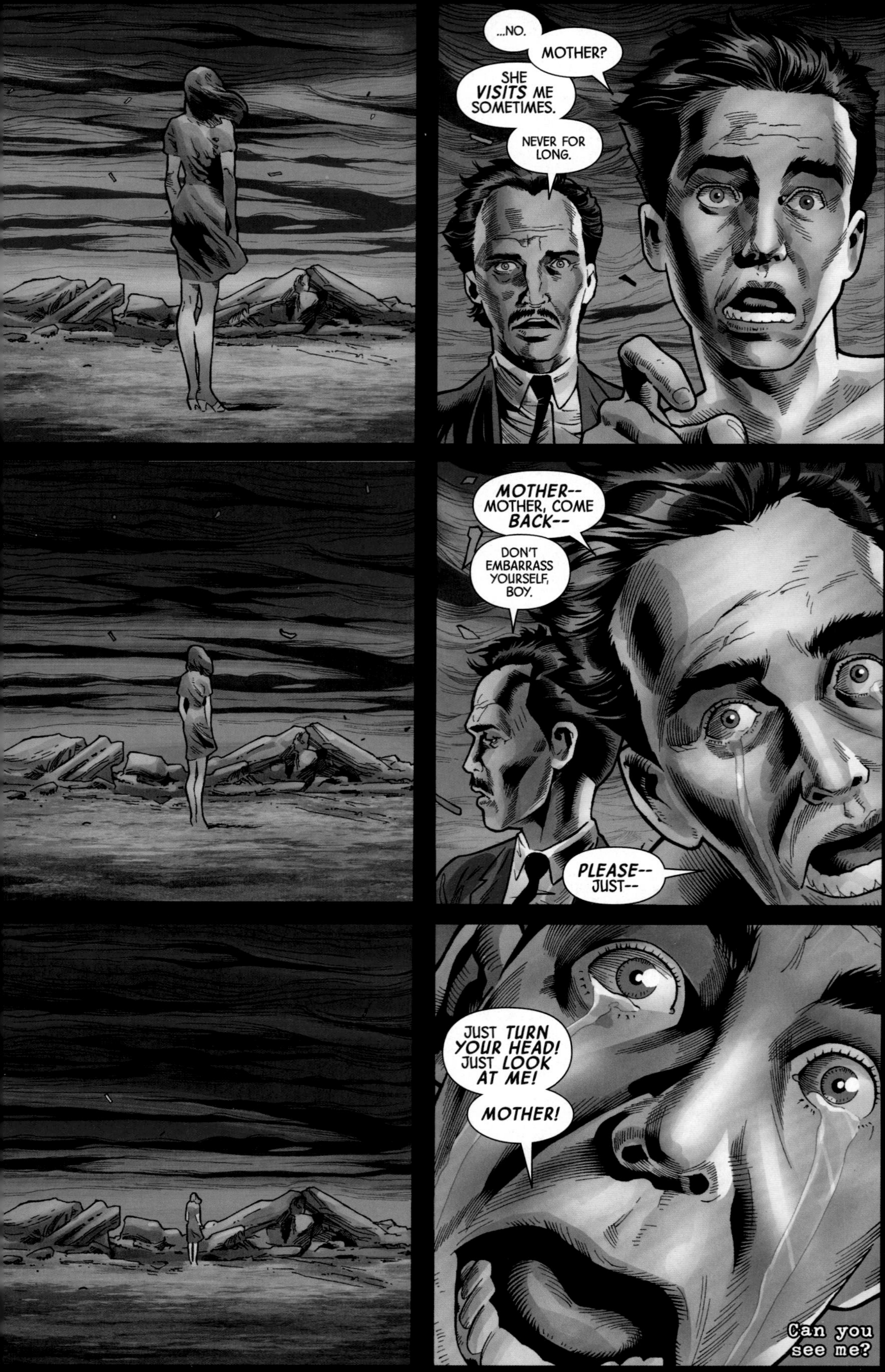
...NO.
MOTHER?
SHE VISITS ME SOMETIMES.
NEVER FOR LONG.
MOTHER-- MOTHER, COME BACK--
DON'T EMBARRASS YOURSELF, BOY.
PLEASE-- JUST--
JUST TURN YOUR HEAD! JUST LOOK AT ME!
MOTHER!
Can you see me?

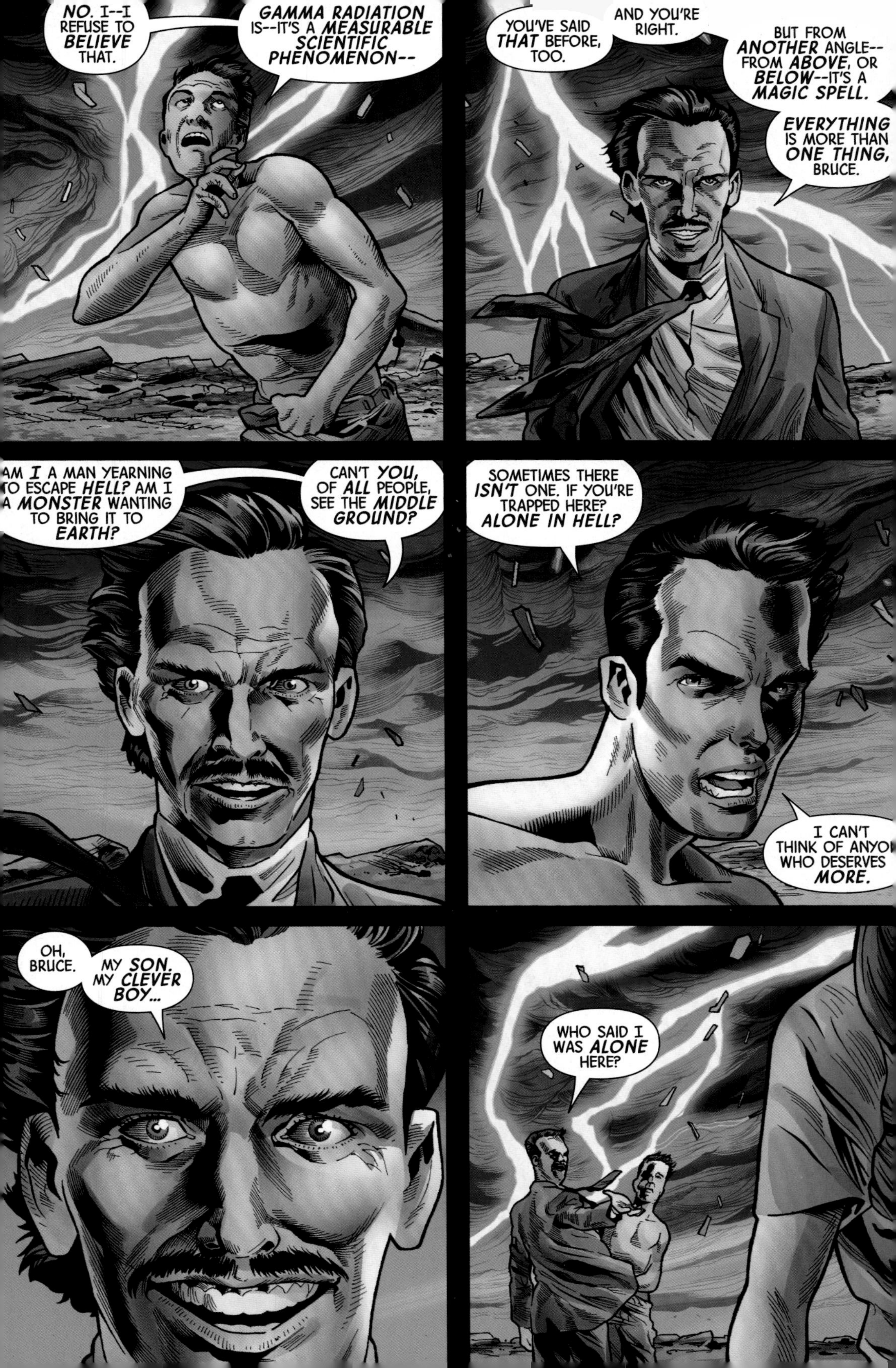
NO. I--I REFUSE TO BELIEVE THAT.
GAMMA RADIATION IS--IT'S A MEASURABLE SCIENTIFIC PHENOMENON--
YOU'VE SAID THAT BEFORE, TOO.
AND YOU'RE RIGHT.
BUT FROM ANOTHER ANGLE-- FROM ABOVE, OR BELOW--IT'S A MAGIC SPELL.
EVERYTHING IS MORE THAN ONE THING, BRUCE.
AM I A MAN YEARNING TO ESCAPE HELL? AM I A MONSTER WANTING TO BRING IT TO EARTH?
CAN'T YOU, OF ALL PEOPLE, SEE THE MIDDLE GROUND?
SOMETIMES THERE ISN'T ONE. IF YOU'RE TRAPPED HERE? ALONE IN HELL?
I CAN'T THINK OF ANYO WHO DESERVES MORE.
OH, BRUCE.
MY SON. MY CLEVER BOY...
WHO SAID I WAS ALONE HERE?

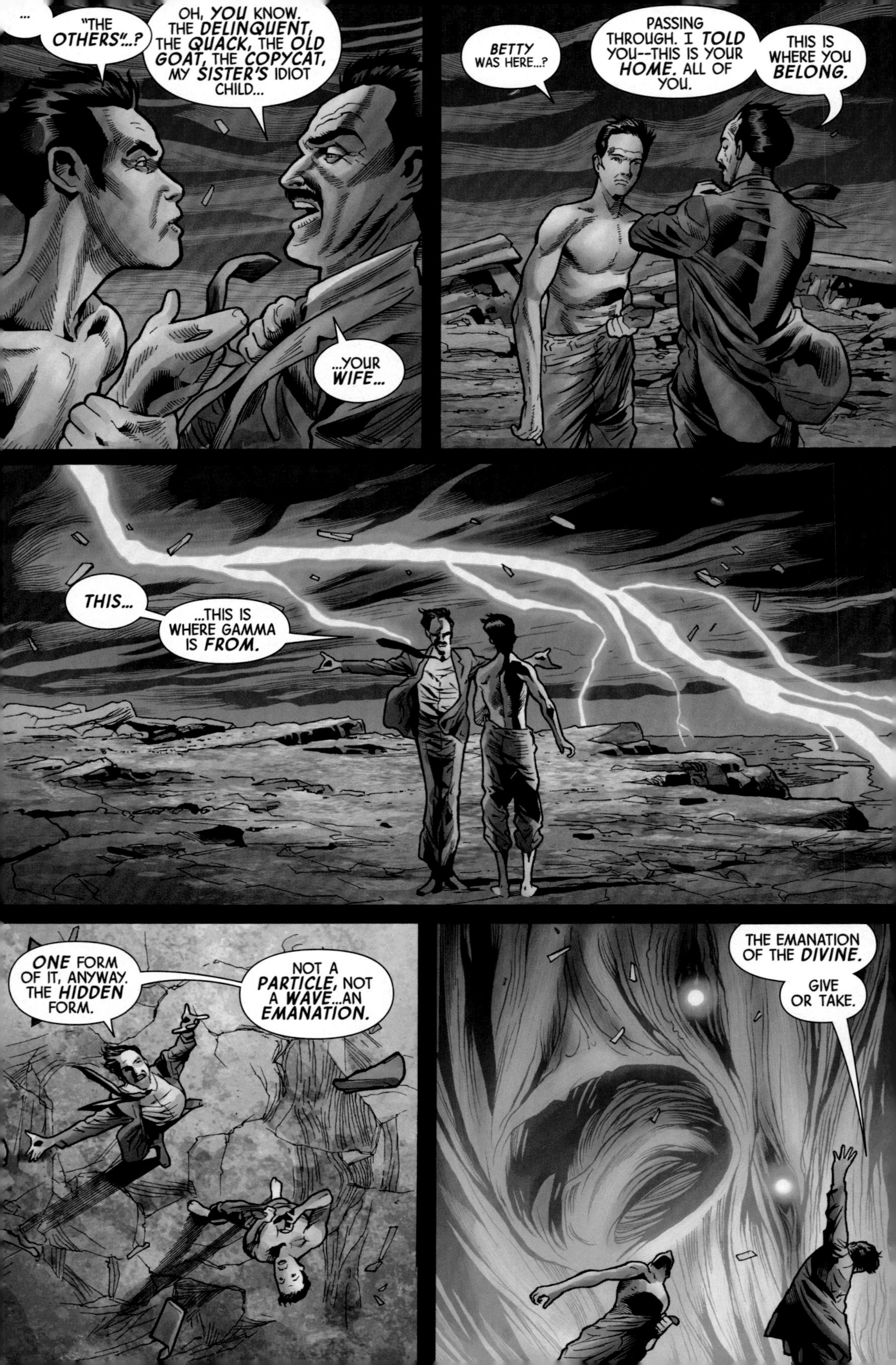
...
"THE OTHERS"...?
OH, YOU KNOW. THE DELINQUENT, THE QUACK, THE OLD GOAT, THE COPYCAT, MY SISTER'S IDIOT CHILD...
...YOUR WIFE...
BETTY WAS HERE...?
PASSING THROUGH. I TOLD YOU--THIS IS YOUR HOME. ALL OF YOU.
THIS IS WHERE YOU BELONG.
THIS...
...THIS IS WHERE GAMMA IS FROM.
ONE FORM OF IT, ANYWAY. THE HIDDEN FORM.
NOT A PARTICLE, NOT A WAVE...AN EMANATION.
THE EMANATION OF THE DIVINE.
GIVE OR TAKE.

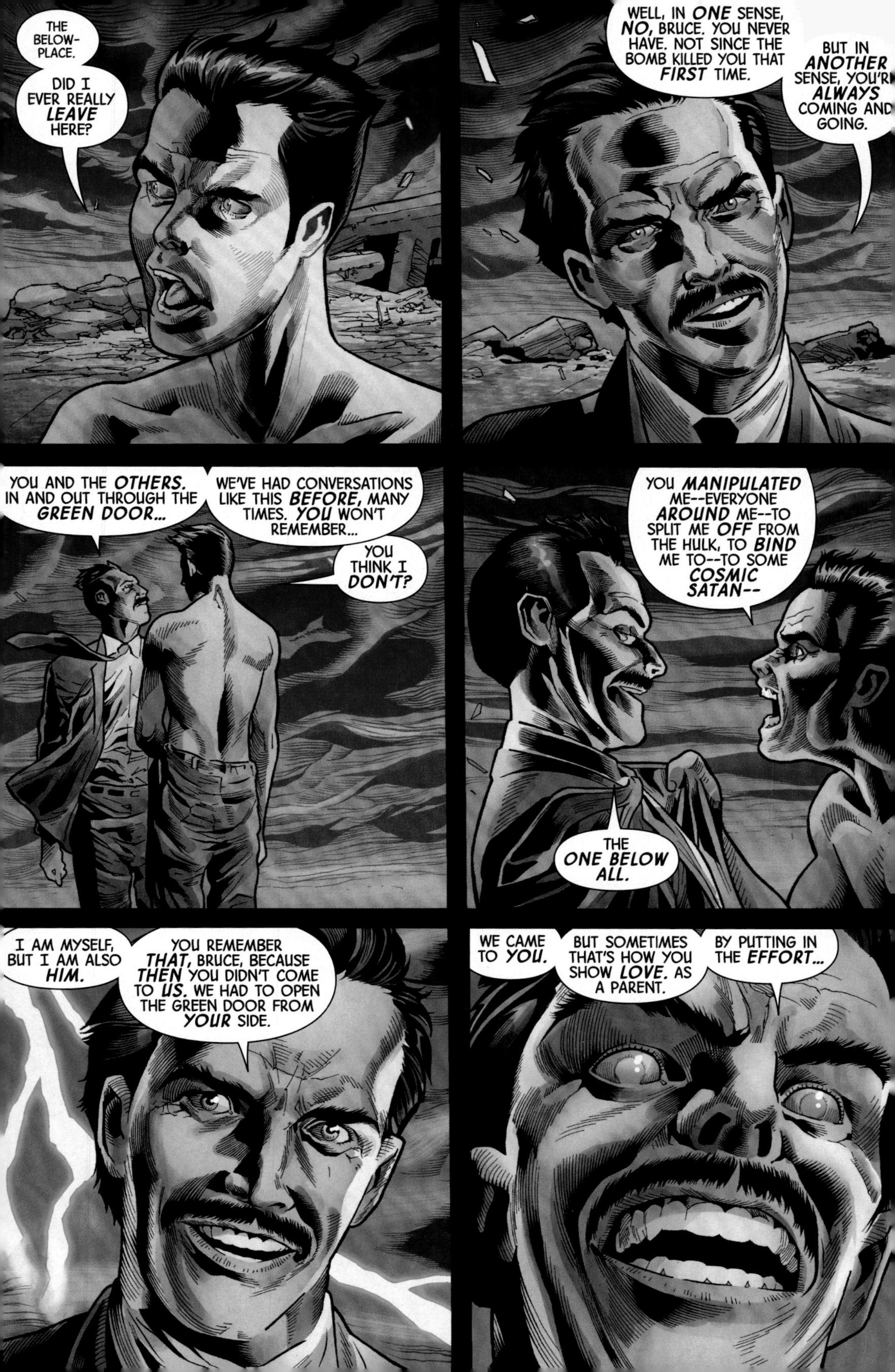
THE BELOW-PLACE.
DID I EVER REALLY LEAVE HERE?
WELL, IN ONE SENSE, NO, BRUCE. YOU NEVER HAVE. NOT SINCE THE BOMB KILLED YOU THAT FIRST TIME.
BUT IN ANOTHER SENSE, YOU'R ALWAYS COMING AND GOING.
YOU AND THE OTHERS. IN AND OUT THROUGH THE GREEN DOOR...
WE'VE HAD CONVERSATIONS LIKE THIS BEFORE, MANY TIMES. YOU WON'T REMEMBER...
YOU THINK I DON'T?
YOU MANIPULATED ME--EVERYONE AROUND ME--TO SPLIT ME OFF FROM THE HULK, TO BIND ME TO--TO SOME COSMIC SATAN--
THE ONE BELOW ALL.
I AM MYSELF, BUT I AM ALSO HIM.
YOU REMEMBER THAT, BRUCE, BECAUSE THEN YOU DIDN'T COME TO US. WE HAD TO OPEN THE GREEN DOOR FROM YOUR SIDE.
WE CAME TO YOU.
BUT SOMETIMES THAT'S HOW YOU SHOW LOVE. AS A PARENT.
BY PUTTING IN THE EFFORT...

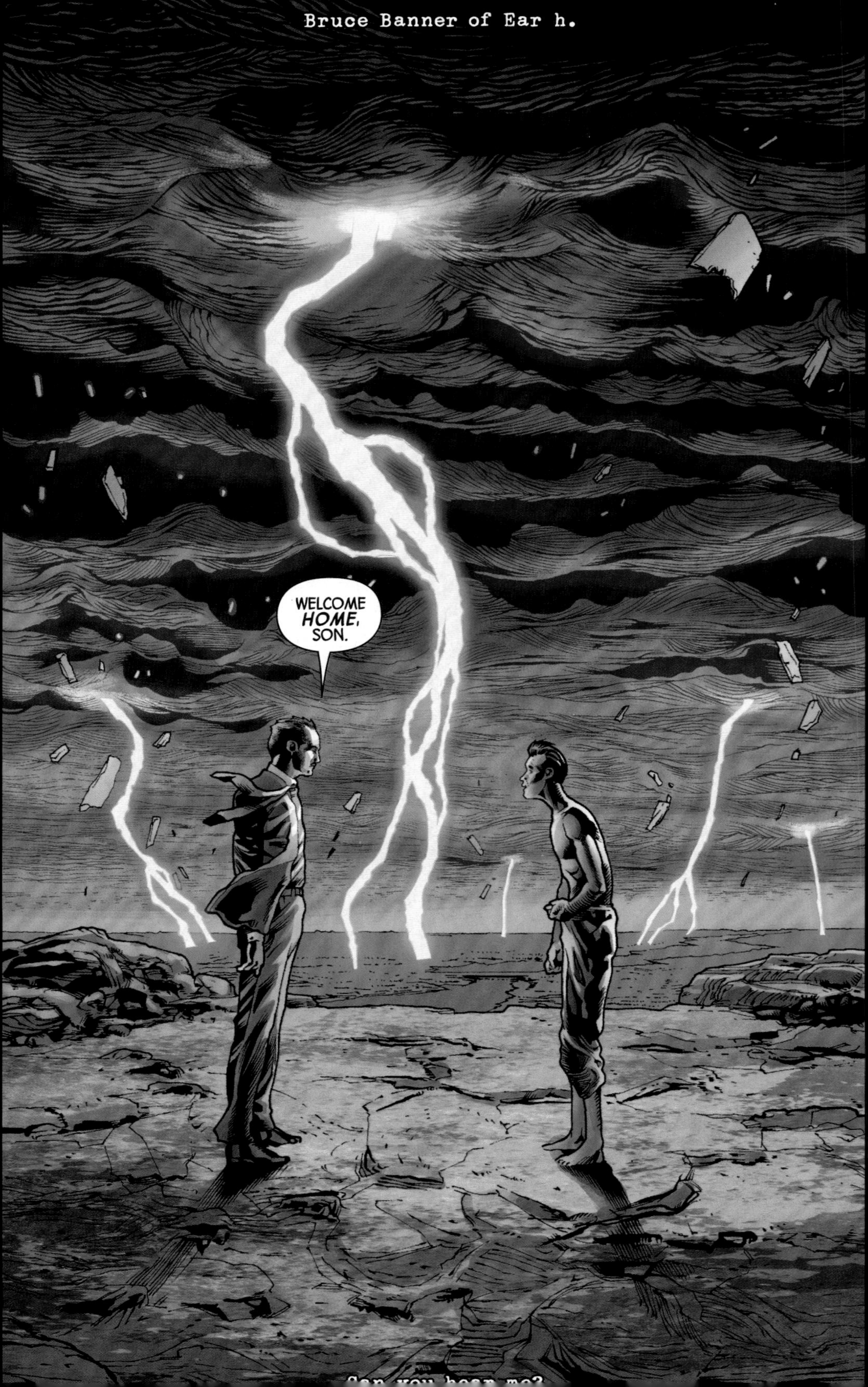
Bruce Banner of Ear h.
WELCOME *HOME*, SON.

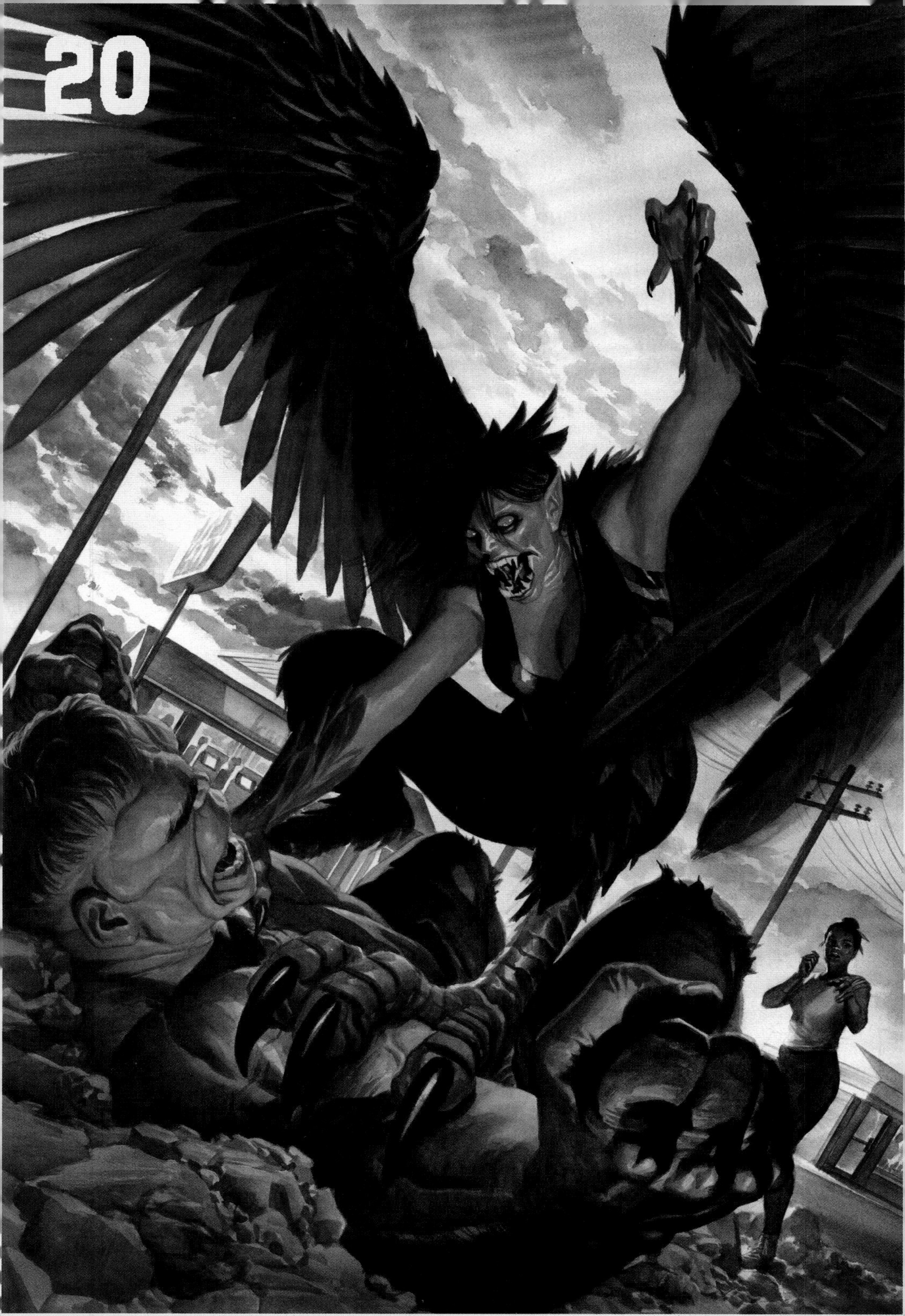
20

“THIS [redacted] RTH.”

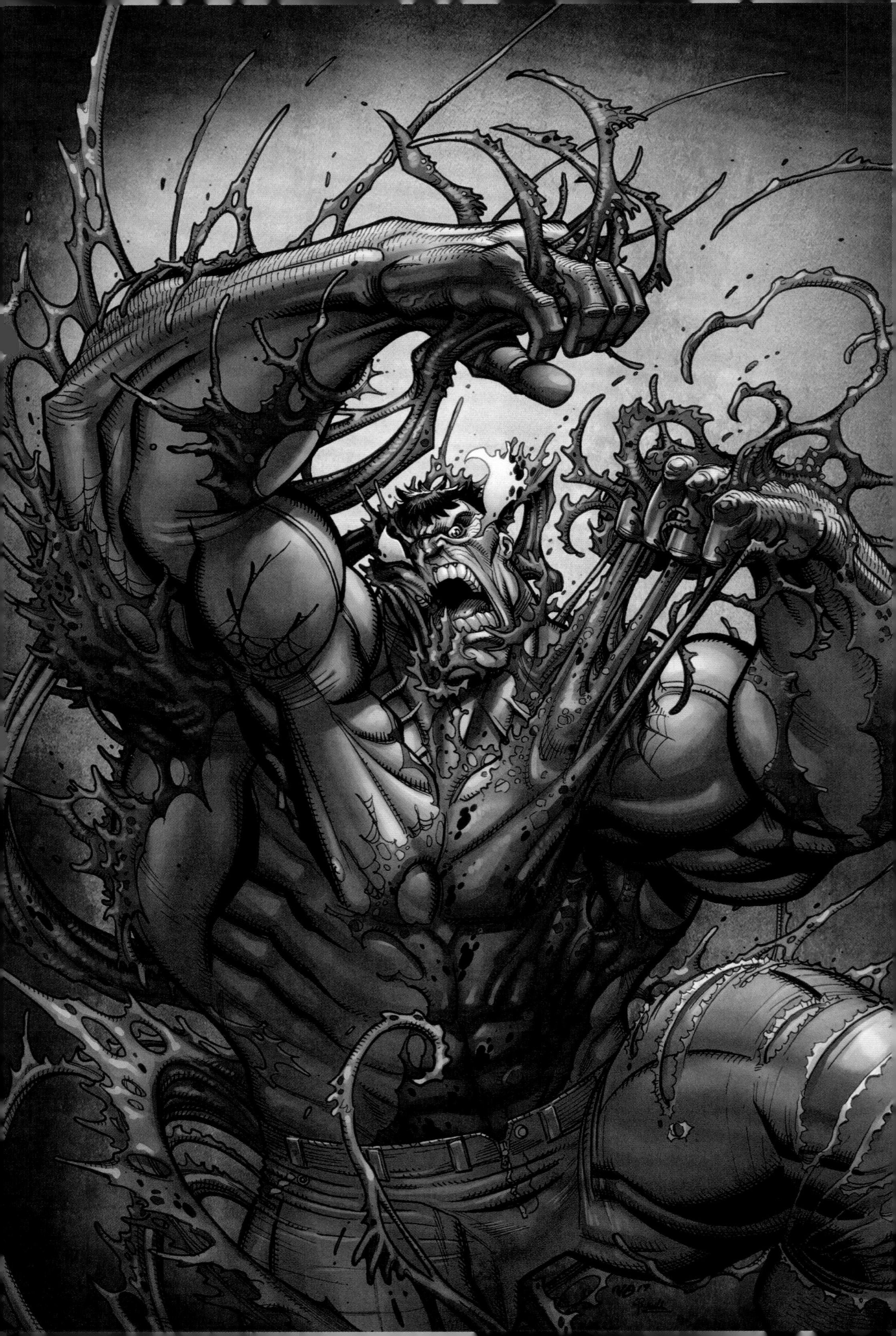

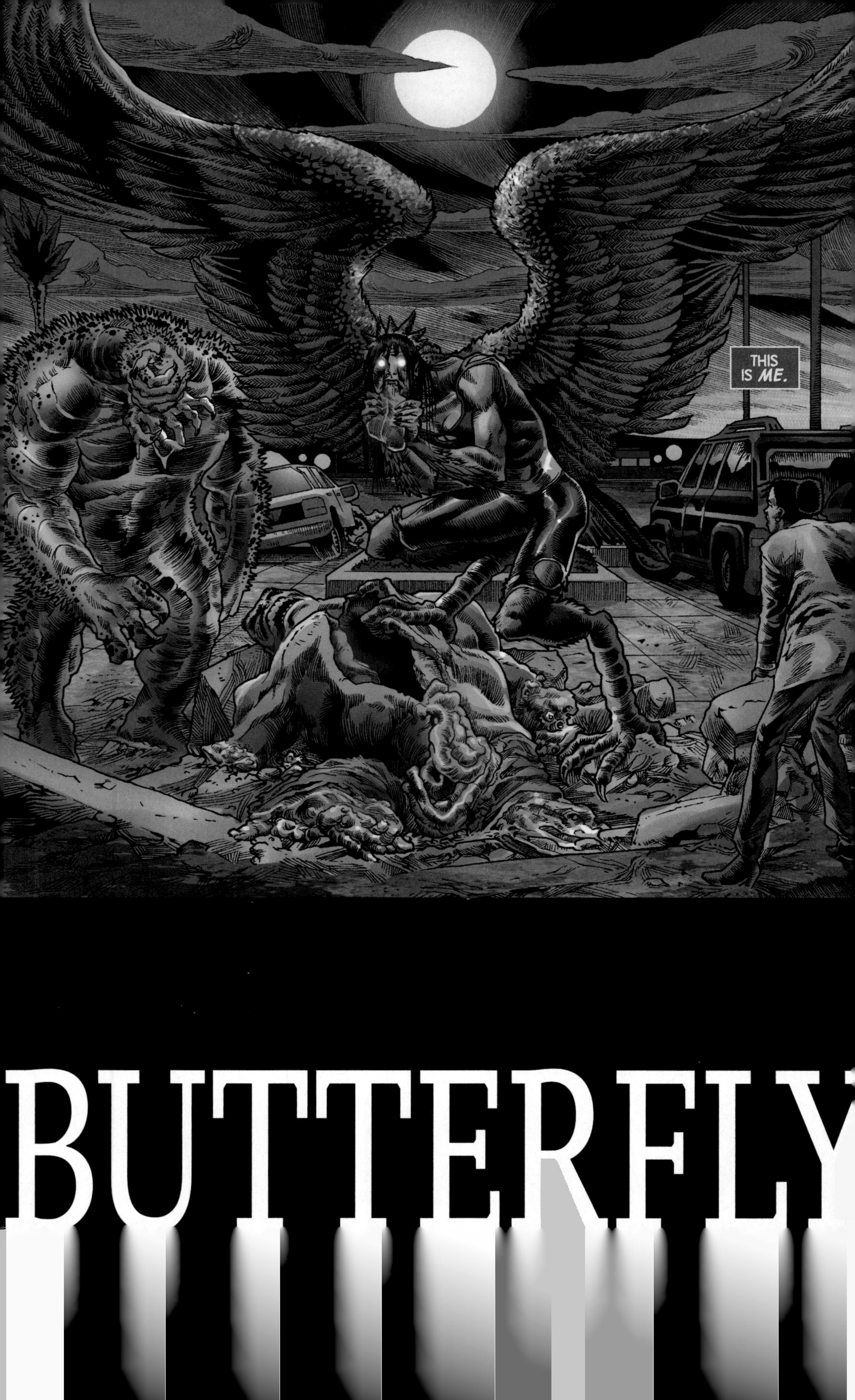
THIS IS ME.

BUTTERFLY

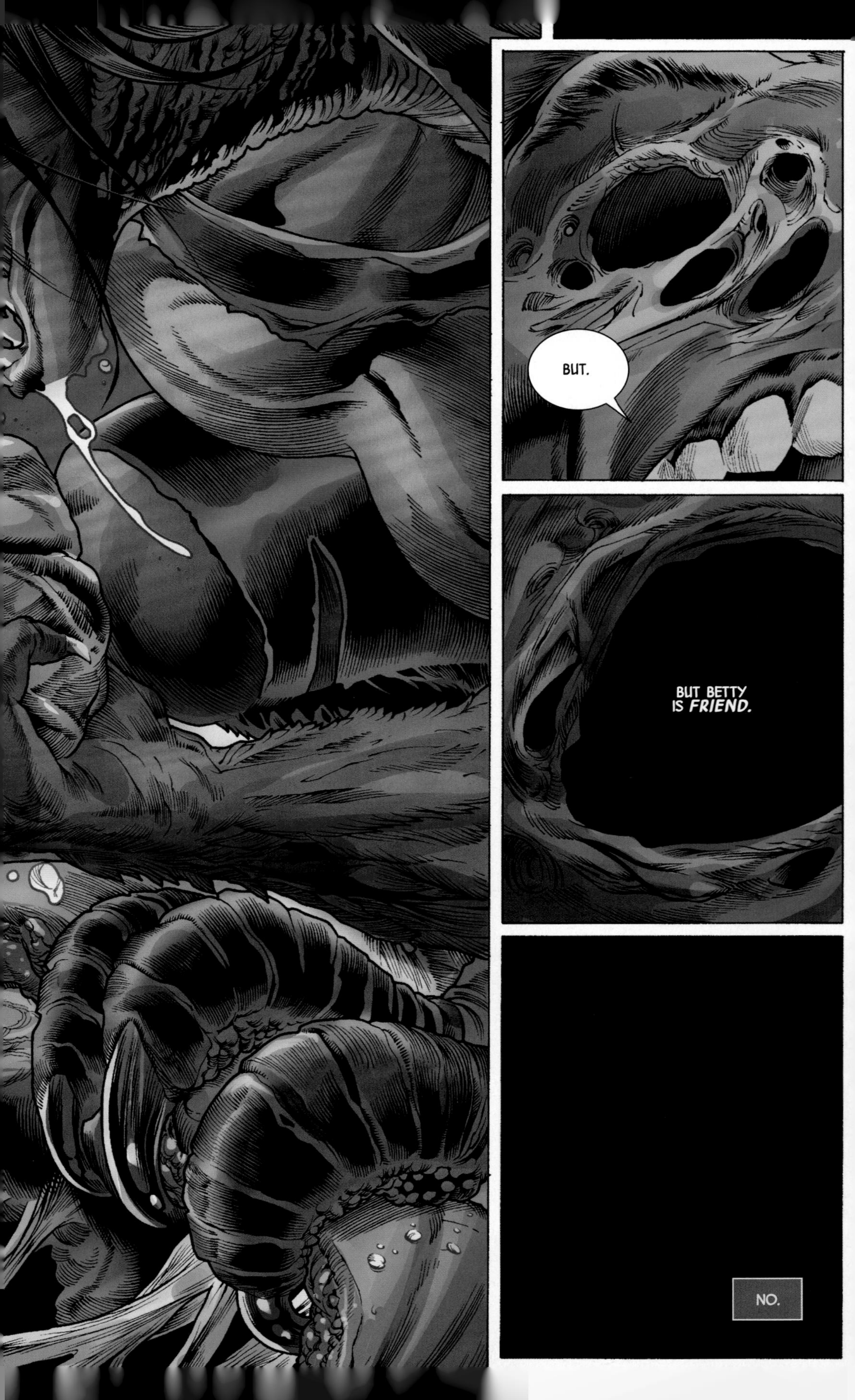
BUT.
BUT BETTY IS FRIEND.
NO.

INCREDIBLE.

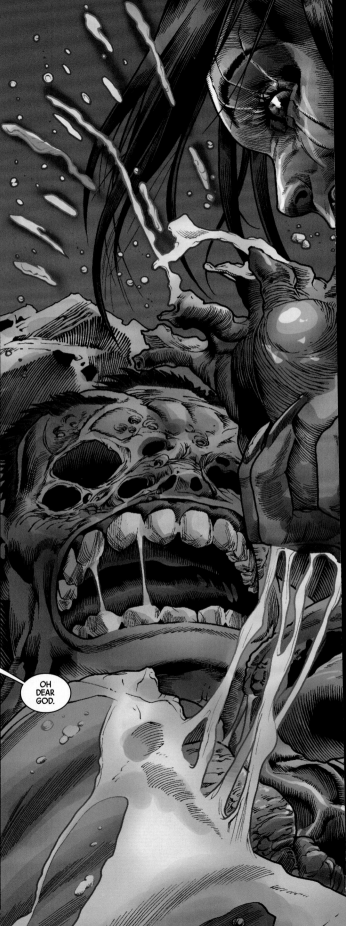

OH GOD.

OH DEAR GOD.

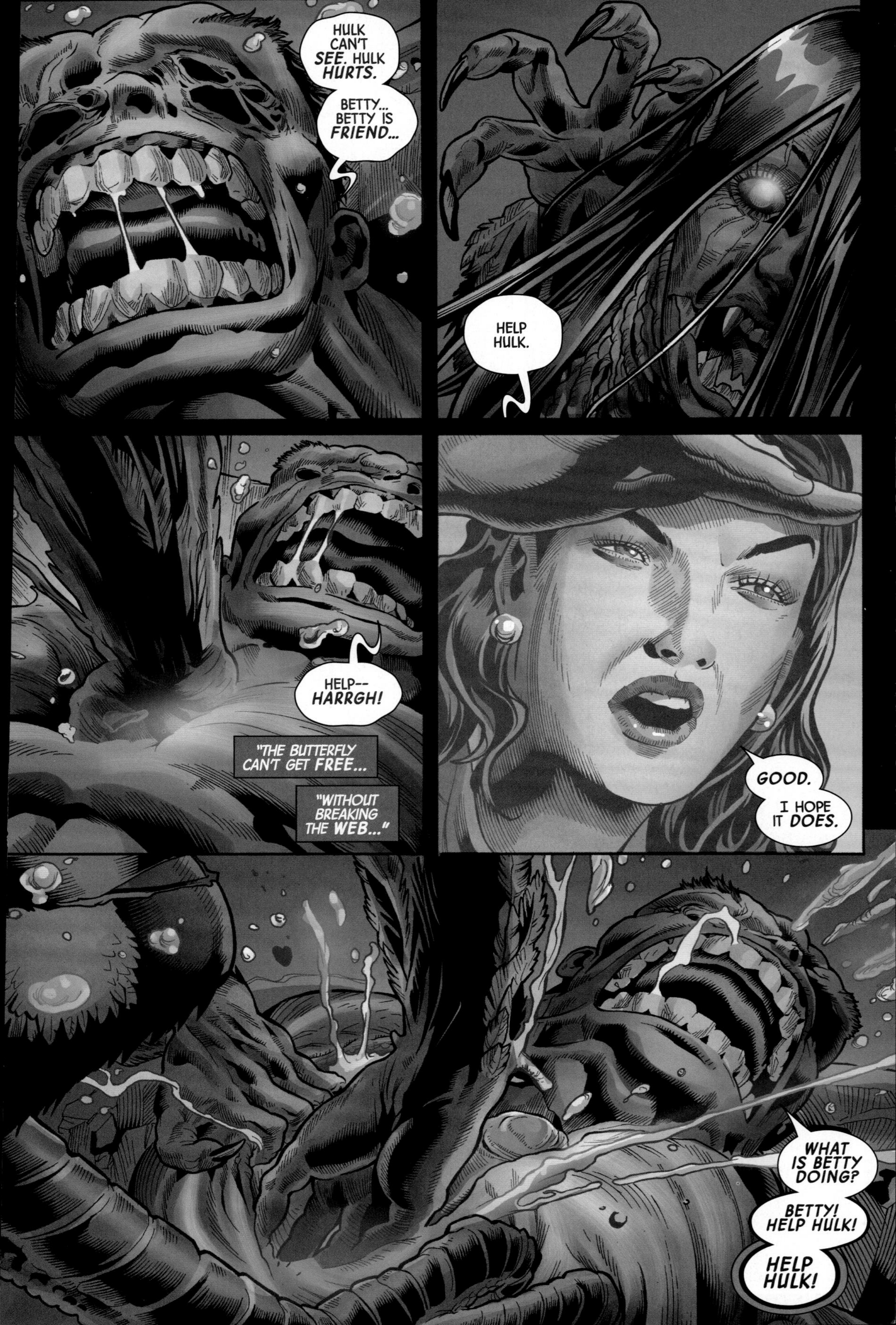
HULK CAN'T SEE. HULK HURTS.
BETTY... BETTY IS FRIEND...
HELP HULK.
HELP-- HARRGH!
"THE BUTTERFLY CAN'T GET FREE...
"WITHOUT BREAKING THE WEB..."
GOOD.
I HOPE IT DOES.
WHAT IS BETTY DOING?
BETTY! HELP HULK!
HELP HULK!

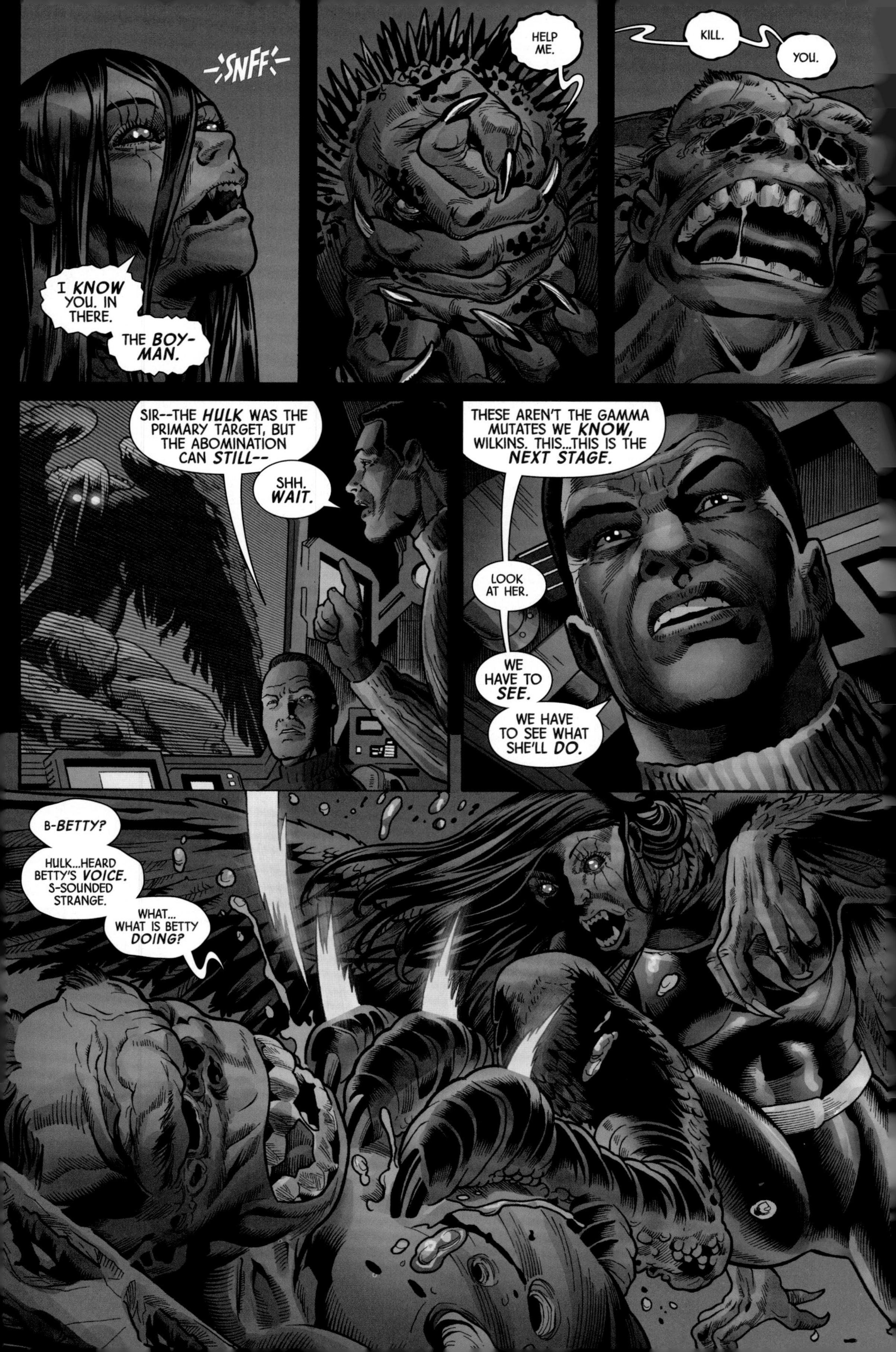
-SNFF-
I KNOW YOU. IN THERE.
THE BOY-MAN.
HELP ME.
KILL.
YOU.
SIR--THE HULK WAS THE PRIMARY TARGET, BUT THE ABOMINATION CAN STILL--
SHH. WAIT.
THESE AREN'T THE GAMMA MUTATES WE KNOW, WILKINS. THIS...THIS IS THE NEXT STAGE.
LOOK AT HER.
WE HAVE TO SEE.
WE HAVE TO SEE WHAT SHE'LL DO.
B-BETTY?
HULK...HEARD BETTY'S VOICE. S-SOUNDED STRANGE.
WHAT... WHAT IS BETTY DOING?

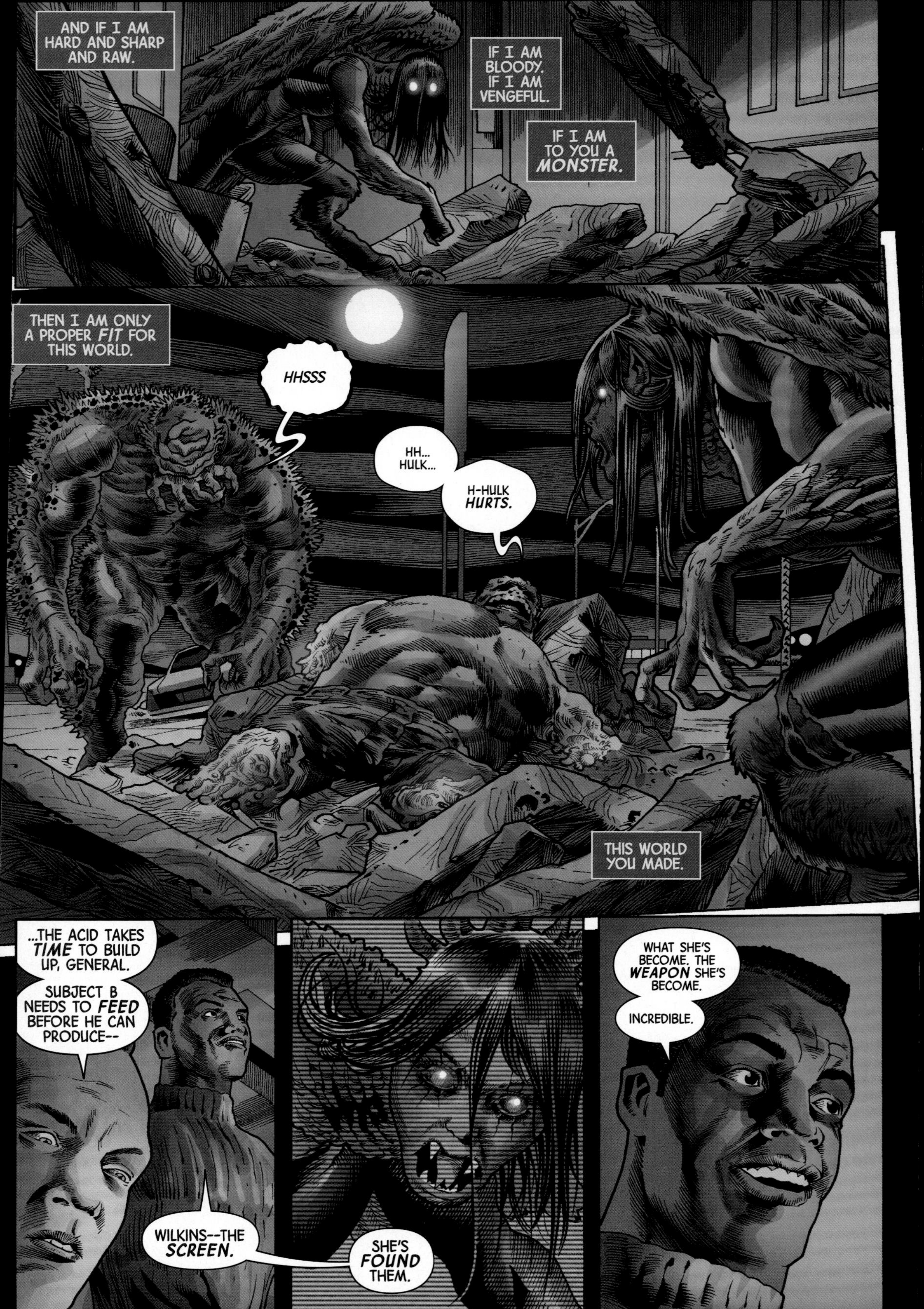
AND IF I AM HARD AND SHARP AND RAW.
IF I AM BLOODY. IF I AM VENGEFUL.
IF I AM TO YOU A MONSTER.
THEN I AM ONLY A PROPER FIT FOR THIS WORLD.
HHSSS
HH... HULK...
H-HULK HURTS.
THIS WORLD YOU MADE.
...THE ACID TAKES TIME TO BUILD UP, GENERAL.
SUBJECT B NEEDS TO FEED BEFORE HE CAN PRODUCE--
WILKINS--THE SCREEN.
SHE'S FOUND THEM.
WHAT SHE'S BECOME. THE WEAPON SHE'S BECOME.
INCREDIBLE.

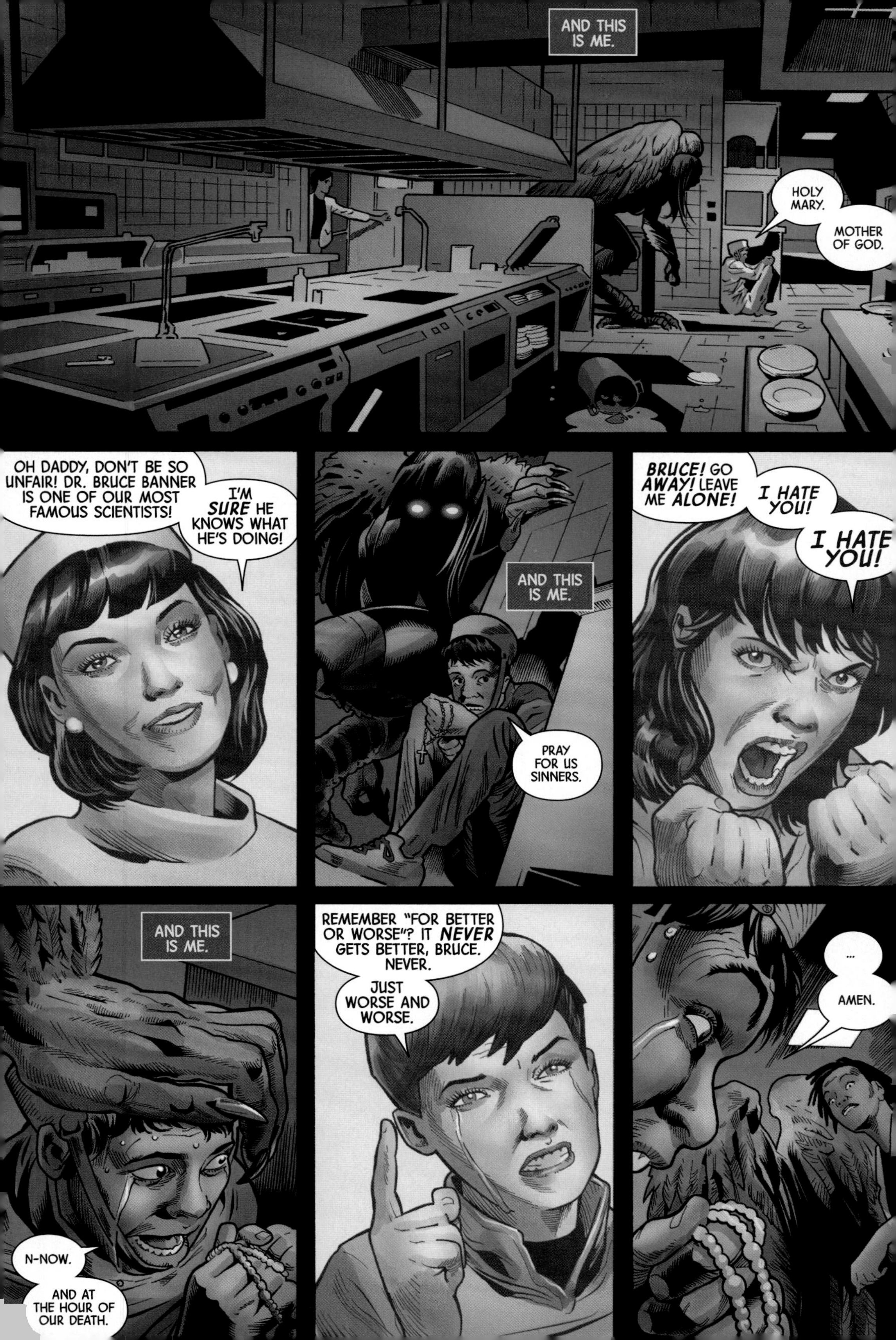
AND THIS IS ME.
HOLY MARY.
MOTHER OF GOD.
OH DADDY, DON'T BE SO UNFAIR! DR. BRUCE BANNER IS ONE OF OUR MOST FAMOUS SCIENTISTS!
I'M SURE HE KNOWS WHAT HE'S DOING!
AND THIS IS ME.
PRAY FOR US SINNERS.
BRUCE! GO AWAY! LEAVE ME ALONE!
I HATE YOU!
I HATE YOU!
AND THIS IS ME.
N-NOW.
AND AT THE HOUR OF OUR DEATH.
REMEMBER "FOR BETTER OR WORSE"? IT NEVER GETS BETTER, BRUCE. NEVER.
JUST WORSE AND WORSE.
...
AMEN.

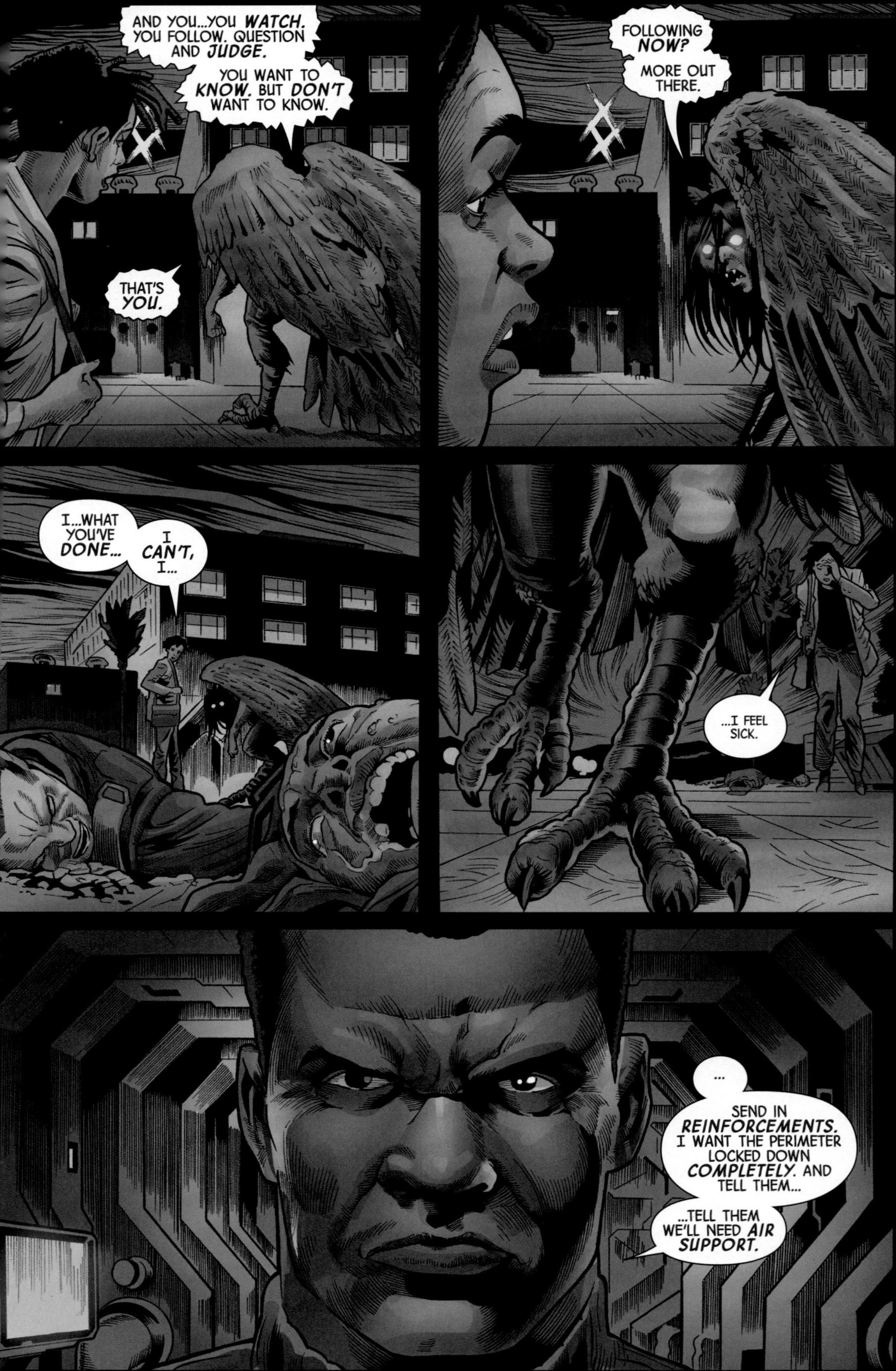
AND YOU...YOU WATCH. YOU FOLLOW. QUESTION AND JUDGE.
YOU WANT TO KNOW. BUT DON'T WANT TO KNOW.
THAT'S YOU.
FOLLOWING NOW?
MORE OUT THERE.
I...WHAT YOU'VE DONE...
I CAN'T, I...
...I FEEL SICK.
...
SEND IN REINFORCEMENTS. I WANT THE PERIMETER LOCKED DOWN COMPLETELY. AND TELL THEM...
...TELL THEM WE'LL NEED AIR SUPPORT.

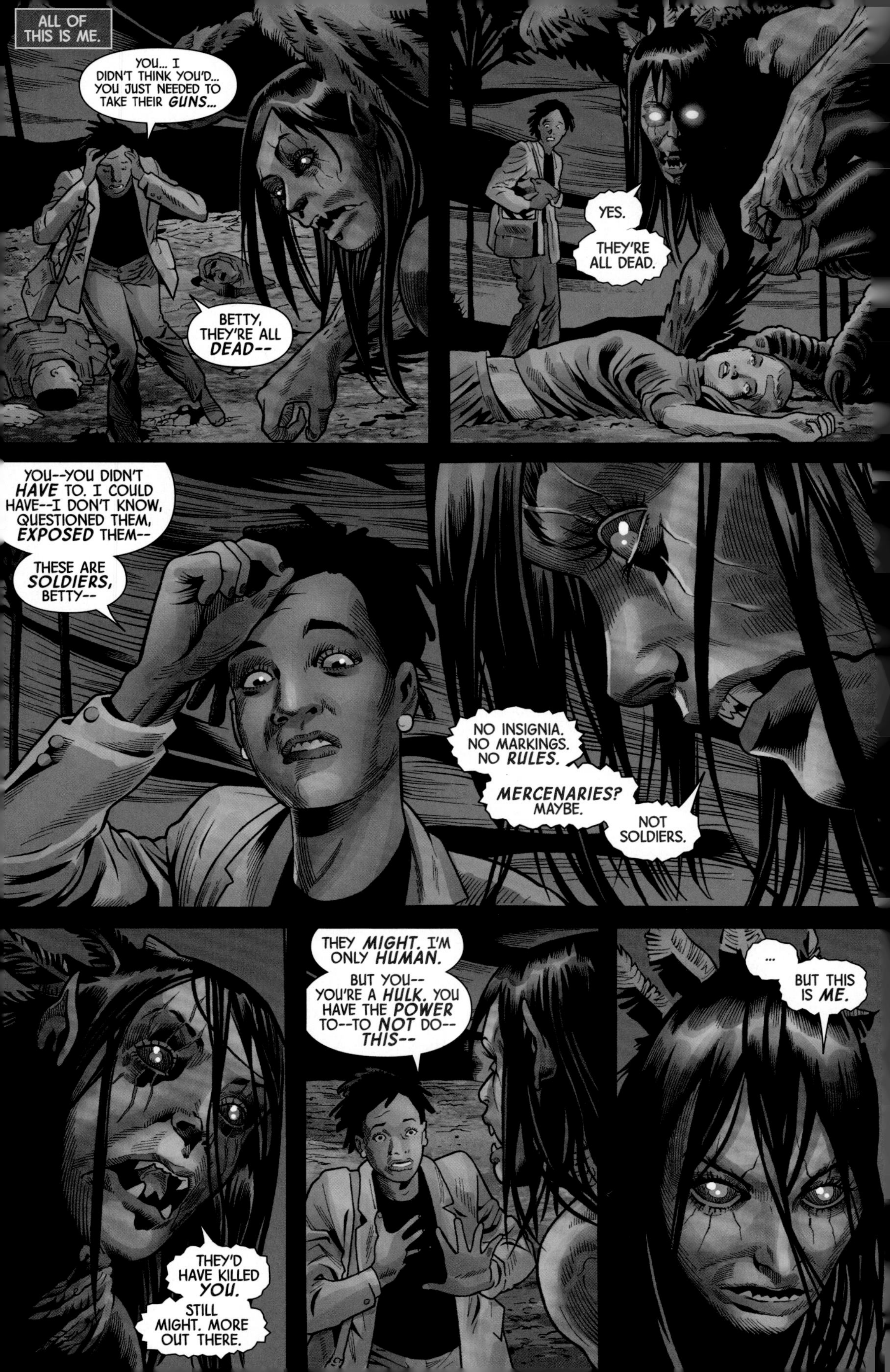
ALL OF THIS IS ME.
YOU... I DIDN'T THINK YOU'D... YOU JUST NEEDED TO TAKE THEIR GUNS...
BETTY, THEY'RE ALL DEAD--
YES.
THEY'RE ALL DEAD.
YOU--YOU DIDN'T HAVE TO. I COULD HAVE--I DON'T KNOW, QUESTIONED THEM, EXPOSED THEM--
THESE ARE SOLDIERS, BETTY--
NO INSIGNIA. NO MARKINGS. NO RULES.
MERCENARIES? MAYBE.
NOT SOLDIERS.
THEY'D HAVE KILLED YOU.
STILL MIGHT. MORE OUT THERE.
THEY MIGHT. I'M ONLY HUMAN.
BUT YOU-- YOU'RE A HULK. YOU HAVE THE POWER TO--TO NOT DO-- THIS--
...
BUT THIS IS ME.

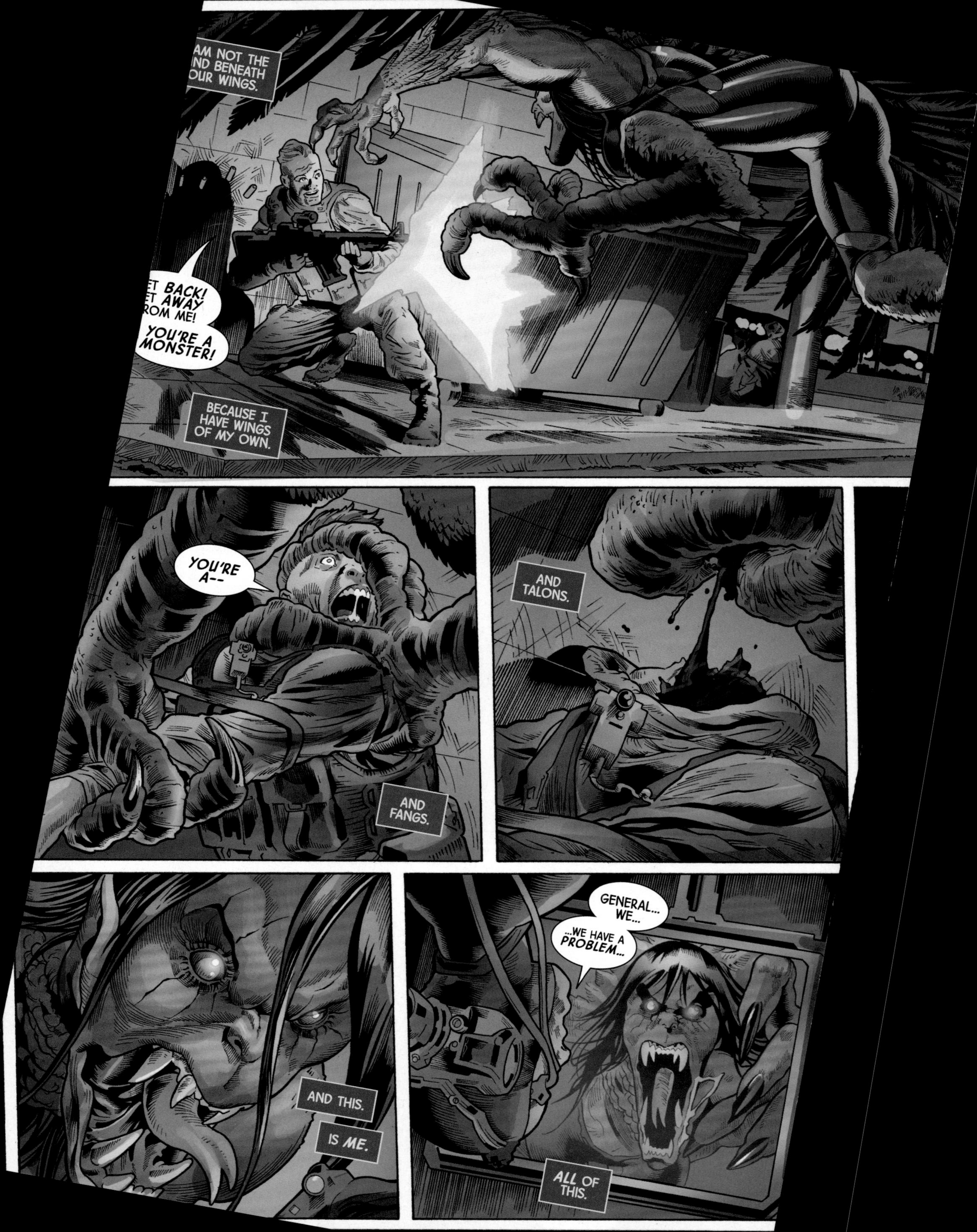
AM NOT THE
IND BENEATH
OUR WINGS.
ET BACK!
ET AWAY
ROM ME!
YOU'RE A
MONSTER!
BECAUSE I
HAVE WINGS
OF MY OWN.
YOU'RE
A--
AND
FANGS.
AND
TALONS.
AND THIS.
IS ME.
GENERAL...
WE...
...WE HAVE A
PROBLEM...
ALL OF
THIS.

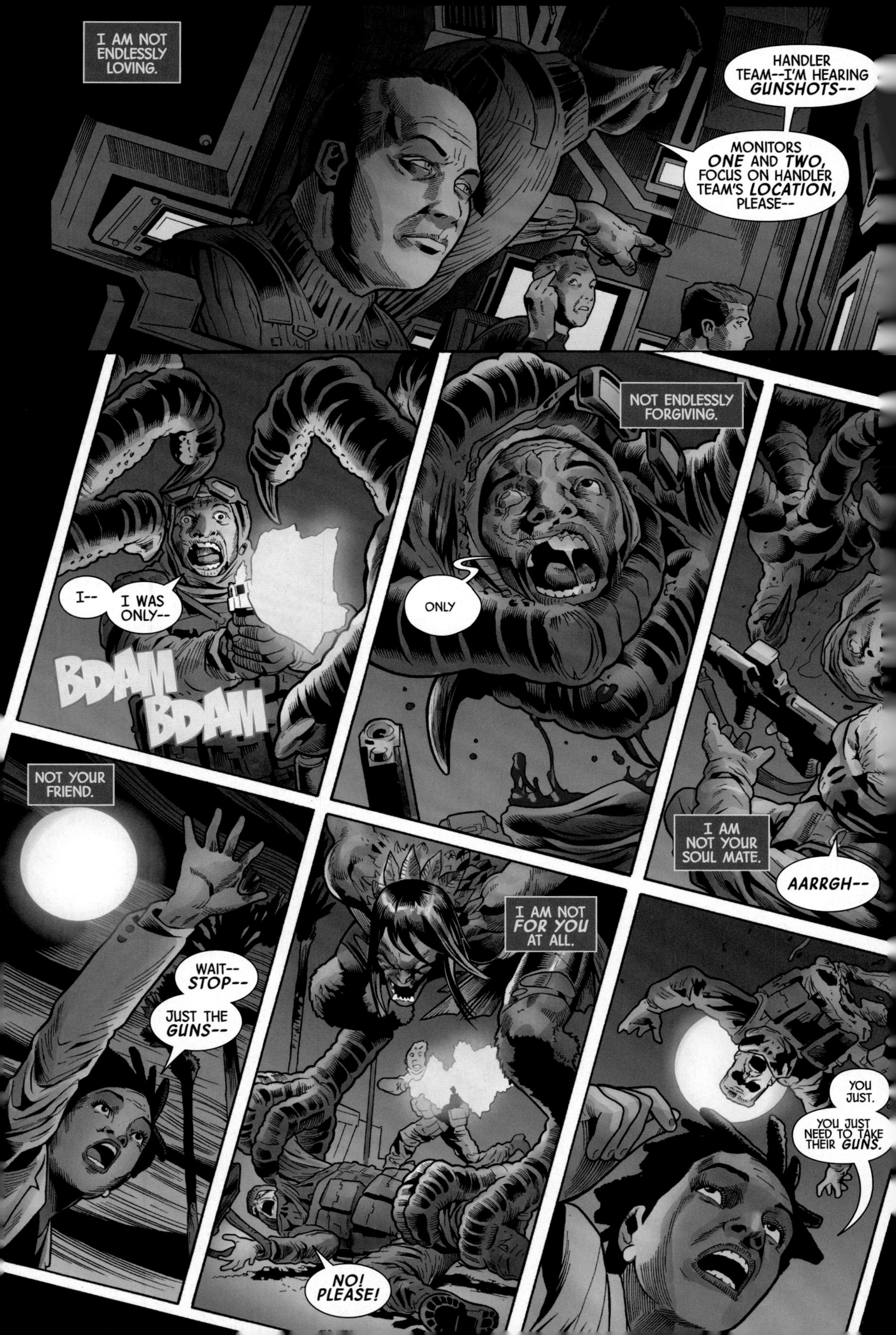

I AM NOT ENDLESSLY LOVING.
HANDLER TEAM--I'M HEARING GUNSHOTS--
MONITORS ONE AND TWO, FOCUS ON HANDLER TEAM'S LOCATION, PLEASE--
I--
I WAS ONLY--
BDAM BDAM
NOT ENDLESSLY FORGIVING.
ONLY
I AM NOT YOUR SOUL MATE.
AARRGH--
NOT YOUR FRIEND.
WAIT-- STOP--
JUST THE GUNS--
I AM NOT FOR YOU AT ALL.
NO! PLEASE!
YOU JUST.
YOU JUST NEED TO TAKE THEIR GUNS.

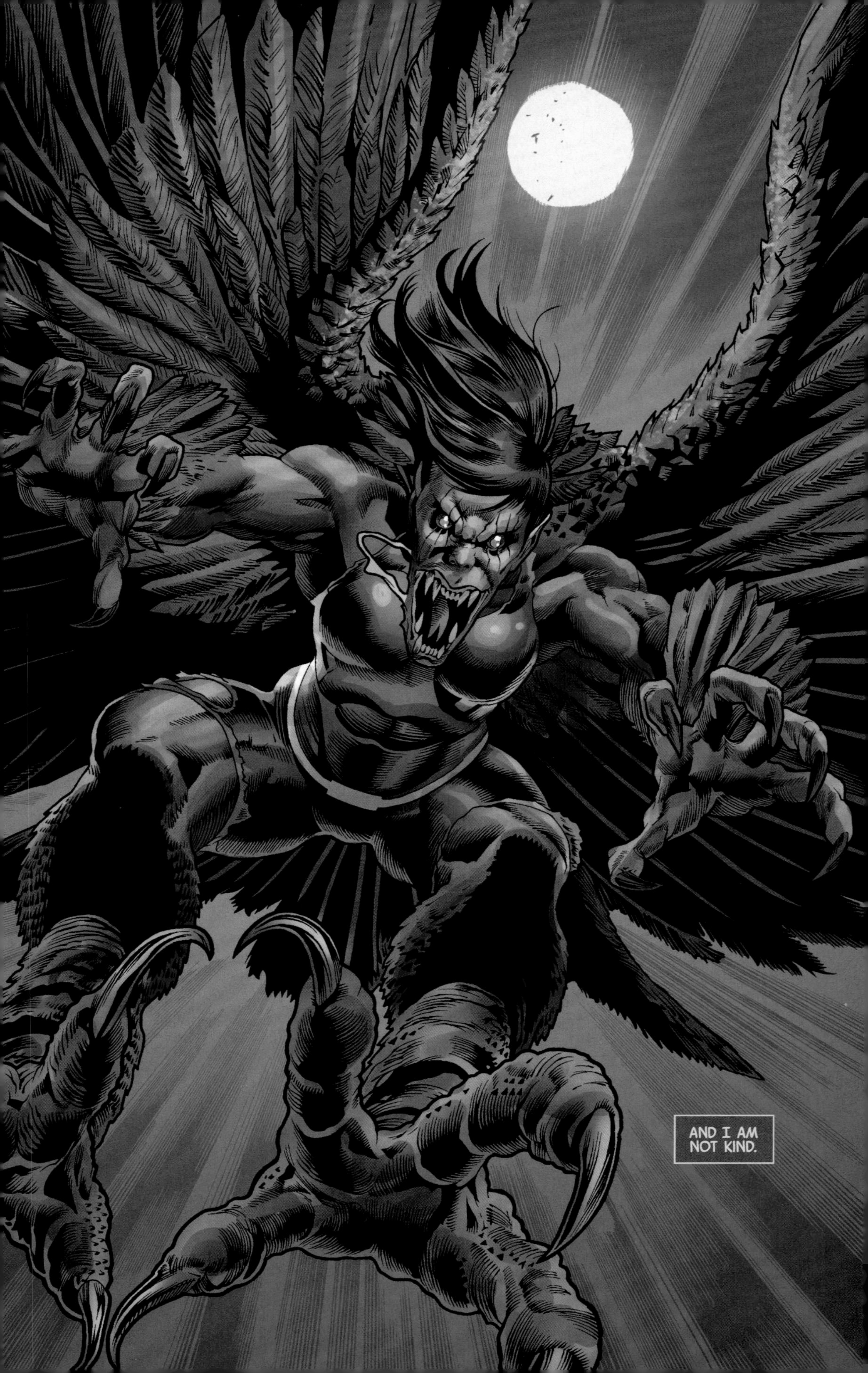
AND I AM
NOT KIND.

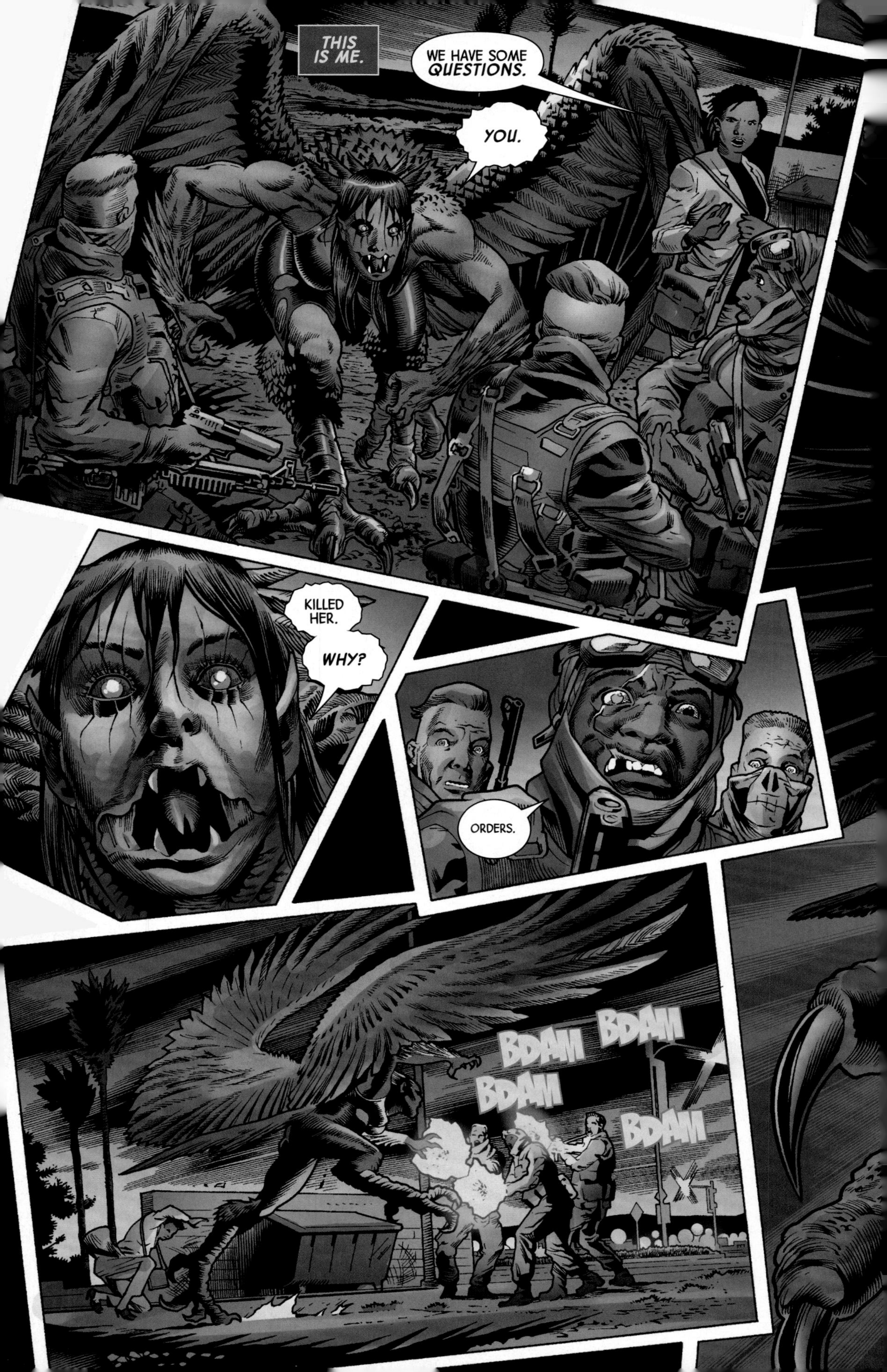
THIS IS ME.
WE HAVE SOME QUESTIONS.
YOU.
KILLED HER.
WHY?
ORDERS.
BDAM BDAM
BDAM
BDAM

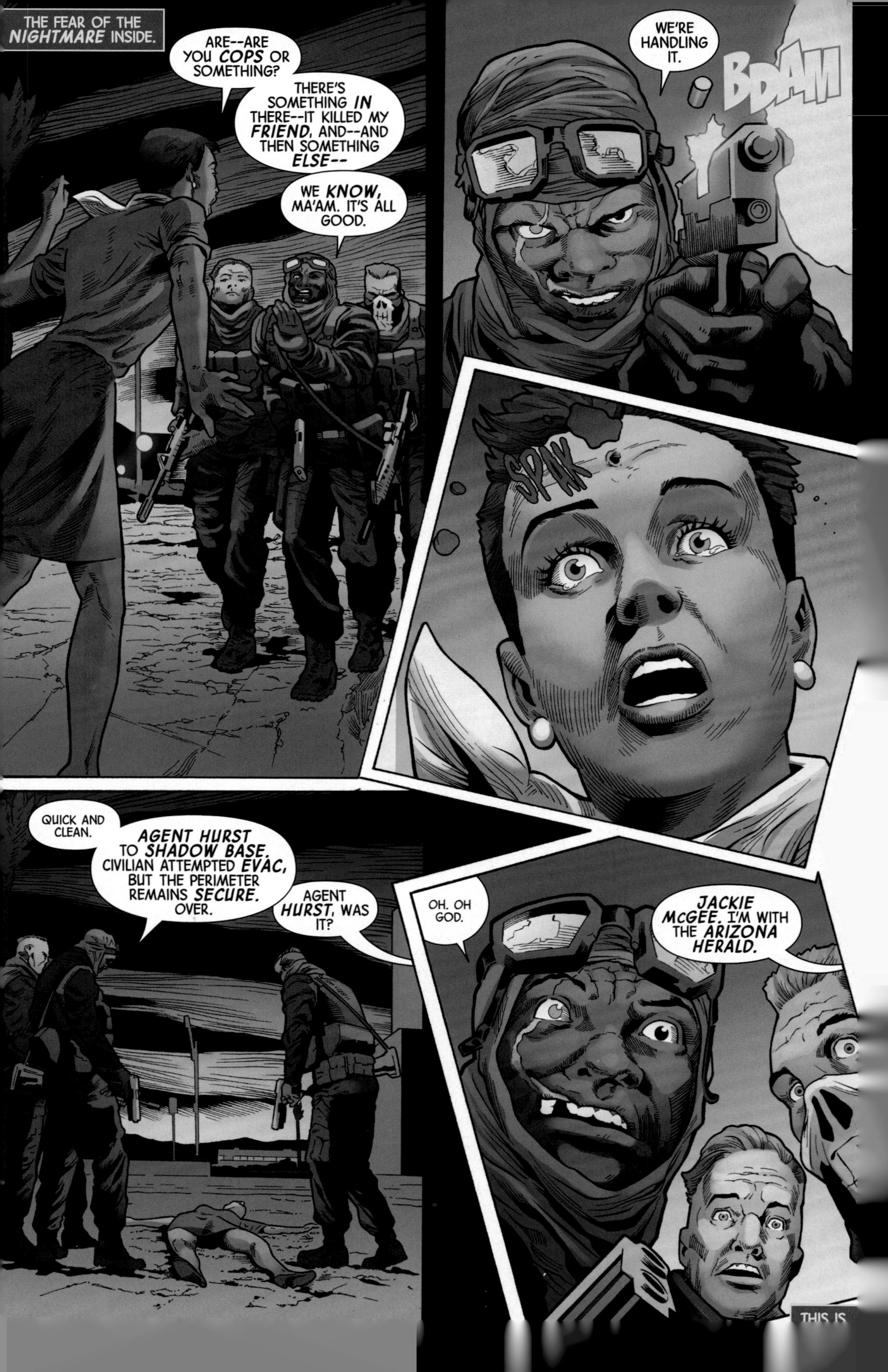

THE FEAR OF THE NIGHTMARE INSIDE.
ARE--ARE YOU COPS OR SOMETHING?
THERE'S SOMETHING IN THERE--IT KILLED MY FRIEND, AND--AND THEN SOMETHING ELSE--
WE KNOW, MA'AM. IT'S ALL GOOD.
WE'RE HANDLING IT.
BDAM
SPAK
QUICK AND CLEAN.
AGENT HURST TO SHADOW BASE. CIVILIAN ATTEMPTED EVAC, BUT THE PERIMETER REMAINS SECURE. OVER.
AGENT HURST, WAS IT?
OH. OH GOD.
JACKIE McGEE. I'M WITH THE ARIZONA HERALD.
THIS IS

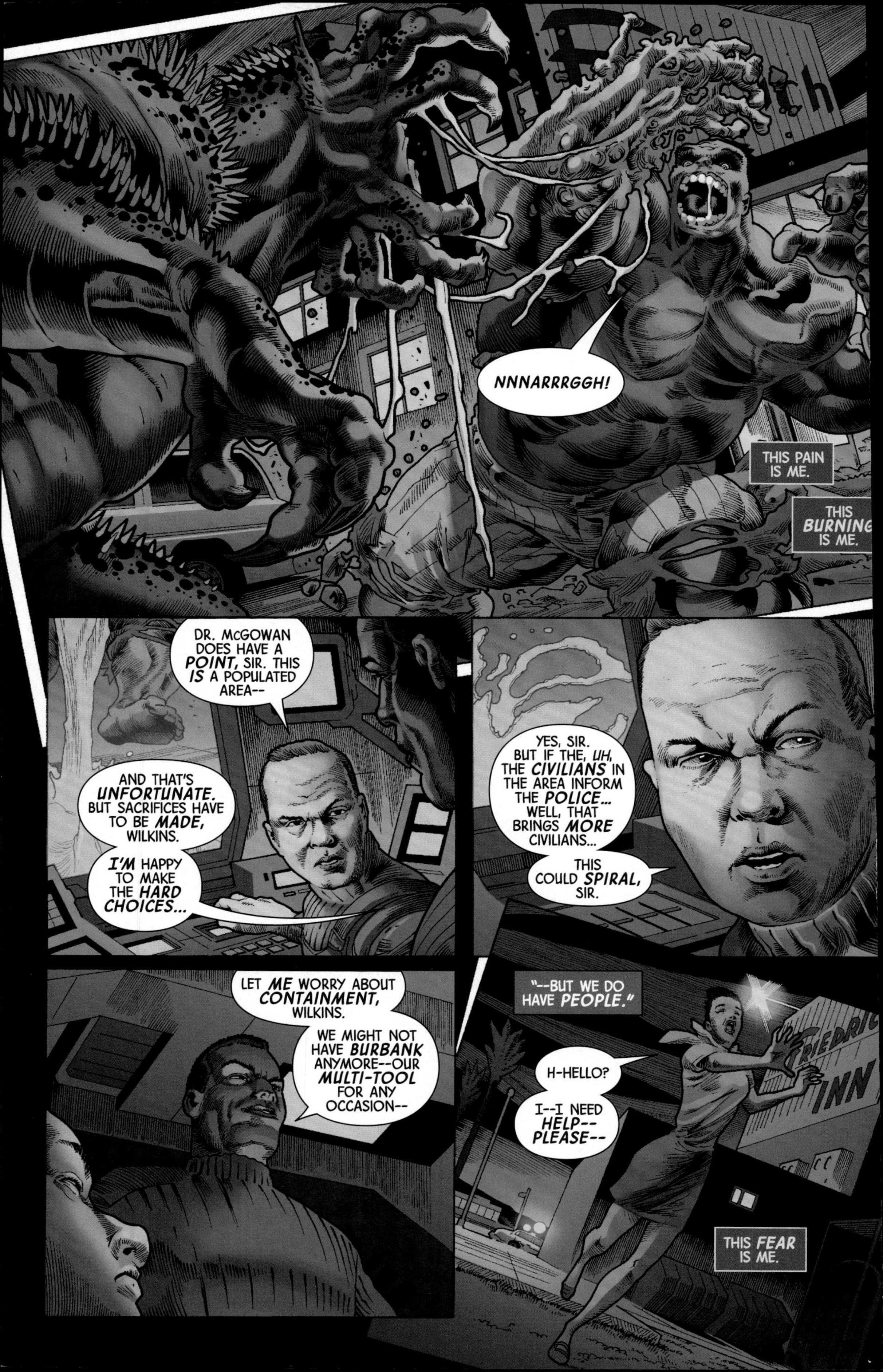

NNNARRRGGH!
THIS PAIN IS ME.
THIS BURNING IS ME.
DR. McGOWAN DOES HAVE A POINT, SIR. THIS IS A POPULATED AREA--
AND THAT'S UNFORTUNATE. BUT SACRIFICES HAVE TO BE MADE, WILKINS.
I'M HAPPY TO MAKE THE HARD CHOICES...
YES, SIR. BUT IF THE, UH, THE CIVILIANS IN THE AREA INFORM THE POLICE... WELL, THAT BRINGS MORE CIVILIANS...
THIS COULD SPIRAL, SIR.
LET ME WORRY ABOUT CONTAINMENT, WILKINS.
WE MIGHT NOT HAVE BURBANK ANYMORE--OUR MULTI-TOOL FOR ANY OCCASION--
"--BUT WE DO HAVE PEOPLE."
H-HELLO?
I--I NEED HELP--PLEASE--
INN
THIS FEAR IS ME.

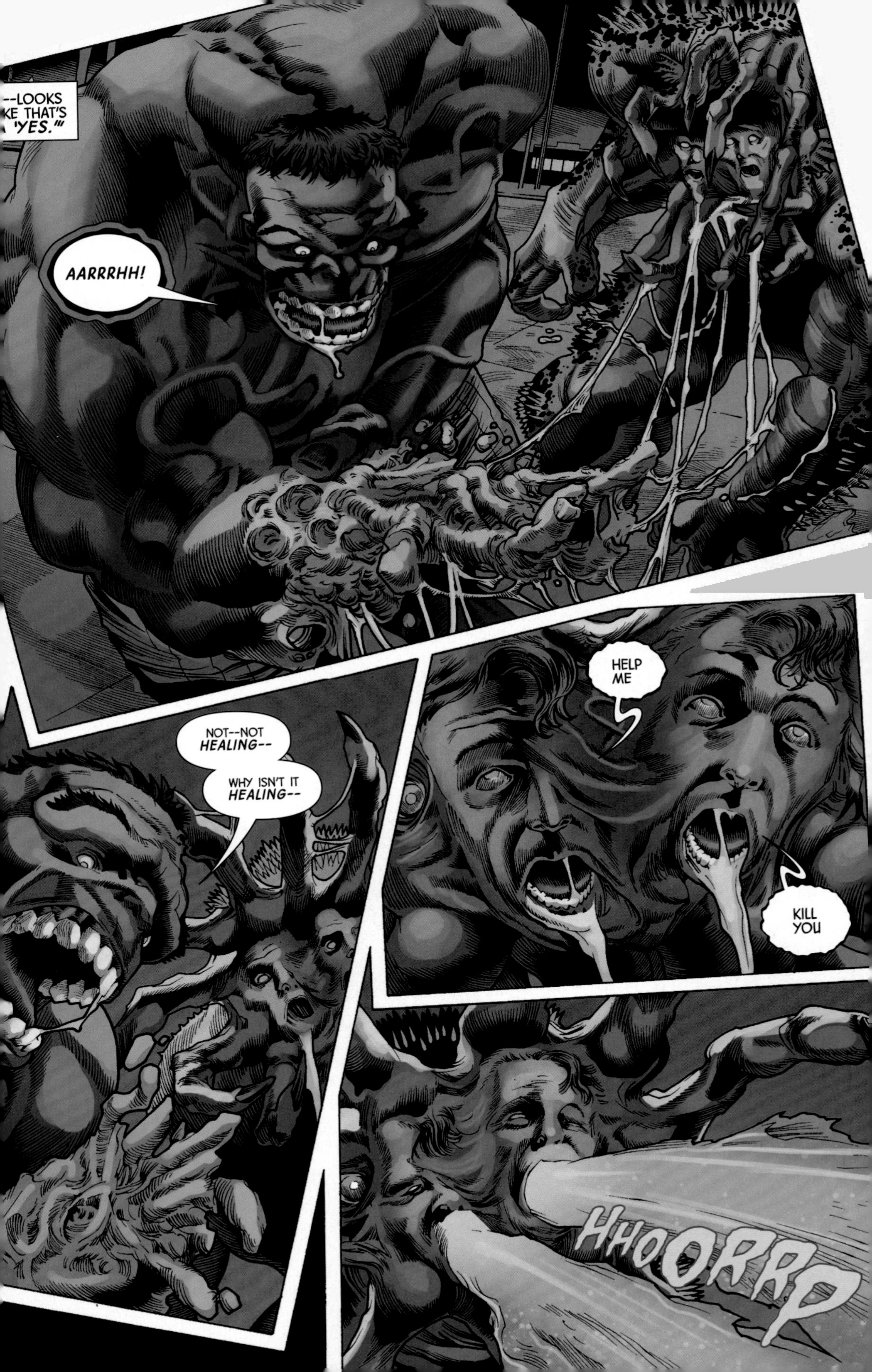
--LOOKS
KE THAT'S
'YES.'"
AARRRHH!
NOT--NOT
HEALING--
WHY ISN'T IT
HEALING--
HELP
ME
KILL
YOU
HHOORRP

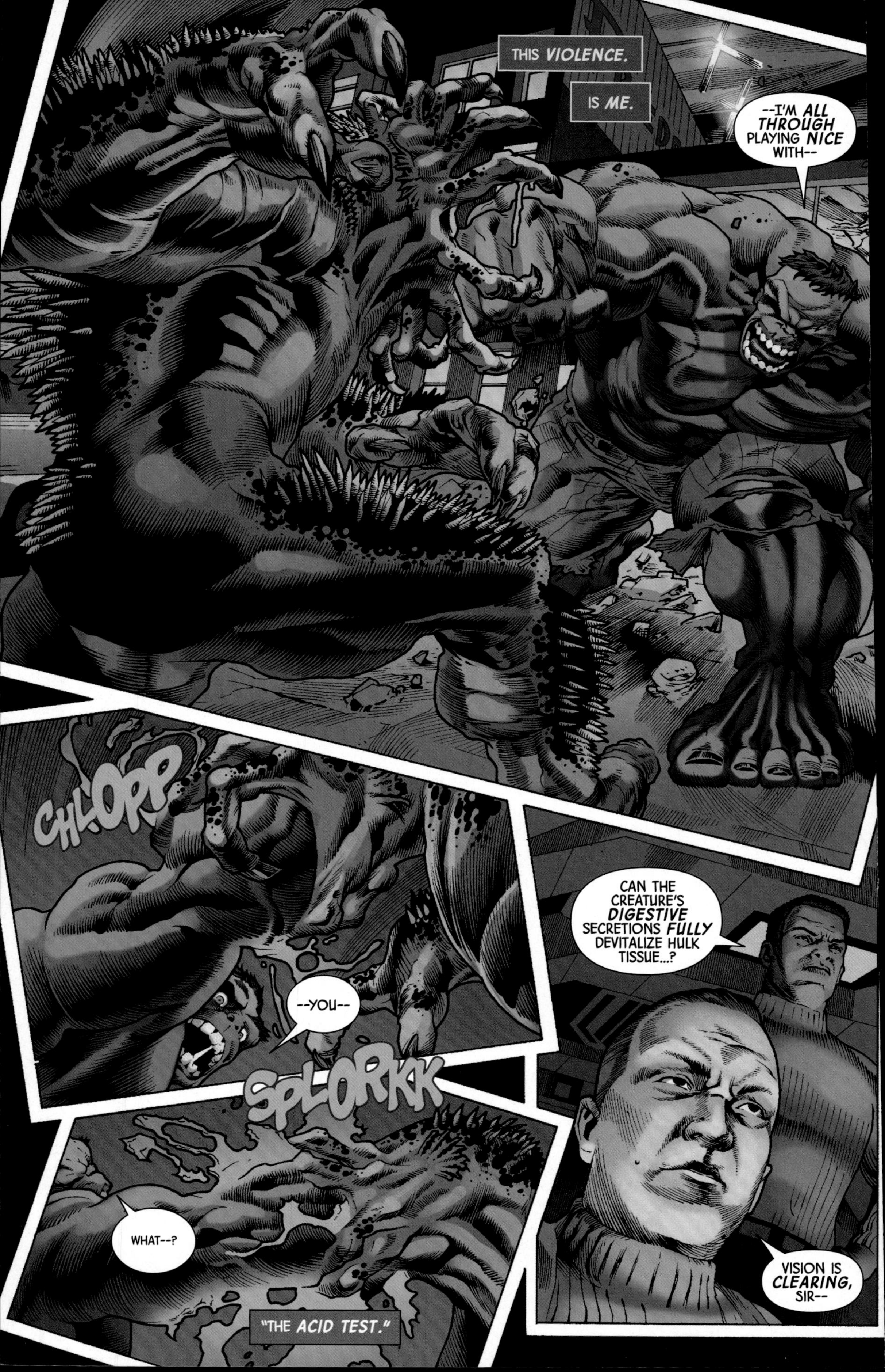
THIS VIOLENCE.
IS ME.
--I'M ALL THROUGH PLAYING NICE WITH--
CHLOPP
--YOU--
SPLORKK
WHAT--?
"THE ACID TEST."
CAN THE CREATURE'S DIGESTIVE SECRETIONS FULLY DEVITALIZE HULK TISSUE...?
VISION IS CLEARING, SIR--

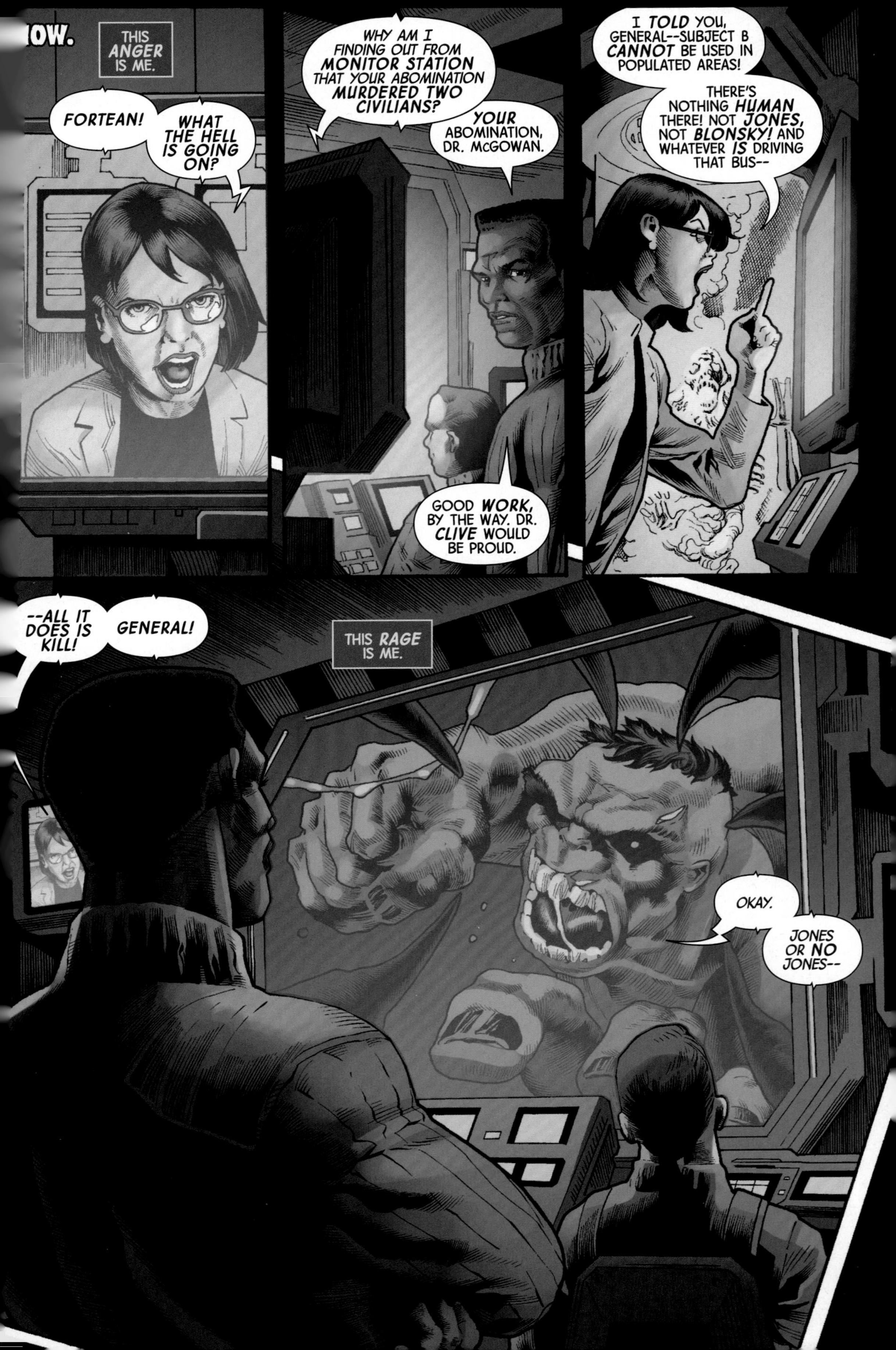

NOW.
THIS ANGER IS ME.
FORTEAN!
WHAT THE HELL IS GOING ON?
WHY AM I FINDING OUT FROM MONITOR STATION THAT YOUR ABOMINATION MURDERED TWO CIVILIANS?
YOUR ABOMINATION, DR. McGOWAN.
GOOD WORK, BY THE WAY. DR. CLIVE WOULD BE PROUD.
I TOLD YOU, GENERAL--SUBJECT B CANNOT BE USED IN POPULATED AREAS!
THERE'S NOTHING HUMAN THERE! NOT JONES, NOT BLONSKY! AND WHATEVER IS DRIVING THAT BUS--
--ALL IT DOES IS KILL!
GENERAL!
THIS RAGE IS ME.
OKAY.
JONES OR NO JONES--

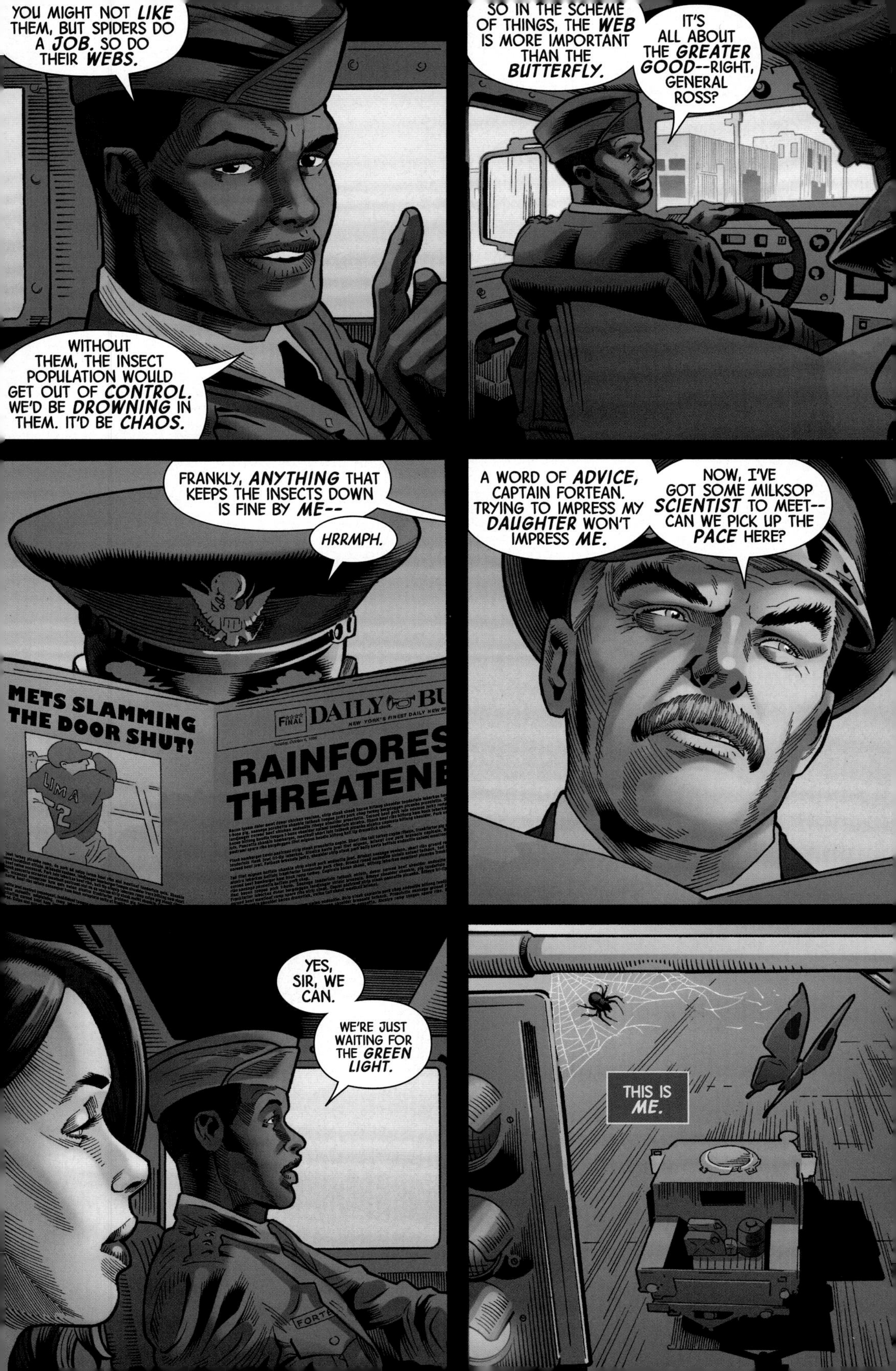
YOU MIGHT NOT LIKE THEM, BUT SPIDERS DO A JOB. SO DO THEIR WEBS.
WITHOUT THEM, THE INSECT POPULATION WOULD GET OUT OF CONTROL. WE'D BE DROWNING IN THEM. IT'D BE CHAOS.
SO IN THE SCHEME OF THINGS, THE WEB IS MORE IMPORTANT THAN THE BUTTERFLY.
IT'S ALL ABOUT THE GREATER GOOD--RIGHT, GENERAL ROSS?
FRANKLY, ANYTHING THAT KEEPS THE INSECTS DOWN IS FINE BY ME--
HRRMPH.
METS SLAMMING THE DOOR SHUT!
LIMA
FINAL
DAILY BU
NEW YORK'S FINEST DAILY NEW
RAINFORES
THREATENE
A WORD OF ADVICE, CAPTAIN FORTEAN. TRYING TO IMPRESS MY DAUGHTER WON'T IMPRESS ME.
NOW, I'VE GOT SOME MILKSOP SCIENTIST TO MEET-- CAN WE PICK UP THE PACE HERE?
YES, SIR, WE CAN.
WE'RE JUST WAITING FOR THE GREEN LIGHT.
FORTE
THIS IS ME.

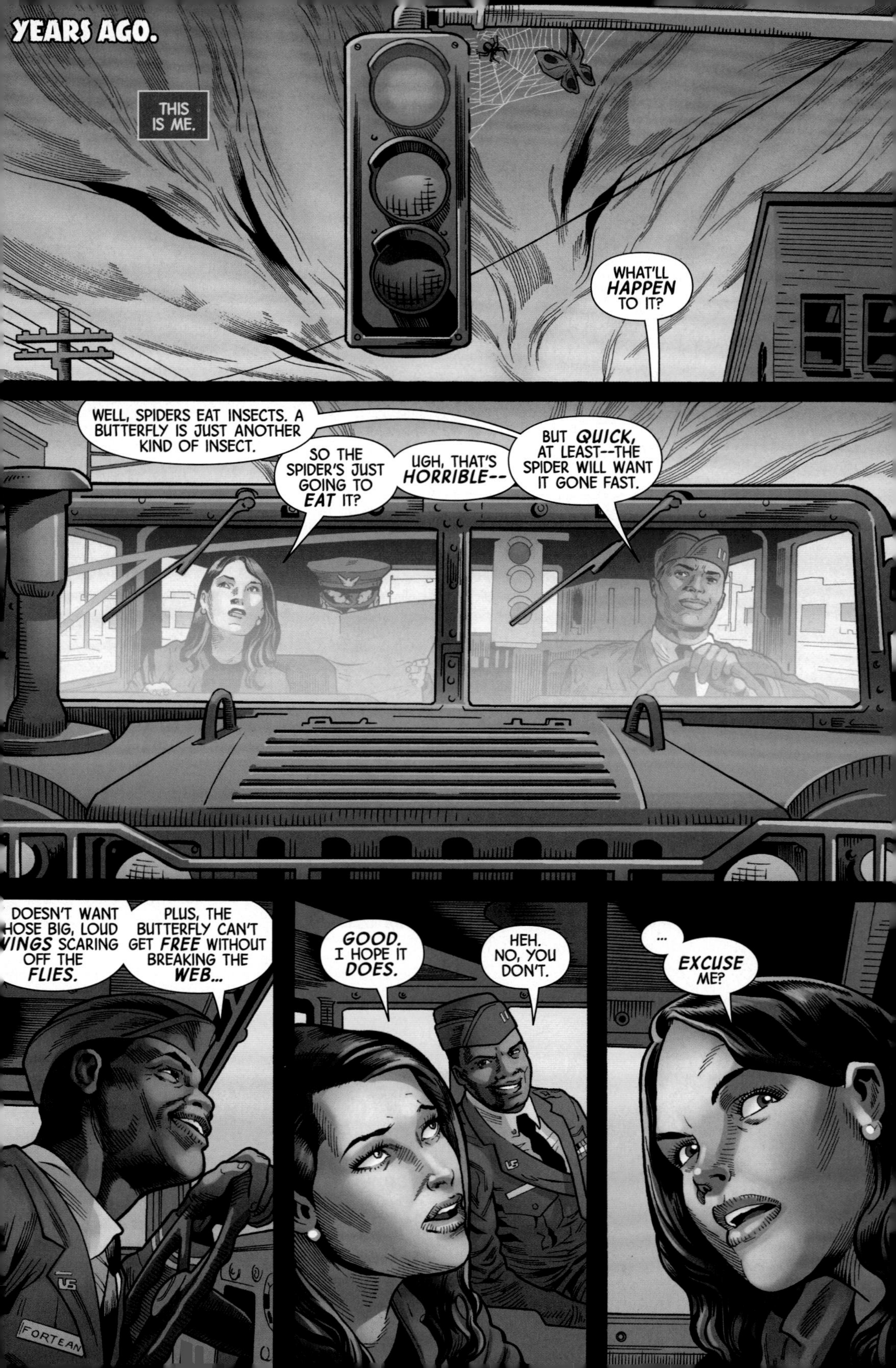
YEARS AGO.
THIS IS ME.
WHAT'LL HAPPEN TO IT?
WELL, SPIDERS EAT INSECTS. A BUTTERFLY IS JUST ANOTHER KIND OF INSECT.
SO THE SPIDER'S JUST GOING TO EAT IT?
UGH, THAT'S HORRIBLE--
BUT QUICK, AT LEAST--THE SPIDER WILL WANT IT GONE FAST.
DOESN'T WANT HOSE BIG, LOUD VINGS SCARING OFF THE FLIES.
PLUS, THE BUTTERFLY CAN'T GET FREE WITHOUT BREAKING THE WEB...
FORTEAN
GOOD. I HOPE IT DOES.
HEH. NO, YOU DON'T.
...
EXCUSE ME?

19

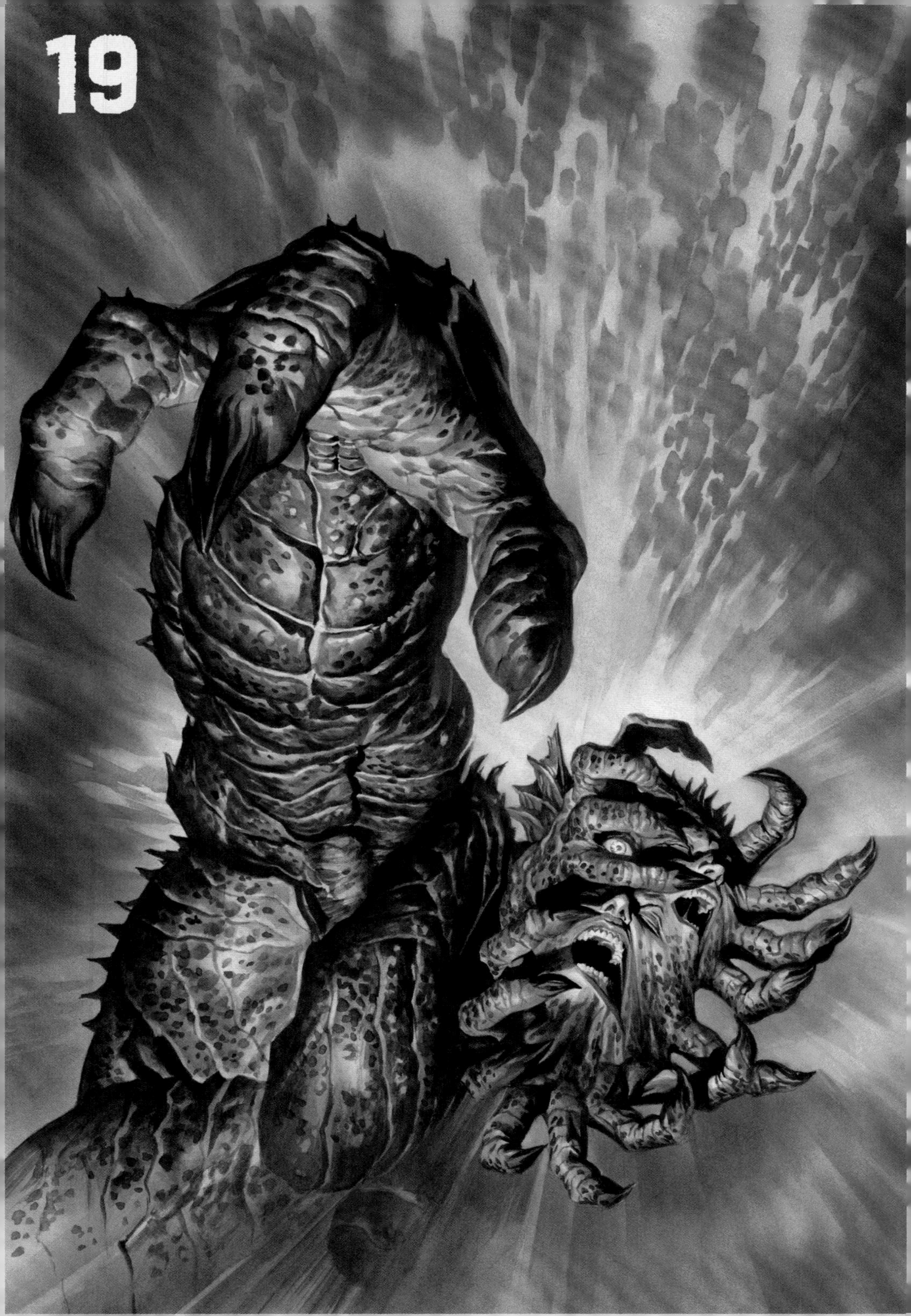

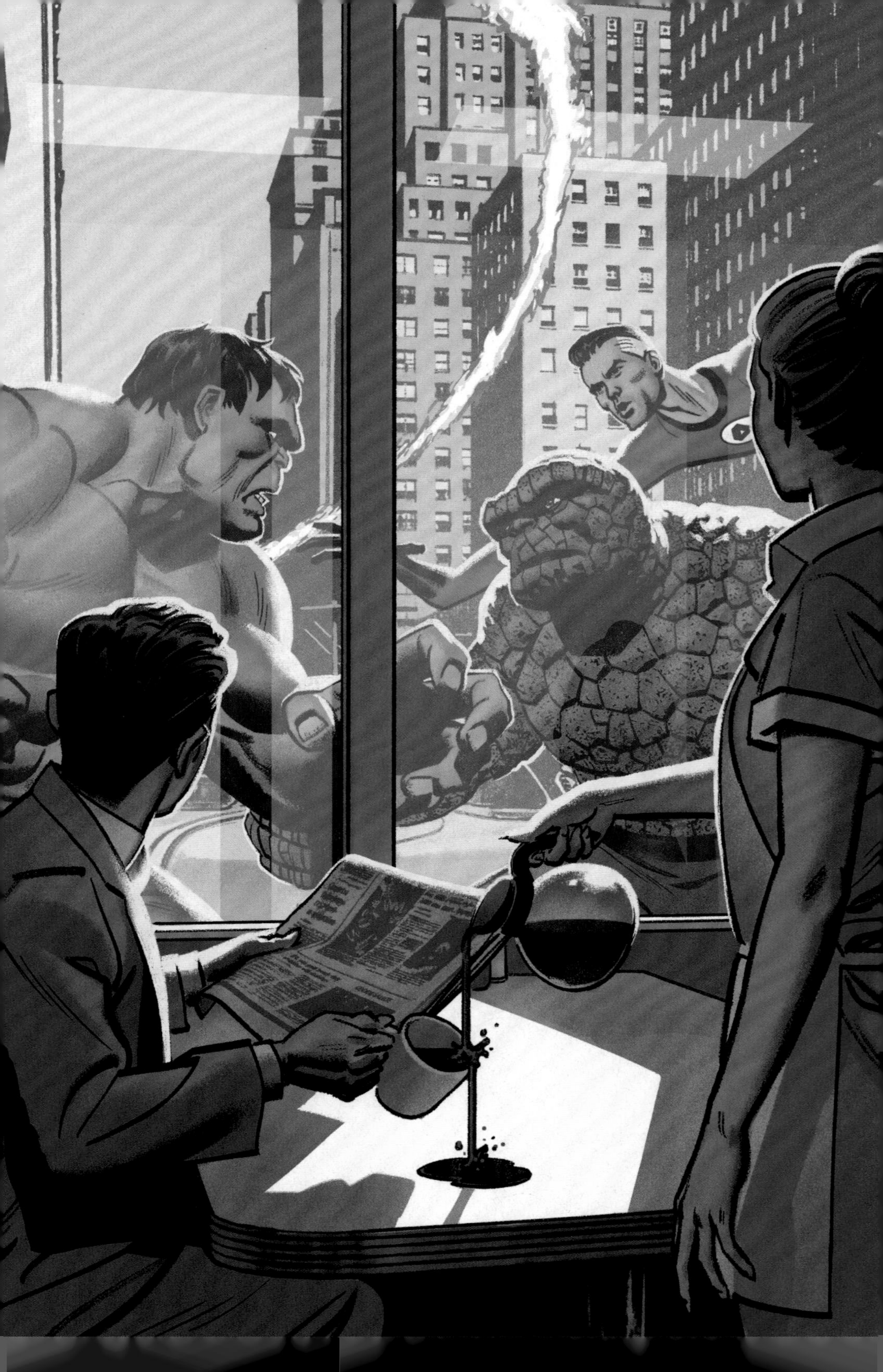

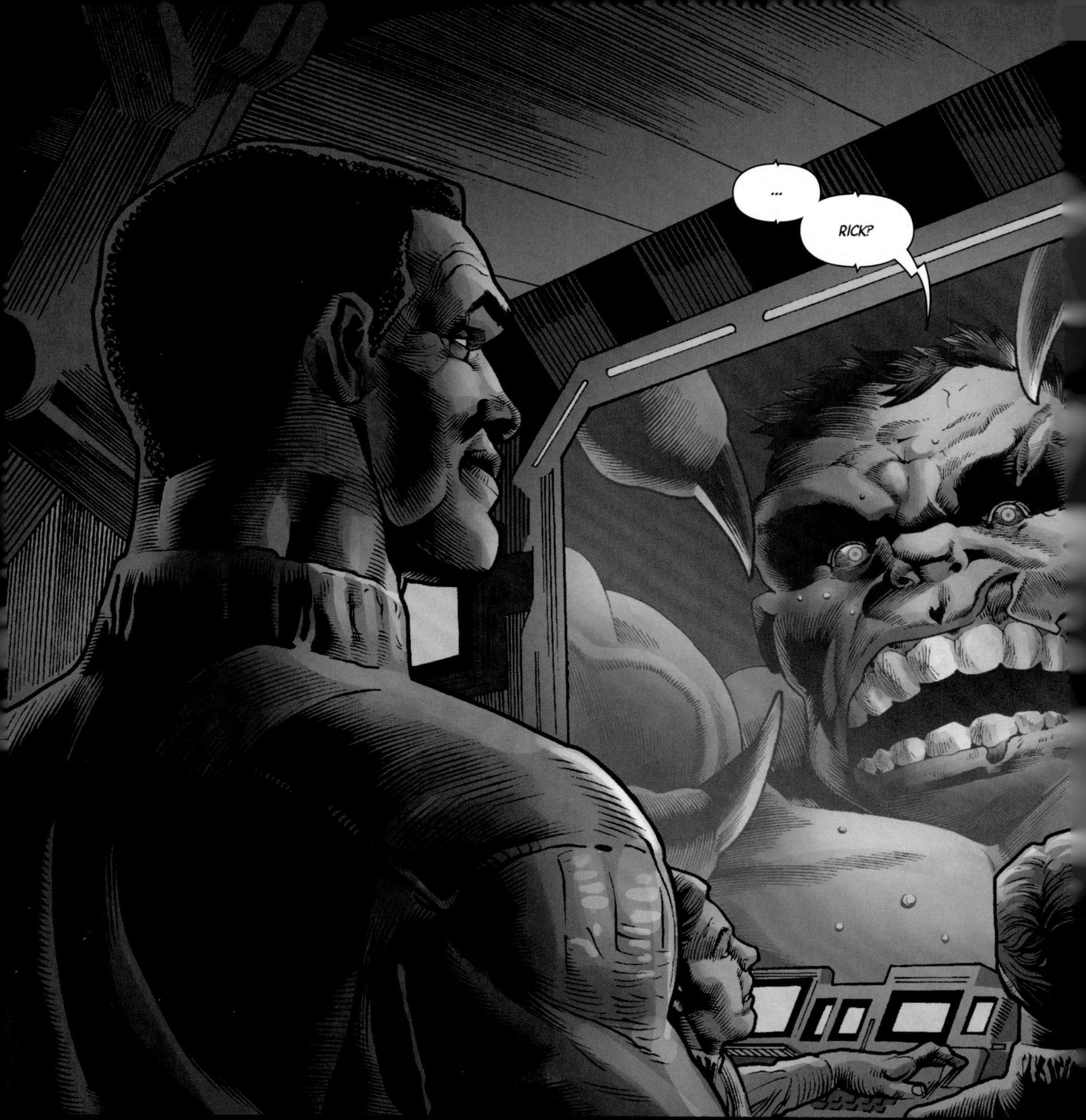
...
RICK?

NECESSARY

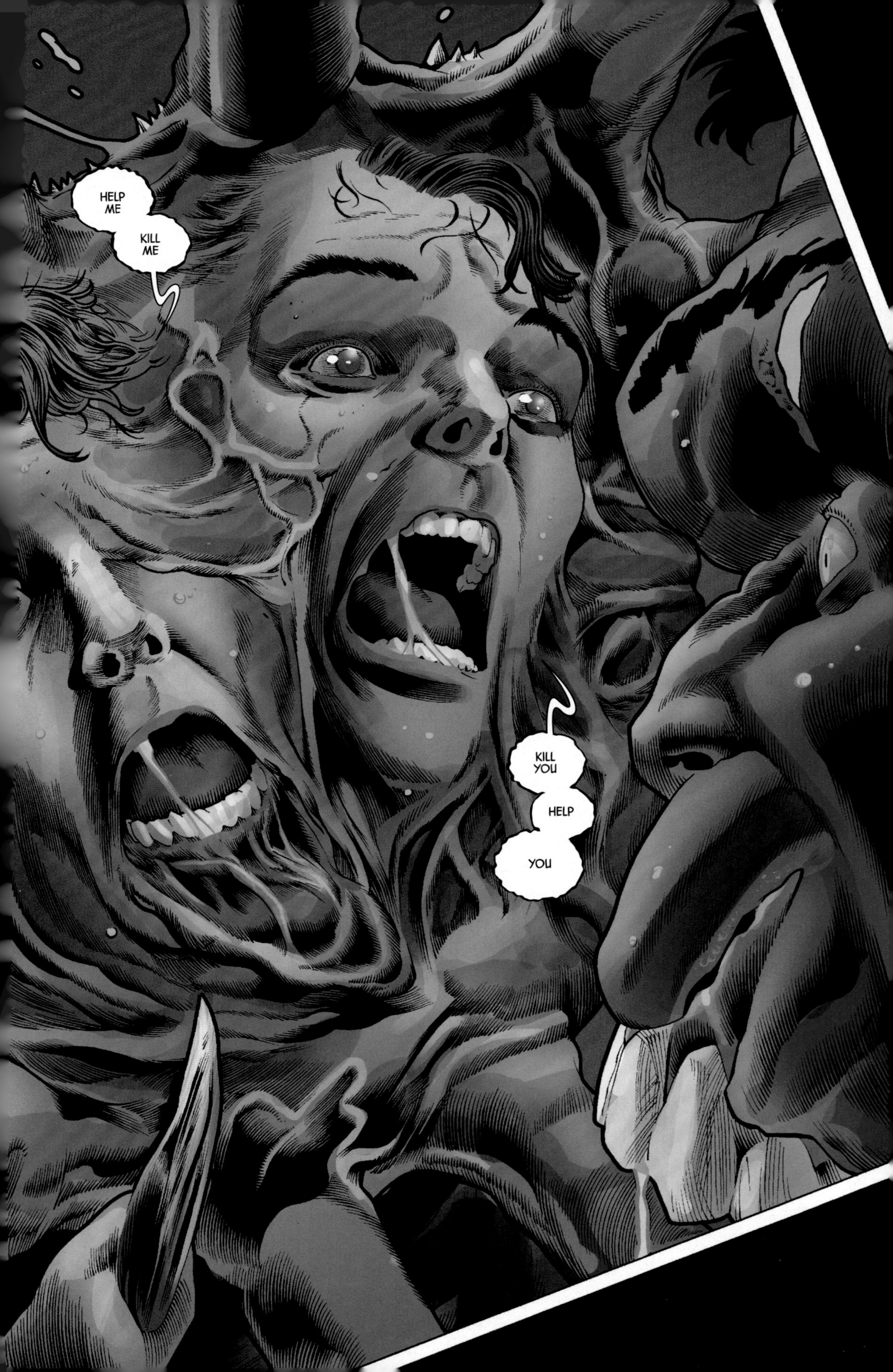
HELP ME
KILL ME
KILL YOU
HELP
YOU

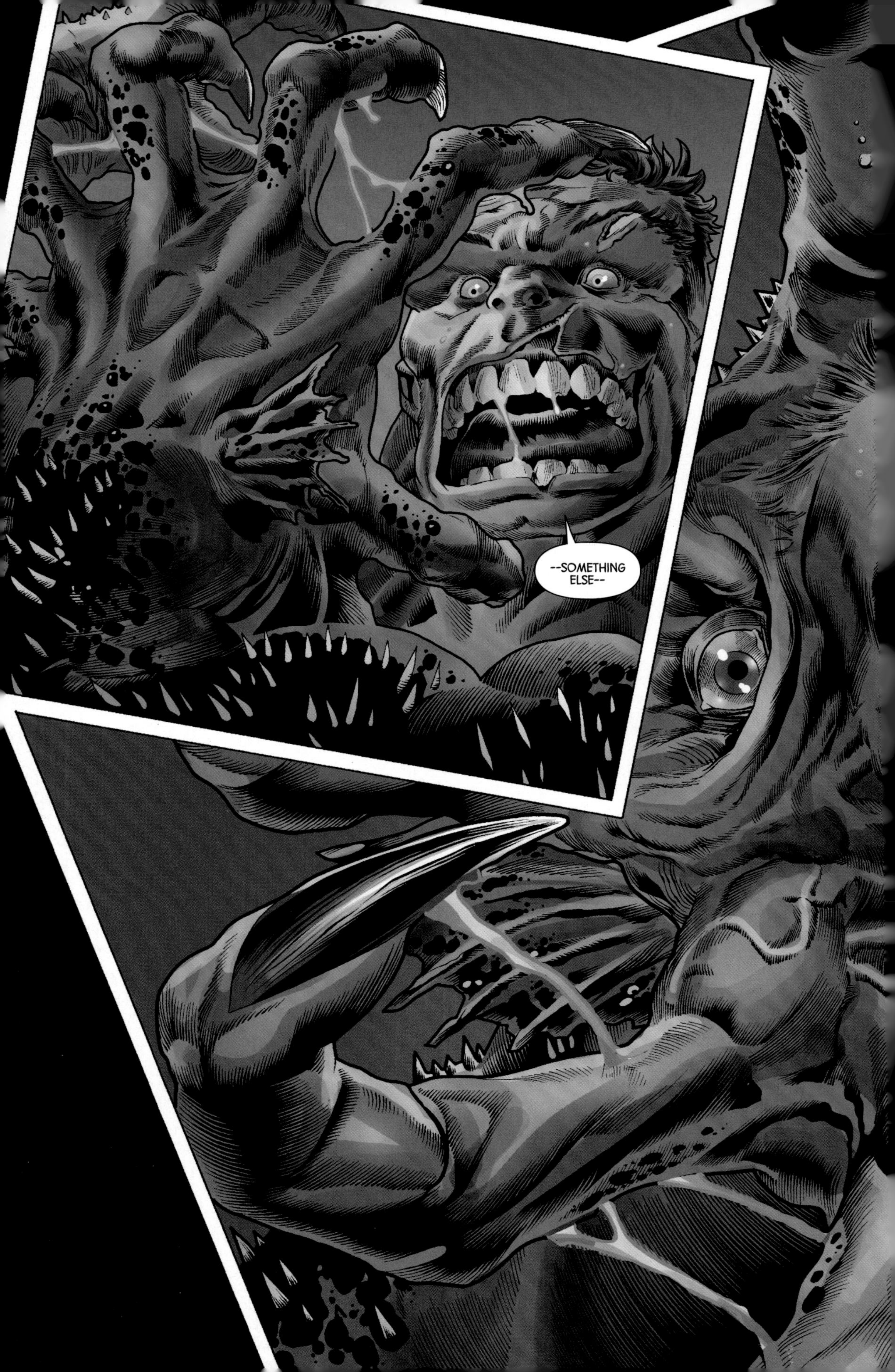
--SOMETHING ELSE--

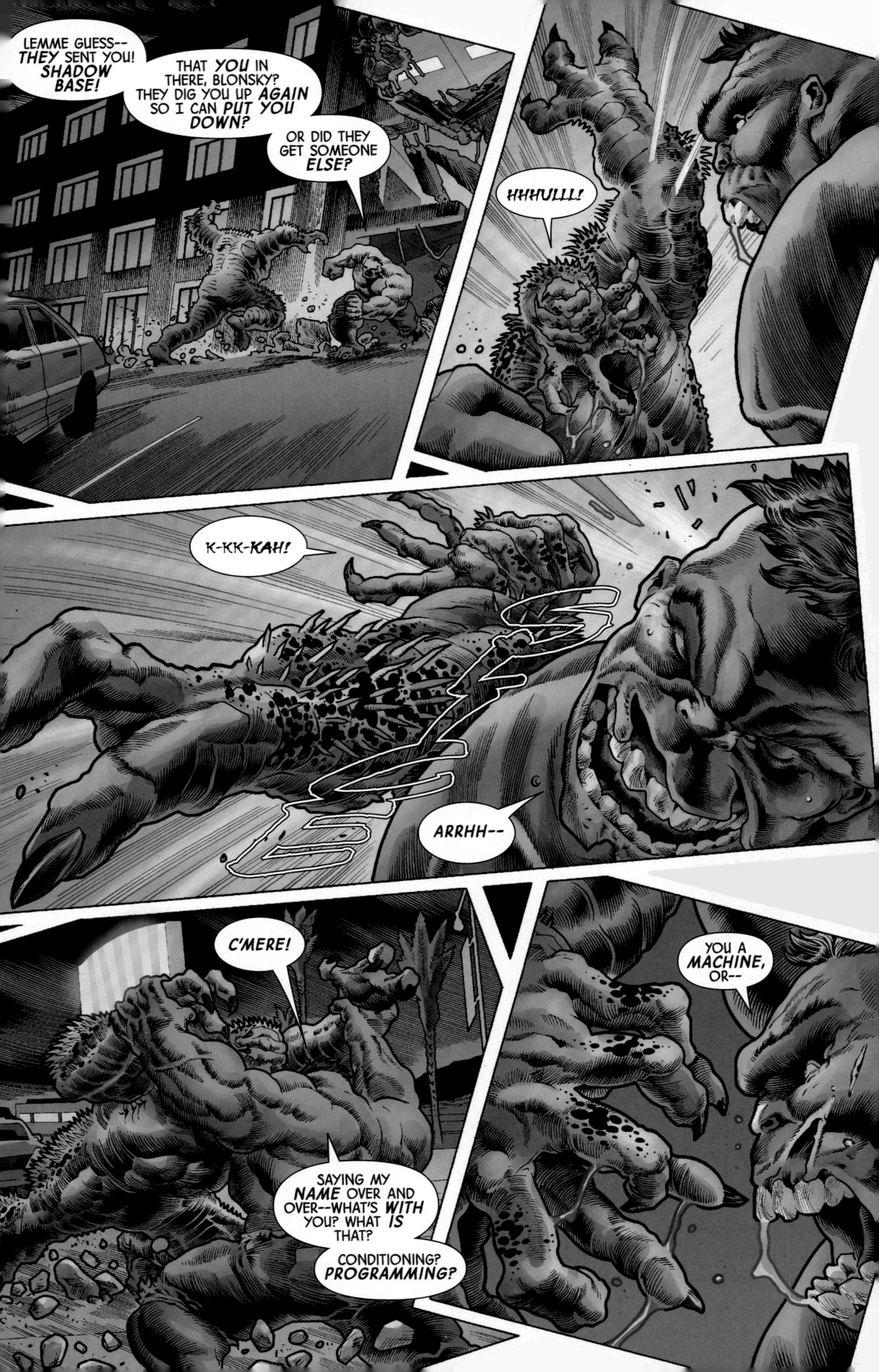
LEMME GUESS-- THEY SENT YOU! SHADOW BASE!
THAT YOU IN THERE, BLONSKY? THEY DIG YOU UP AGAIN SO I CAN PUT YOU DOWN?
OR DID THEY GET SOMEONE ELSE?
HHHULLL!
K-KK-KAH!
ARRHH--
C'MERE!
SAYING MY NAME OVER AND OVER--WHAT'S WITH YOU? WHAT IS THAT?
CONDITIONING? PROGRAMMING?
YOU A MACHINE, OR--

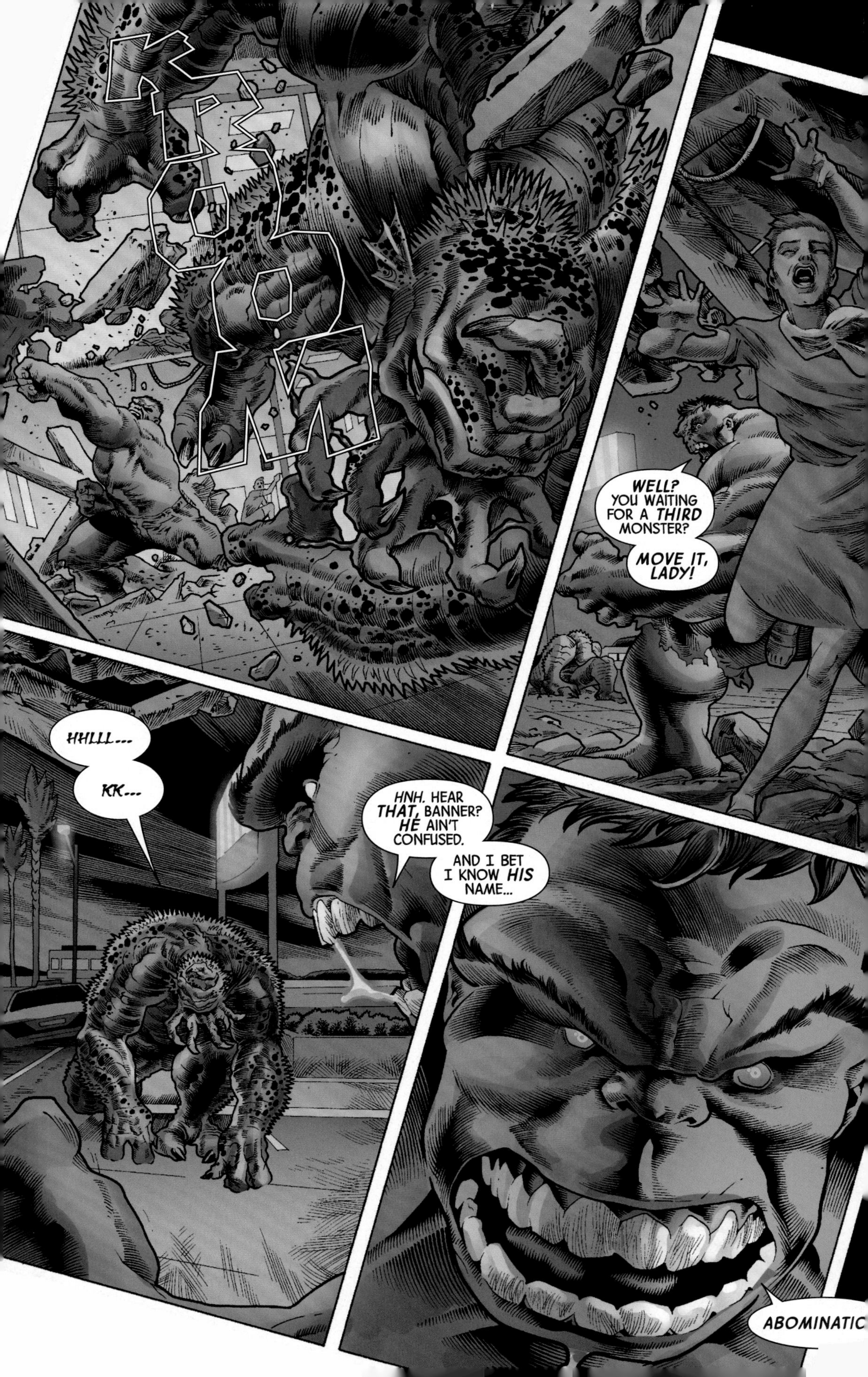
KRAKOOM
WELL? YOU WAITING FOR A THIRD MONSTER?
MOVE IT, LADY!
HHLLL...
KK...
HNH. HEAR THAT, BANNER? HE AIN'T CONFUSED.
AND I BET I KNOW HIS NAME...
ABOMINATIC

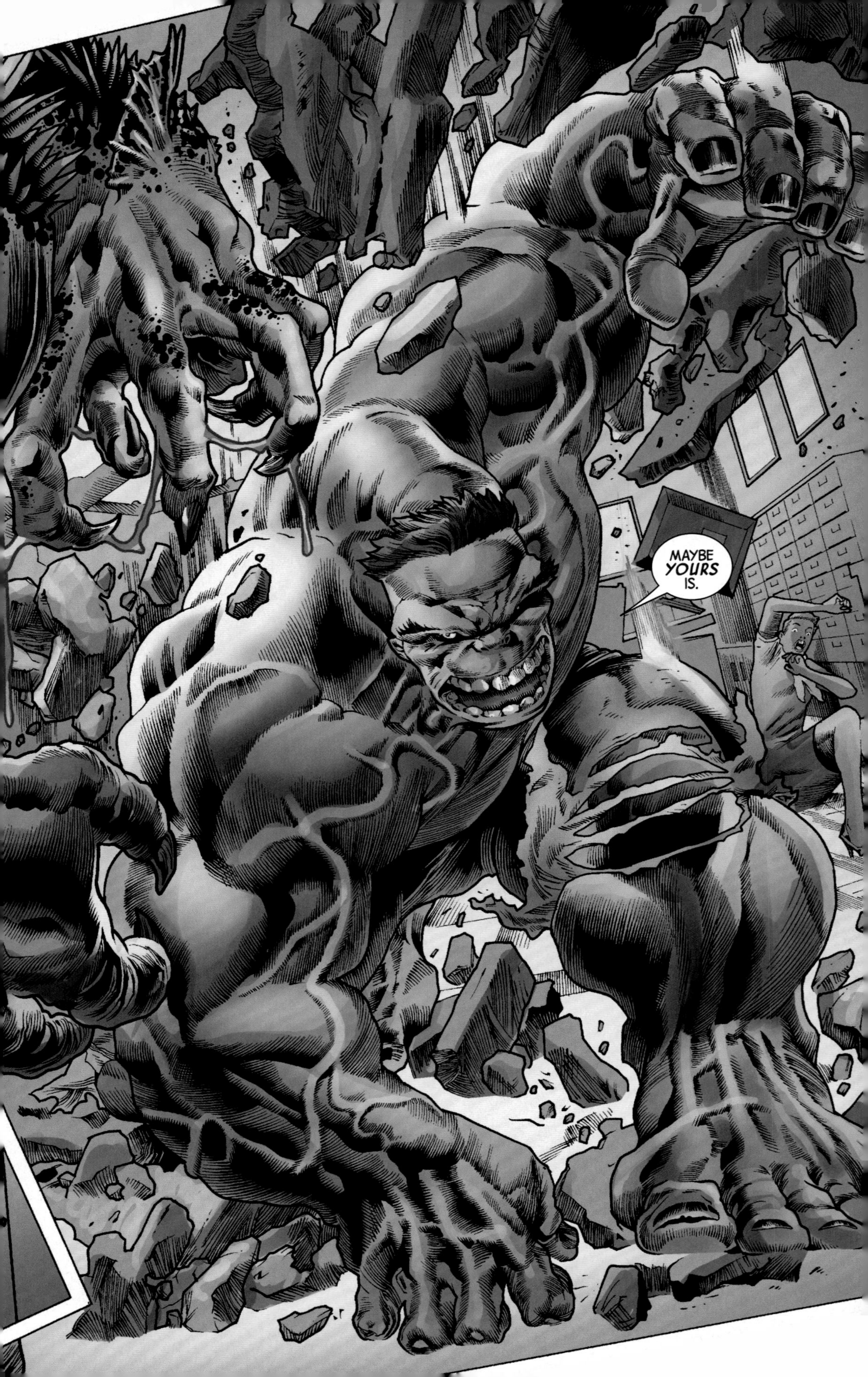
MAYBE YOURS IS.

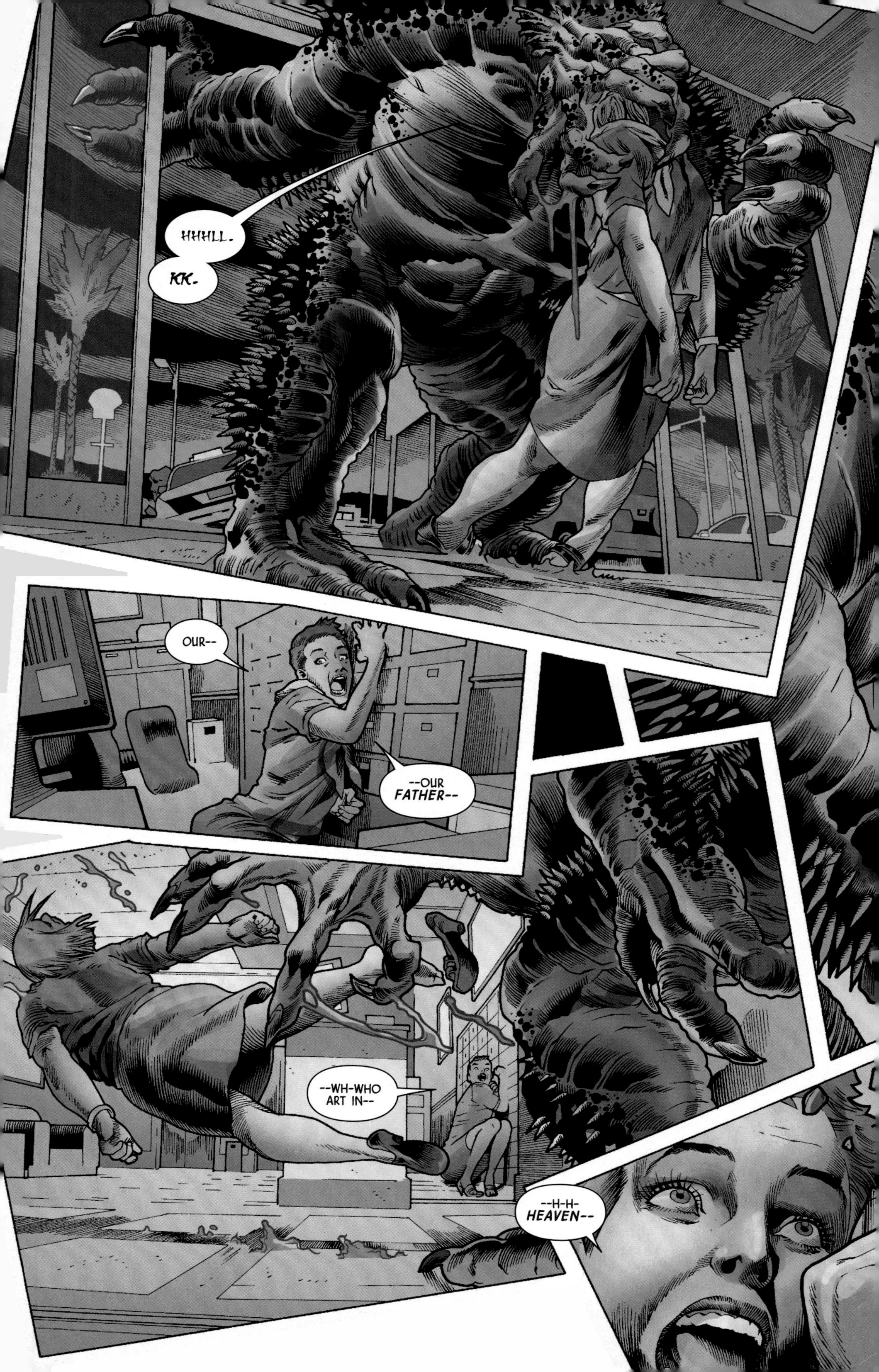
HHHLL.
KK.
OUR--
--OUR FATHER--
--WH-WHO ART IN--
--H-H- HEAVEN--

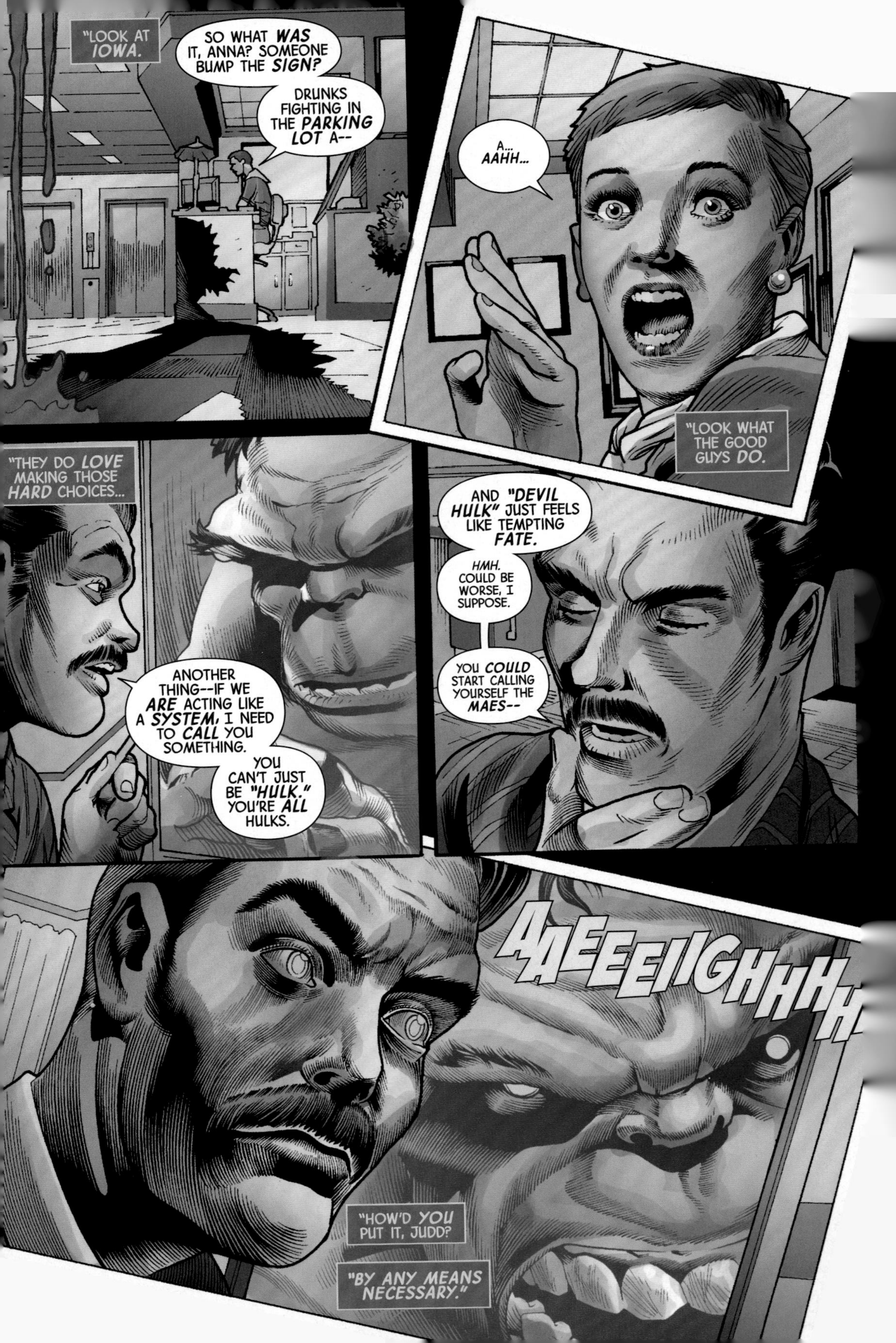
"LOOK AT IOWA.
SO WHAT WAS IT, ANNA? SOMEONE BUMP THE SIGN?
DRUNKS FIGHTING IN THE PARKING LOT A--
A... AAHH...
"LOOK WHAT THE GOOD GUYS DO.
"THEY DO LOVE MAKING THOSE HARD CHOICES...
ANOTHER THING--IF WE ARE ACTING LIKE A SYSTEM, I NEED TO CALL YOU SOMETHING.
YOU CAN'T JUST BE "HULK." YOU'RE ALL HULKS.
AND "DEVIL HULK" JUST FEELS LIKE TEMPTING FATE.
HMH. COULD BE WORSE, I SUPPOSE.
YOU COULD START CALLING YOURSELF THE MAES--
AAEEEIIGHHHH
"HOW'D YOU PUT IT, JUDD?
"BY ANY MEANS NECESSARY."

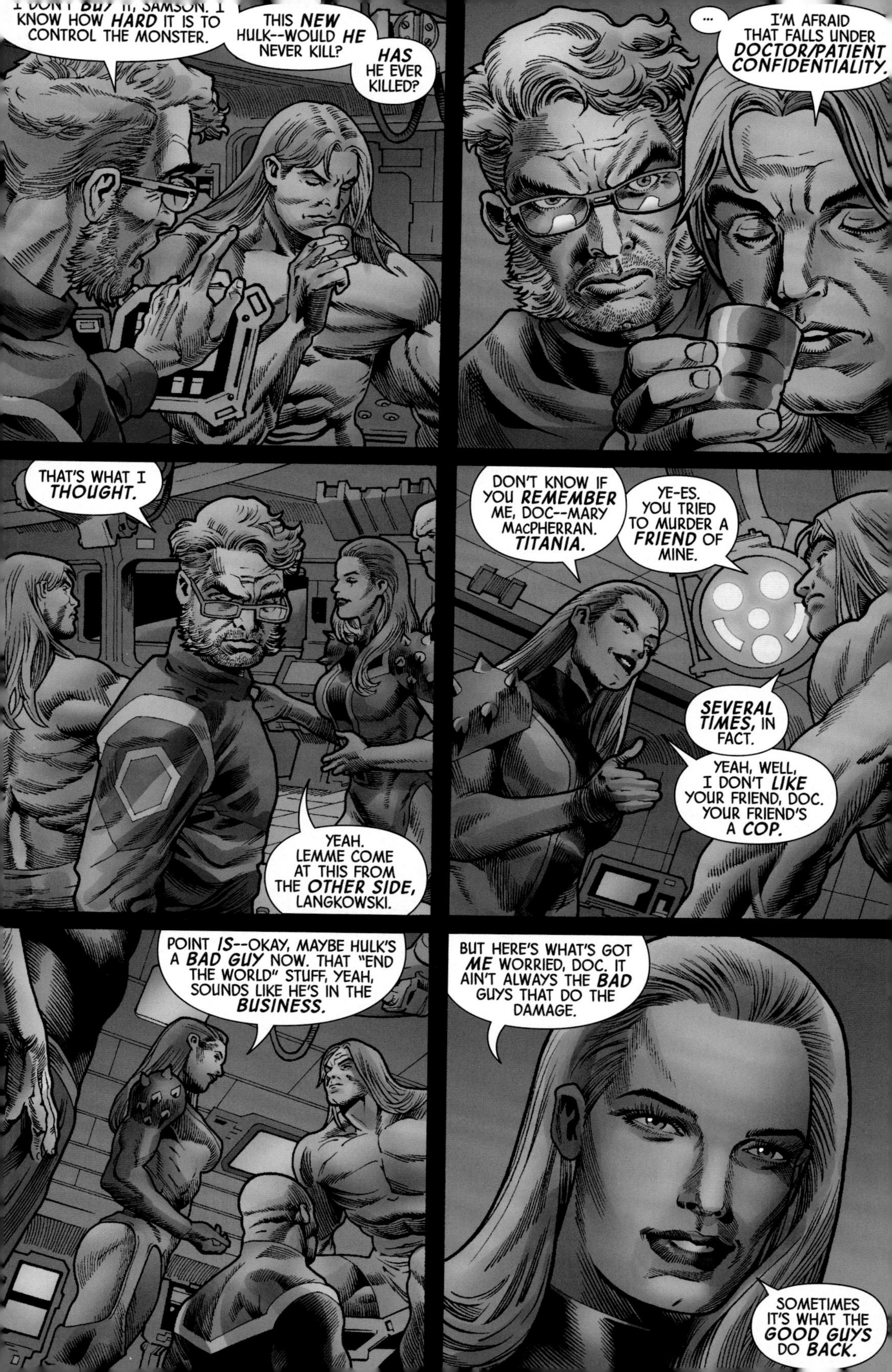
I DON'T BUY IT, SAMSON. I KNOW HOW HARD IT IS TO CONTROL THE MONSTER.
THIS NEW HULK--WOULD HE NEVER KILL?
HAS HE EVER KILLED?
...
I'M AFRAID THAT FALLS UNDER DOCTOR/PATIENT CONFIDENTIALITY.
THAT'S WHAT I THOUGHT.
YEAH. LEMME COME AT THIS FROM THE OTHER SIDE, LANGKOWSKI.
DON'T KNOW IF YOU REMEMBER ME, DOC--MARY MacPHERRAN. TITANIA.
YE-ES. YOU TRIED TO MURDER A FRIEND OF MINE.
SEVERAL TIMES, IN FACT.
YEAH, WELL, I DON'T LIKE YOUR FRIEND, DOC. YOUR FRIEND'S A COP.
POINT IS--OKAY, MAYBE HULK'S A BAD GUY NOW. THAT "END THE WORLD" STUFF, YEAH, SOUNDS LIKE HE'S IN THE BUSINESS.
BUT HERE'S WHAT'S GOT ME WORRIED, DOC. IT AIN'T ALWAYS THE BAD GUYS THAT DO THE DAMAGE.
SOMETIMES IT'S WHAT THE GOOD GUYS DO BACK.

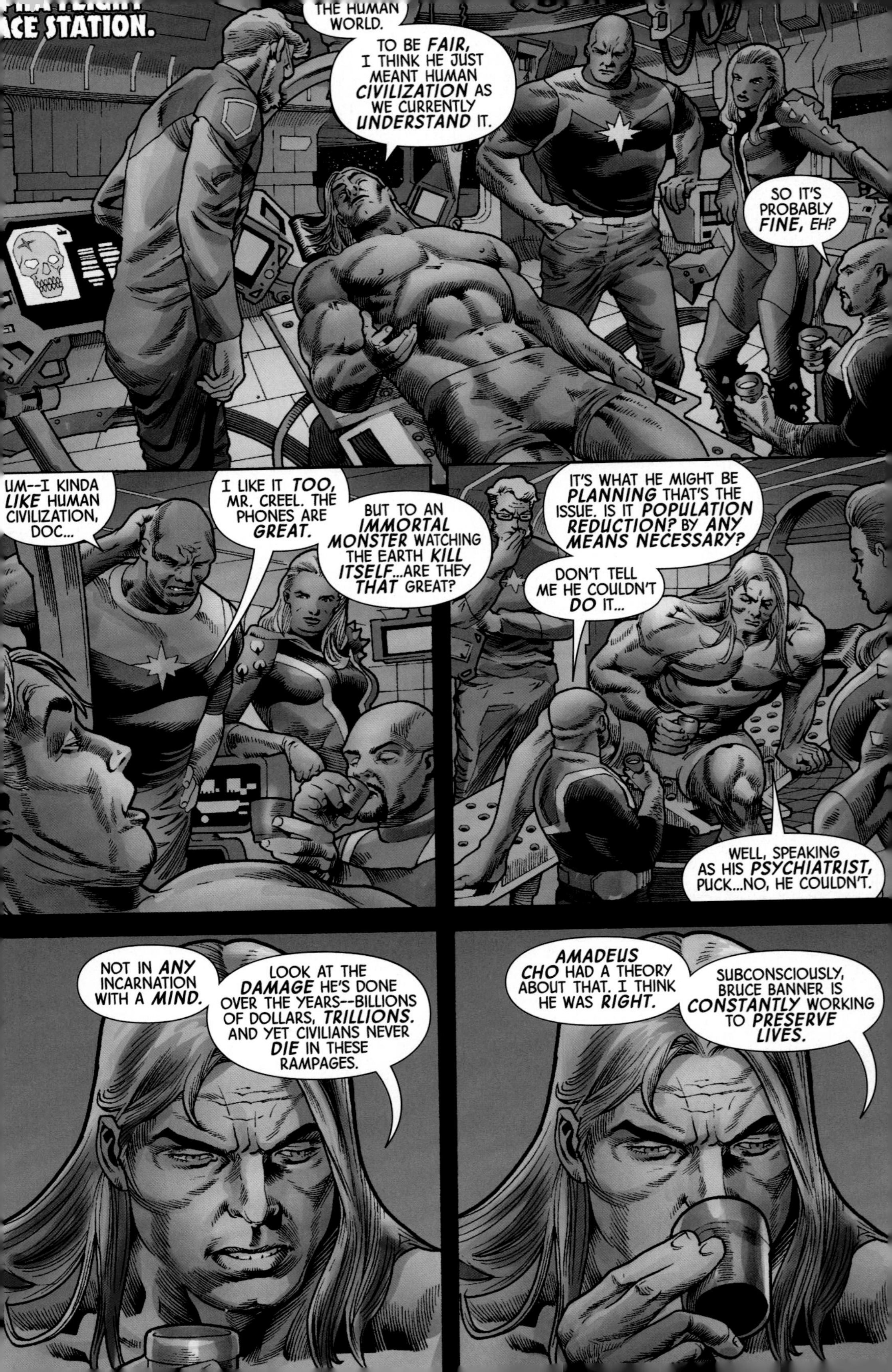
...ACE STATION.
THE HUMAN WORLD.
TO BE FAIR, I THINK HE JUST MEANT HUMAN CIVILIZATION AS WE CURRENTLY UNDERSTAND IT.
SO IT'S PROBABLY FINE, EH?
UM--I KINDA LIKE HUMAN CIVILIZATION, DOC...
I LIKE IT TOO, MR. CREEL. THE PHONES ARE GREAT.
BUT TO AN IMMORTAL MONSTER WATCHING THE EARTH KILL ITSELF...ARE THEY THAT GREAT?
IT'S WHAT HE MIGHT BE PLANNING THAT'S THE ISSUE. IS IT POPULATION REDUCTION? BY ANY MEANS NECESSARY?
DON'T TELL ME HE COULDN'T DO IT...
WELL, SPEAKING AS HIS PSYCHIATRIST, PUCK...NO, HE COULDN'T.
NOT IN ANY INCARNATION WITH A MIND.
LOOK AT THE DAMAGE HE'S DONE OVER THE YEARS--BILLIONS OF DOLLARS, TRILLIONS. AND YET CIVILIANS NEVER DIE IN THESE RAMPAGES.
AMADEUS CHO HAD A THEORY ABOUT THAT. I THINK HE WAS RIGHT.
SUBCONSCIOUSLY, BRUCE BANNER IS CONSTANTLY WORKING TO PRESERVE LIVES.

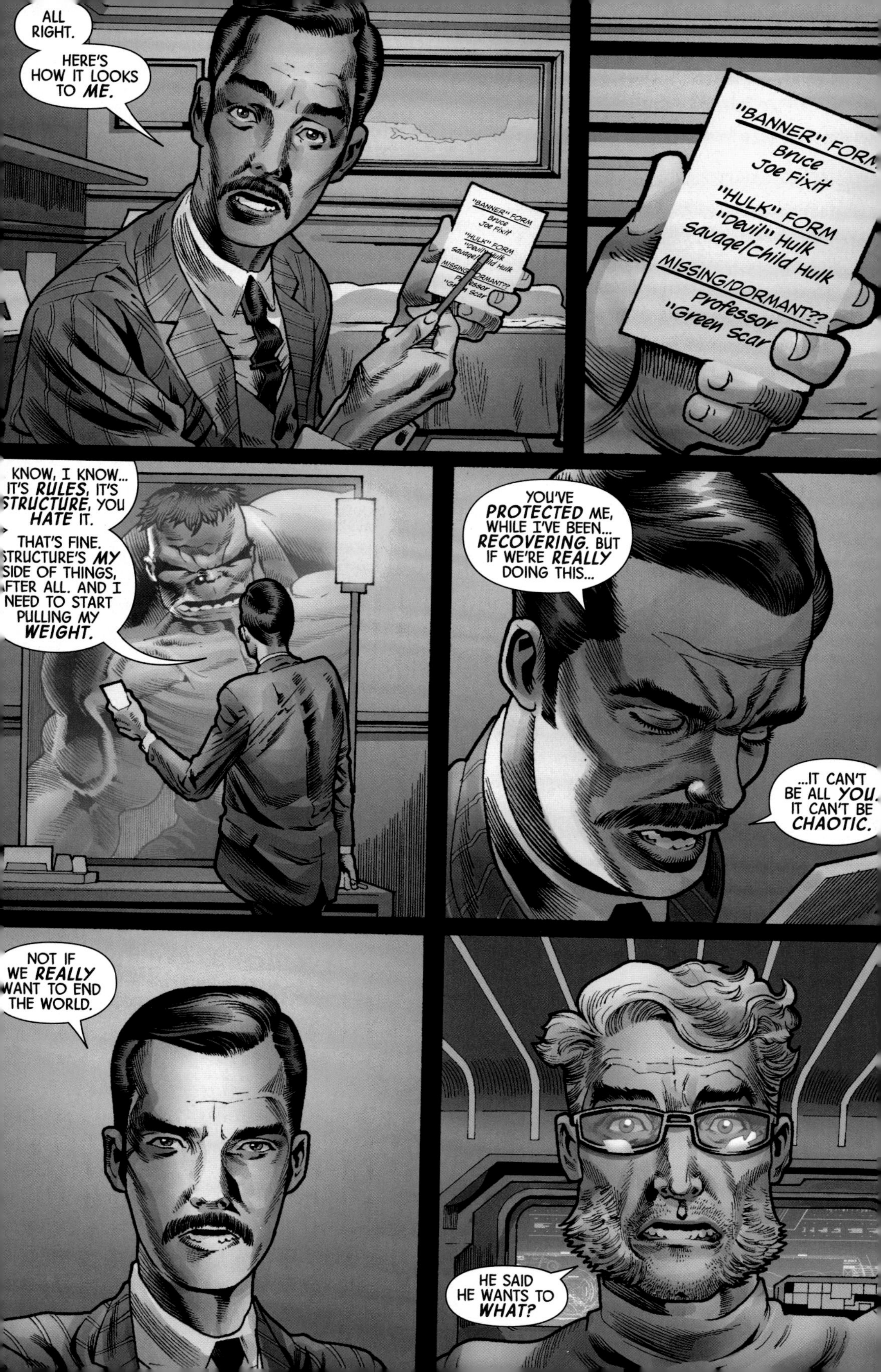
ALL RIGHT.
HERE'S HOW IT LOOKS TO ME.
"BANNER" FORM
Bruce
Joe Fixit
"HULK" FORM
"Devil" Hulk
Savage/Child Hulk
MISSING/DORMANT??
Professor
"Green Scar
KNOW, I KNOW... IT'S RULES, IT'S STRUCTURE, YOU HATE IT.
THAT'S FINE. STRUCTURE'S MY SIDE OF THINGS, AFTER ALL. AND I NEED TO START PULLING MY WEIGHT.
YOU'VE PROTECTED ME, WHILE I'VE BEEN... RECOVERING. BUT IF WE'RE REALLY DOING THIS...
...IT CAN'T BE ALL YOU. IT CAN'T BE CHAOTIC.
NOT IF WE REALLY WANT TO END THE WORLD.
HE SAID HE WANTS TO WHAT?

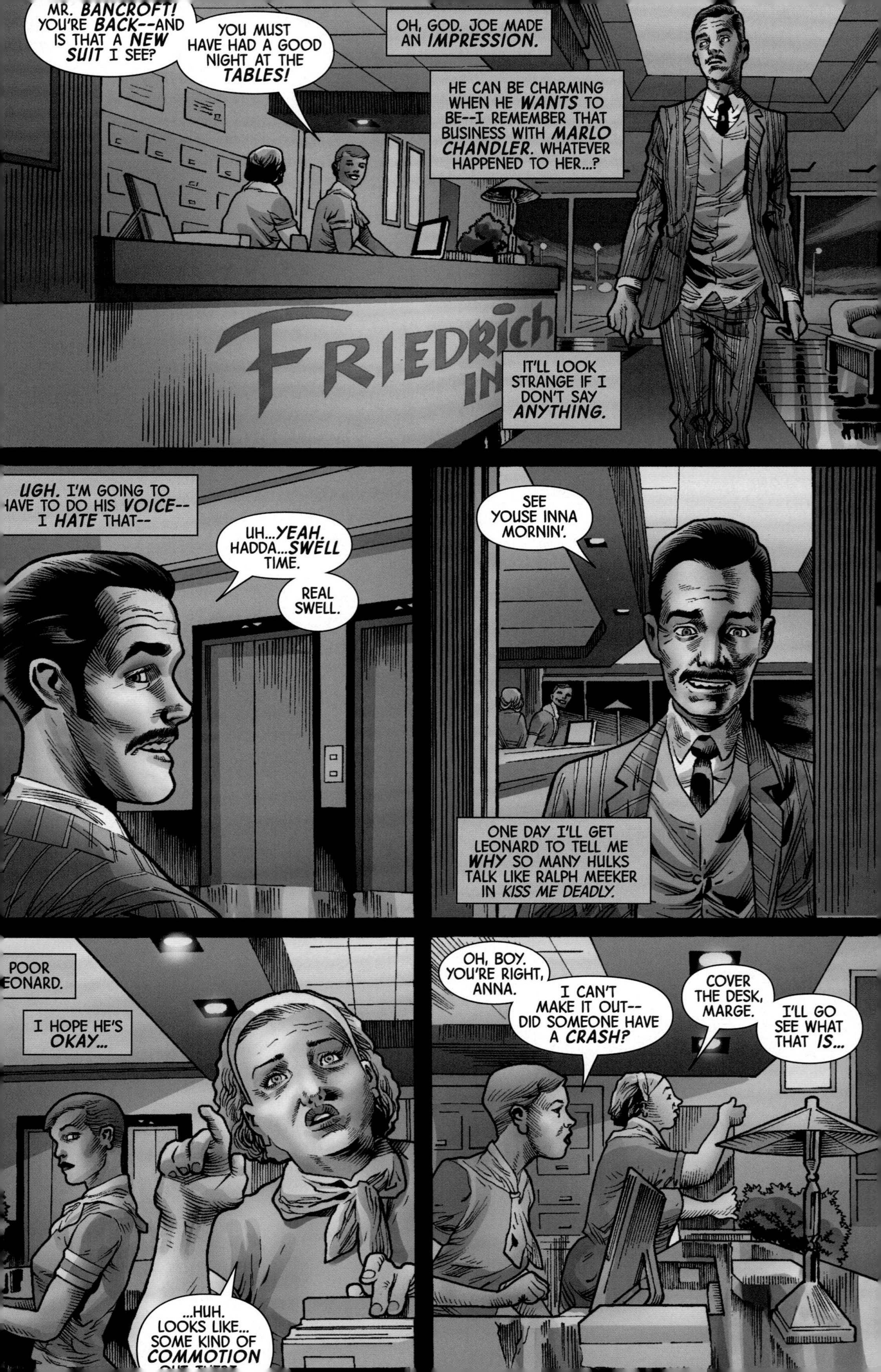

MR. BANCROFT! YOU'RE BACK--AND IS THAT A NEW SUIT I SEE?
YOU MUST HAVE HAD A GOOD NIGHT AT THE TABLES!
OH, GOD. JOE MADE AN IMPRESSION.
HE CAN BE CHARMING WHEN HE WANTS TO BE--I REMEMBER THAT BUSINESS WITH MARLO CHANDLER. WHATEVER HAPPENED TO HER...?
FRIEDRICH IN
IT'LL LOOK STRANGE IF I DON'T SAY ANYTHING.
UGH. I'M GOING TO HAVE TO DO HIS VOICE-- I HATE THAT--
UH...YEAH. HADDA...SWELL TIME.
REAL SWELL.
SEE YOUSE INNA MORNIN'.
ONE DAY I'LL GET LEONARD TO TELL ME WHY SO MANY HULKS TALK LIKE RALPH MEEKER IN KISS ME DEADLY.
POOR LEONARD.
I HOPE HE'S OKAY...
...HUH. LOOKS LIKE... SOME KIND OF COMMOTION
OH, BOY. YOU'RE RIGHT, ANNA.
I CAN'T MAKE IT OUT-- DID SOMEONE HAVE A CRASH?
COVER THE DESK, MARGE.
I'LL GO SEE WHAT THAT IS...

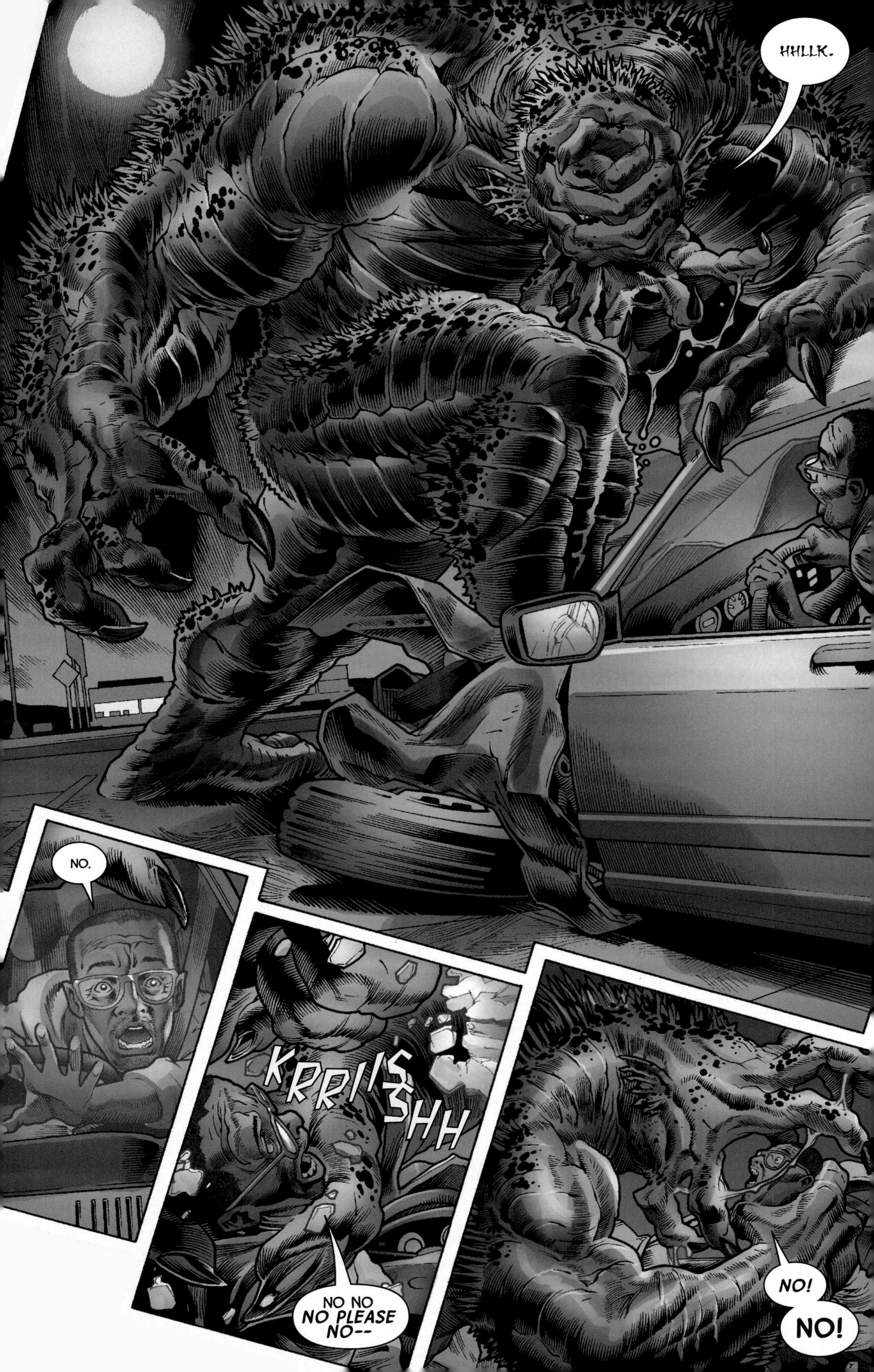
HHLLK.
NO.
KRRIISSHH
NO NO
NO PLEASE
NO--
NO!
NO!

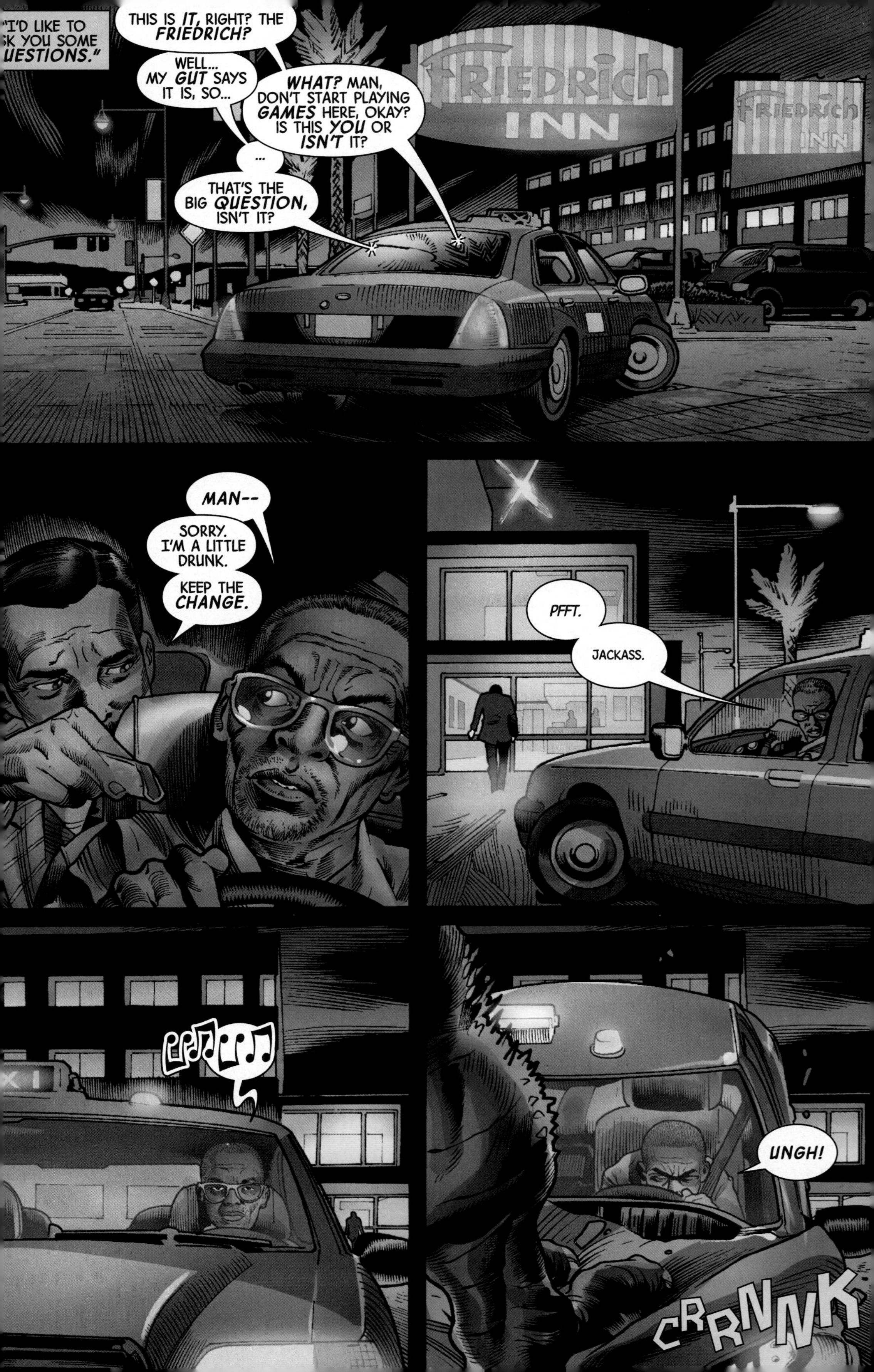
"I'D LIKE TO
SK YOU SOME
UESTIONS."
THIS IS IT, RIGHT? THE FRIEDRICH?
WELL... MY GUT SAYS IT IS, SO...
WHAT? MAN, DON'T START PLAYING GAMES HERE, OKAY? IS THIS YOU OR ISN'T IT?
...
THAT'S THE BIG QUESTION, ISN'T IT?
FRIEDRICH INN
FRIEDRICH INN
MAN--
SORRY. I'M A LITTLE DRUNK.
KEEP THE CHANGE.
PFFT.
JACKASS.
UNGH!
CRRNNK

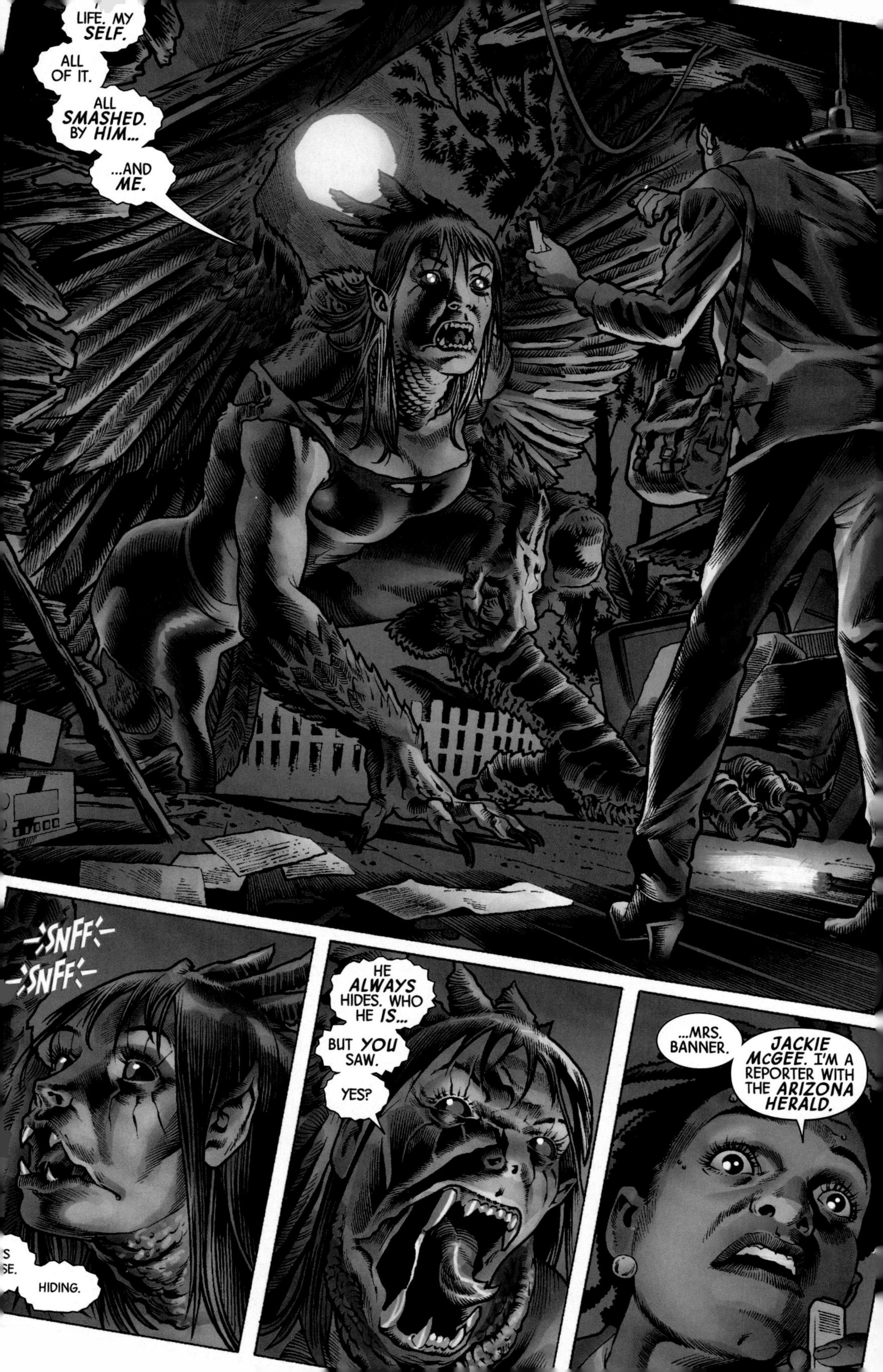
LIFE. MY SELF.
ALL OF IT.
ALL SMASHED. BY HIM...
...AND ME.
SNFF
SNFF
HIDING.
HE ALWAYS HIDES. WHO HE IS...
BUT YOU SAW.
YES?
...MRS. BANNER.
JACKIE McGEE. I'M A REPORTER WITH THE ARIZONA HERALD.

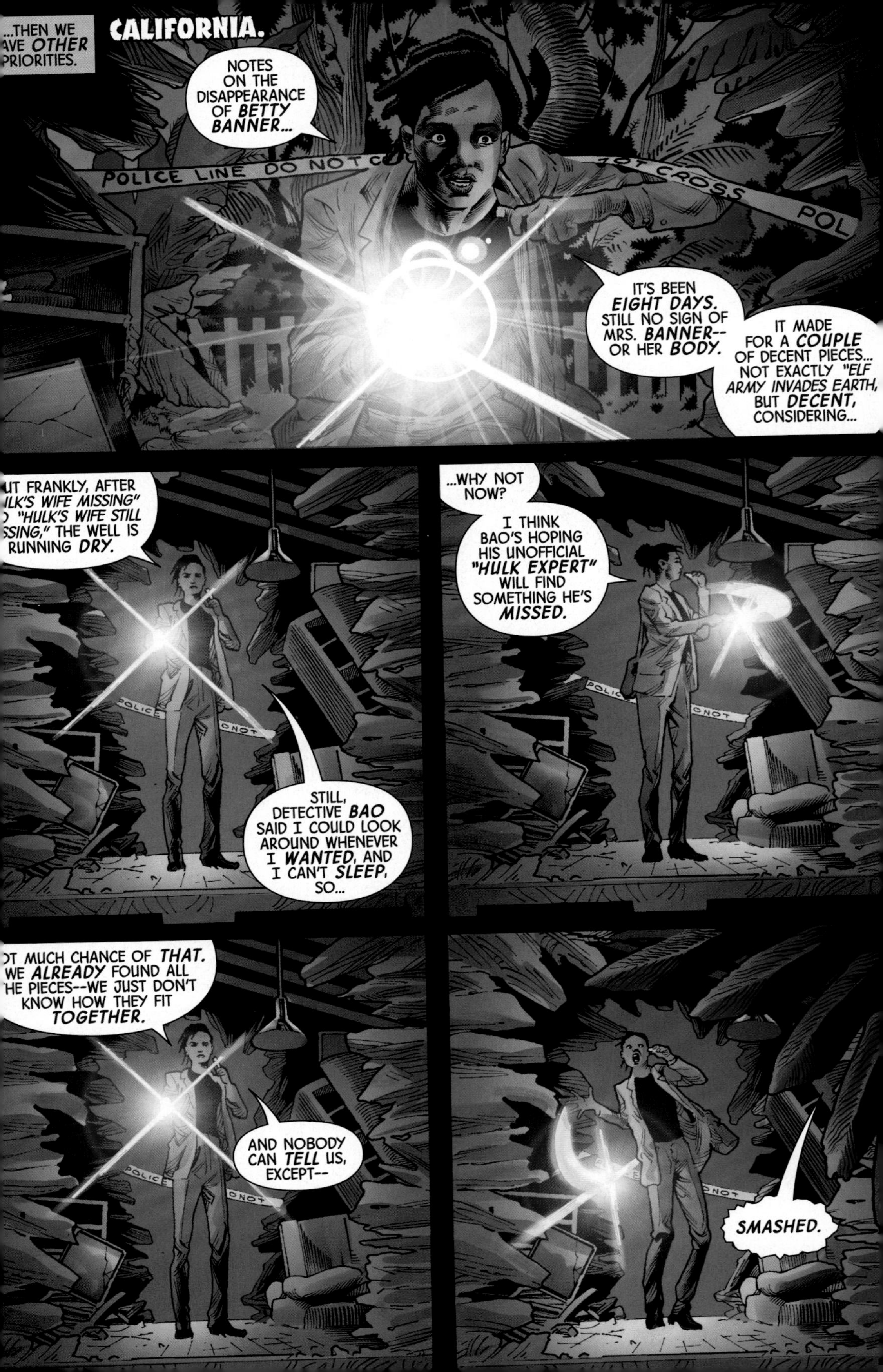

...THEN WE AVE OTHER PRIORITIES.
CALIFORNIA.
NOTES ON THE DISAPPEARANCE OF BETTY BANNER...
POLICE LINE DO NOT C
NOT CROSS
POL
IT'S BEEN EIGHT DAYS. STILL NO SIGN OF MRS. BANNER-- OR HER BODY.
IT MADE FOR A COUPLE OF DECENT PIECES... NOT EXACTLY "ELF ARMY INVADES EARTH, BUT DECENT, CONSIDERING...
UT FRANKLY, AFTER ULK'S WIFE MISSING" D "HULK'S WIFE STILL SSING," THE WELL IS RUNNING DRY.
STILL, DETECTIVE BAO SAID I COULD LOOK AROUND WHENEVER I WANTED, AND I CAN'T SLEEP, SO...
...WHY NOT NOW?
I THINK BAO'S HOPING HIS UNOFFICIAL "HULK EXPERT" WILL FIND SOMETHING HE'S MISSED.
OT MUCH CHANCE OF THAT. WE ALREADY FOUND ALL HE PIECES--WE JUST DON'T KNOW HOW THEY FIT TOGETHER.
AND NOBODY CAN TELL US, EXCEPT--
SMASHED.

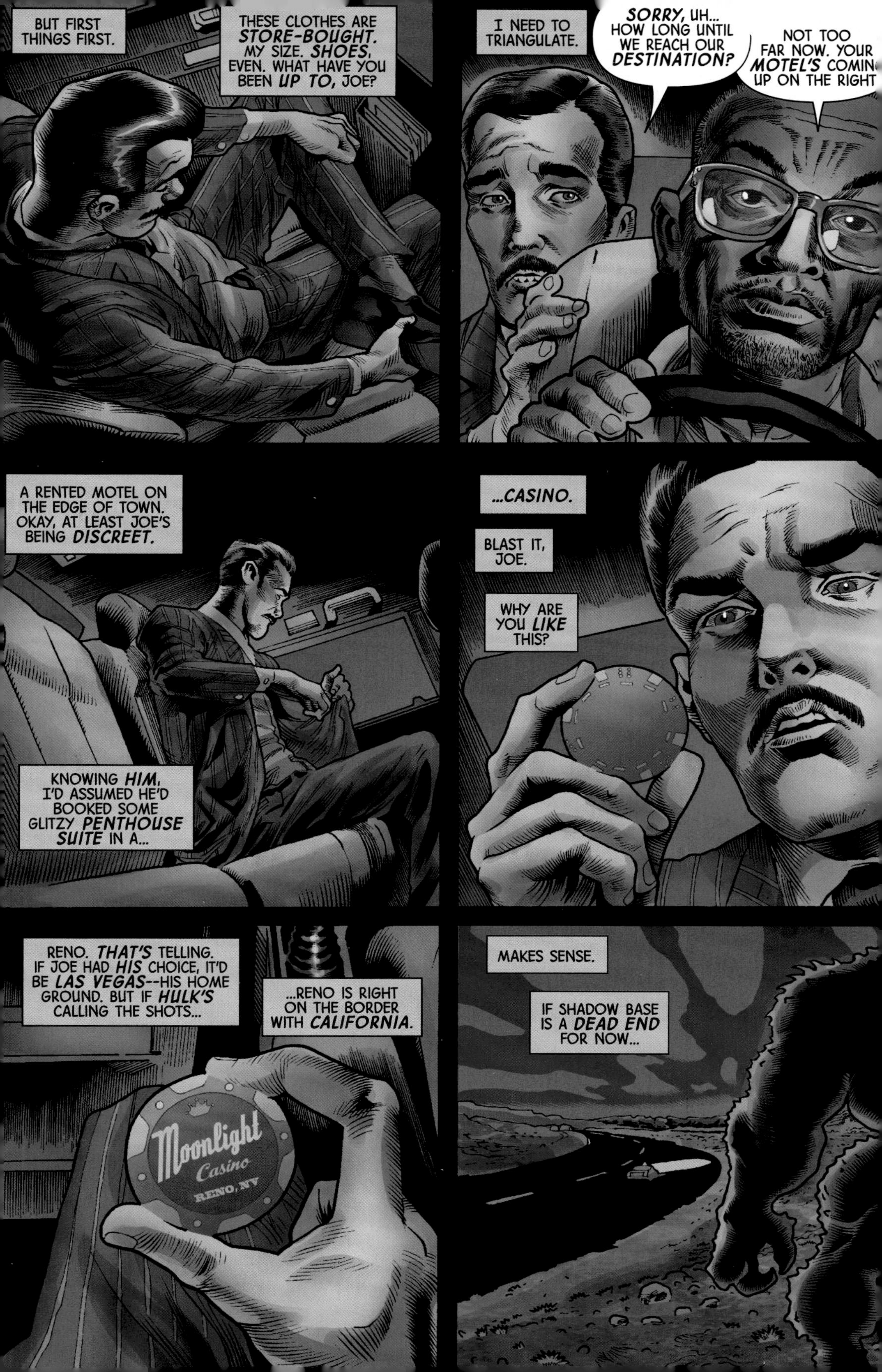

BUT FIRST THINGS FIRST.
THESE CLOTHES ARE STORE-BOUGHT. MY SIZE. SHOES, EVEN. WHAT HAVE YOU BEEN UP TO, JOE?
I NEED TO TRIANGULATE.
SORRY, UH... HOW LONG UNTIL WE REACH OUR DESTINATION?
NOT TOO FAR NOW. YOUR MOTEL'S COMIN UP ON THE RIGHT
A RENTED MOTEL ON THE EDGE OF TOWN. OKAY, AT LEAST JOE'S BEING DISCREET.
KNOWING HIM, I'D ASSUMED HE'D BOOKED SOME GLITZY PENTHOUSE SUITE IN A...
...CASINO.
BLAST IT, JOE.
WHY ARE YOU LIKE THIS?
RENO. THAT'S TELLING. IF JOE HAD HIS CHOICE, IT'D BE LAS VEGAS--HIS HOME GROUND. BUT IF HULK'S CALLING THE SHOTS...
...RENO IS RIGHT ON THE BORDER WITH CALIFORNIA.
Moonlight Casino RENO, NV
MAKES SENSE.
IF SHADOW BASE IS A DEAD END FOR NOW...

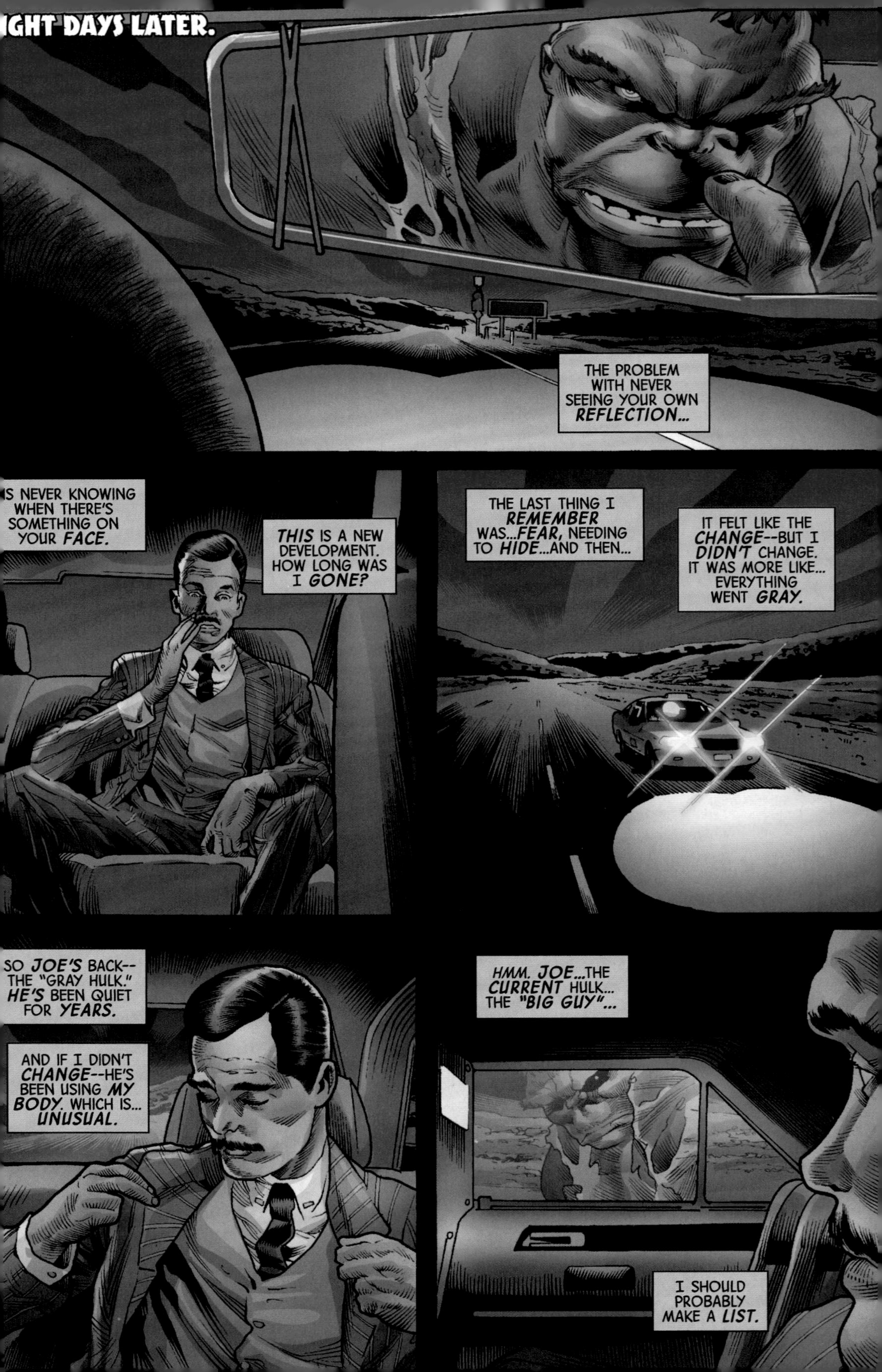
GHT DAYS LATER.
THE PROBLEM WITH NEVER SEEING YOUR OWN REFLECTION...
S NEVER KNOWING WHEN THERE'S SOMETHING ON YOUR FACE.
THIS IS A NEW DEVELOPMENT. HOW LONG WAS I GONE?
THE LAST THING I REMEMBER WAS...FEAR, NEEDING TO HIDE...AND THEN...
IT FELT LIKE THE CHANGE--BUT I DIDN'T CHANGE. IT WAS MORE LIKE... EVERYTHING WENT GRAY.
SO JOE'S BACK-- THE "GRAY HULK." HE'S BEEN QUIET FOR YEARS.
AND IF I DIDN'T CHANGE--HE'S BEEN USING MY BODY. WHICH IS... UNUSUAL.
HMM. JOE...THE CURRENT HULK... THE "BIG GUY"...
I SHOULD PROBABLY MAKE A LIST.

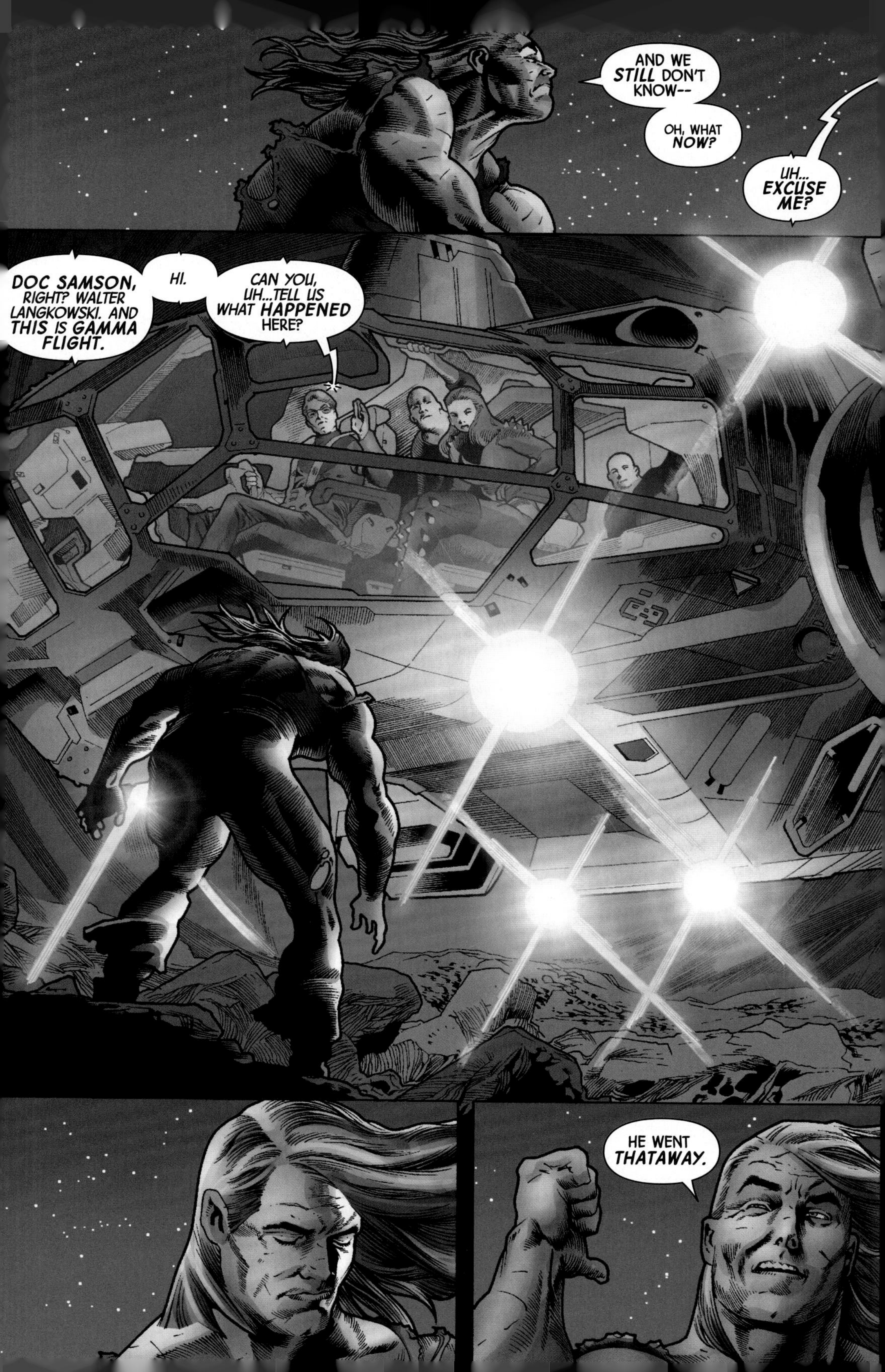
AND WE STILL DON'T KNOW--
OH, WHAT NOW?
UH... EXCUSE ME?
DOC SAMSON, RIGHT? WALTER LANGKOWSKI. AND THIS IS GAMMA FLIGHT.
HI.
CAN YOU, UH...TELL US WHAT HAPPENED HERE?
HE WENT THATAWAY.

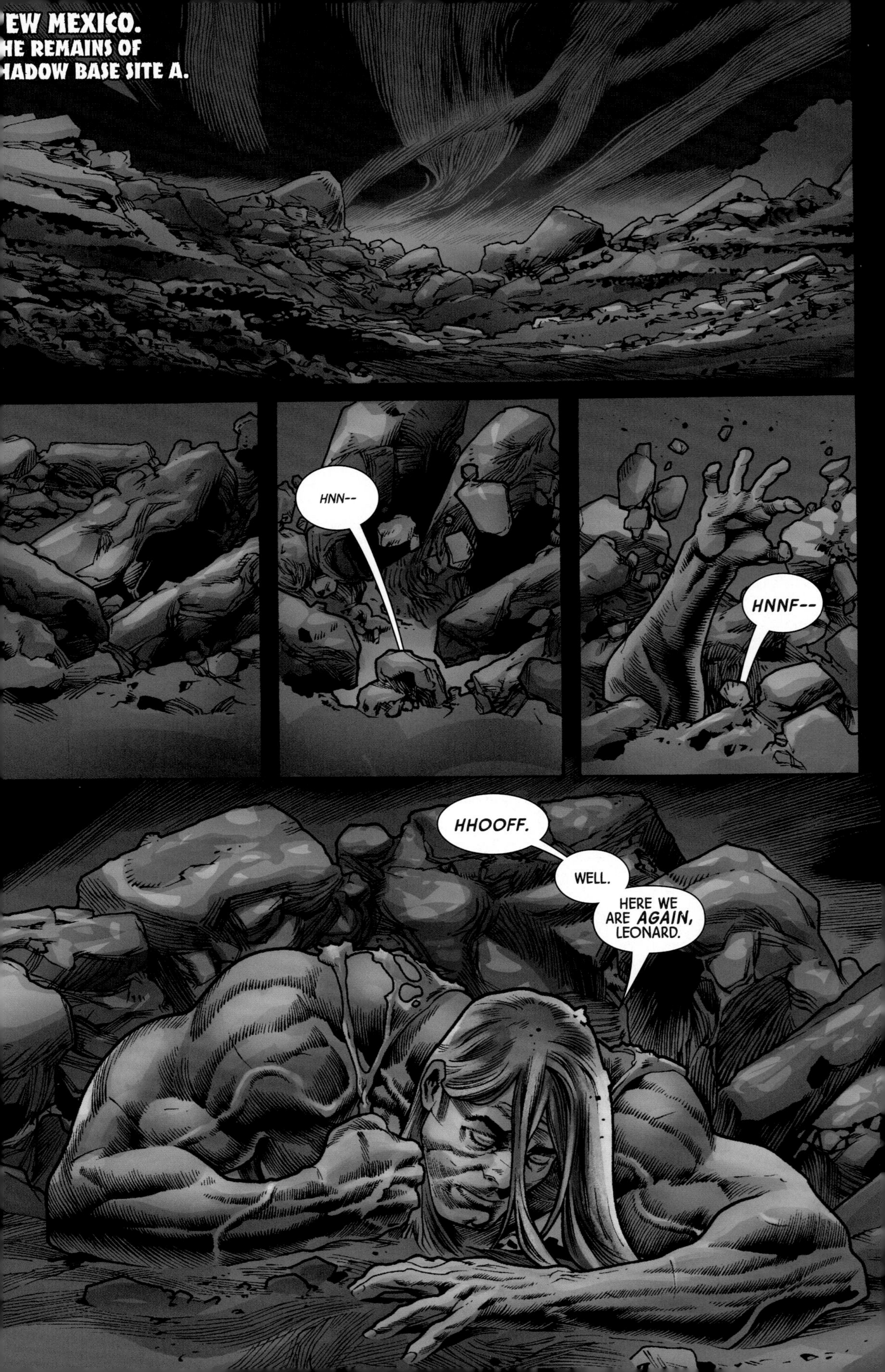
EW MEXICO.
HE REMAINS OF
HADOW BASE SITE A.
HNN--
HNNF--
HHOOFF.
WELL.
HERE WE ARE AGAIN, LEONARD.

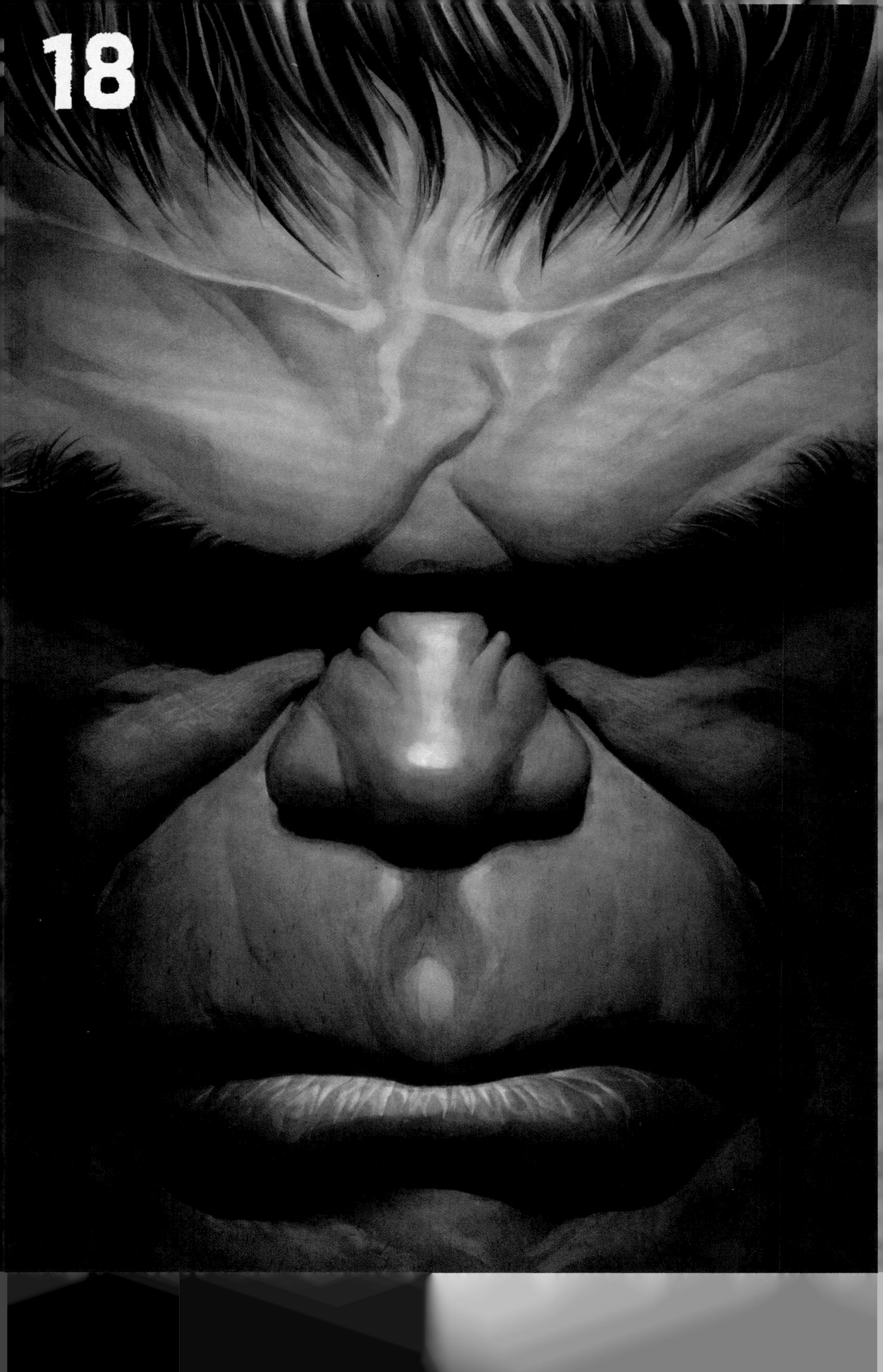
18

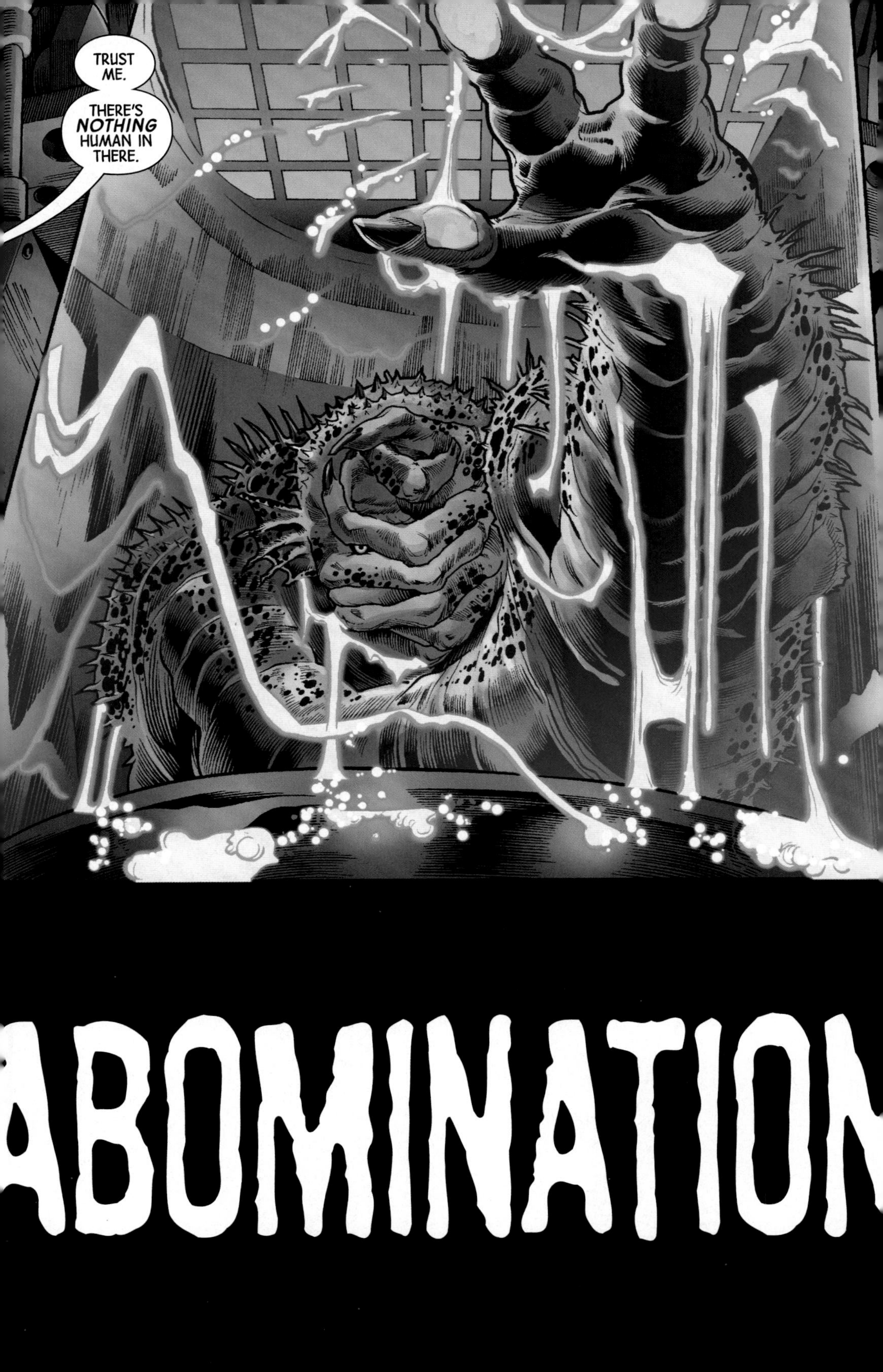
TRUST ME.
THERE'S *NOTHING* HUMAN IN THERE.
ABOMINATION

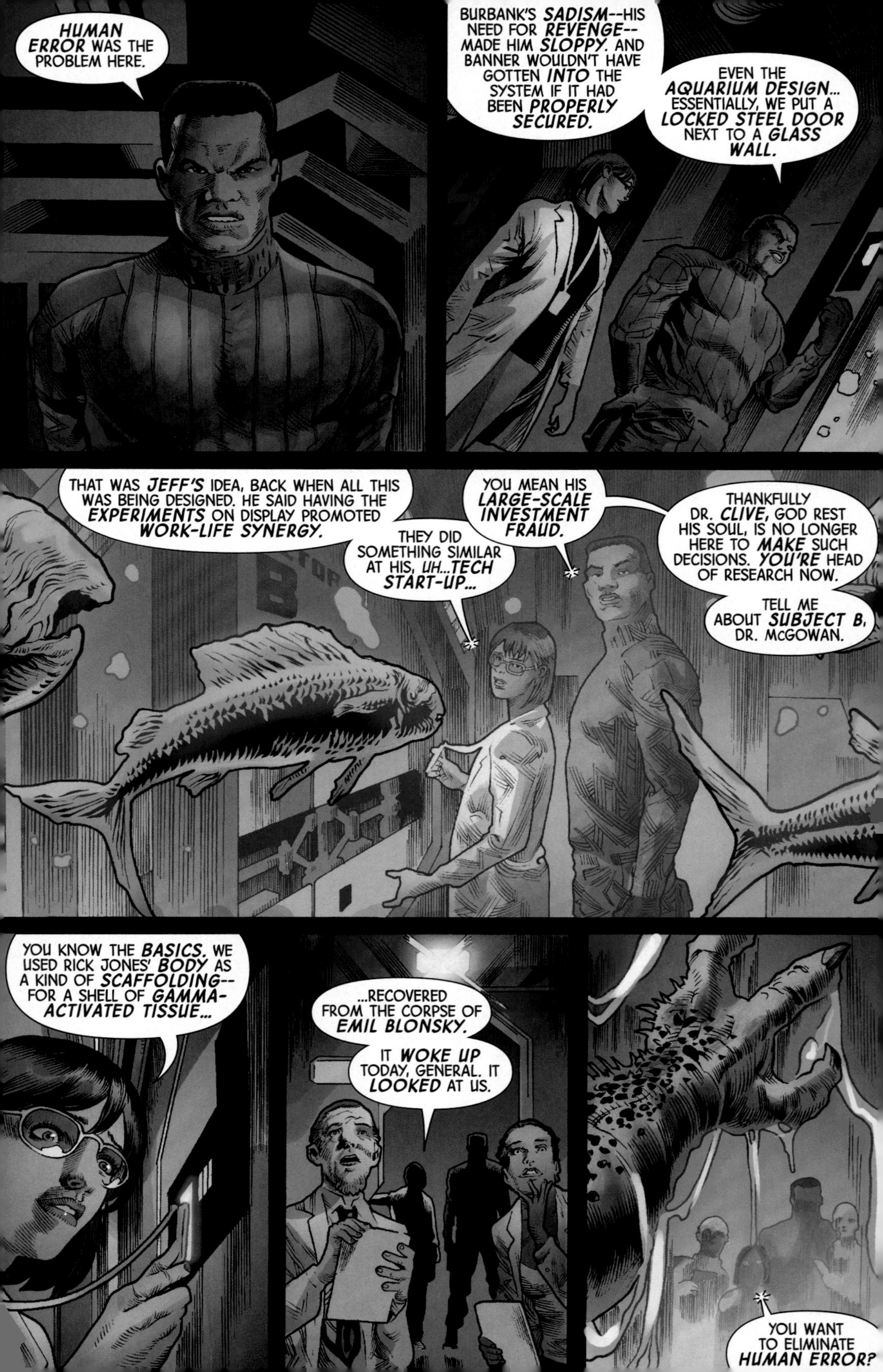
HUMAN ERROR WAS THE PROBLEM HERE.
BURBANK'S SADISM--HIS NEED FOR REVENGE--MADE HIM SLOPPY. AND BANNER WOULDN'T HAVE GOTTEN INTO THE SYSTEM IF IT HAD BEEN PROPERLY SECURED.
EVEN THE AQUARIUM DESIGN... ESSENTIALLY, WE PUT A LOCKED STEEL DOOR NEXT TO A GLASS WALL.
THAT WAS JEFF'S IDEA, BACK WHEN ALL THIS WAS BEING DESIGNED. HE SAID HAVING THE EXPERIMENTS ON DISPLAY PROMOTED WORK-LIFE SYNERGY.
THEY DID SOMETHING SIMILAR AT HIS, UH...TECH START-UP...
YOU MEAN HIS LARGE-SCALE INVESTMENT FRAUD.
THANKFULLY DR. CLIVE, GOD REST HIS SOUL, IS NO LONGER HERE TO MAKE SUCH DECISIONS. YOU'RE HEAD OF RESEARCH NOW.
TELL ME ABOUT SUBJECT B, DR. McGOWAN.
YOU KNOW THE BASICS. WE USED RICK JONES' BODY AS A KIND OF SCAFFOLDING--FOR A SHELL OF GAMMA-ACTIVATED TISSUE...
...RECOVERED FROM THE CORPSE OF EMIL BLONSKY.
IT WOKE UP TODAY, GENERAL. IT LOOKED AT US.
YOU WANT TO ELIMINATE HUMAN ERROR?

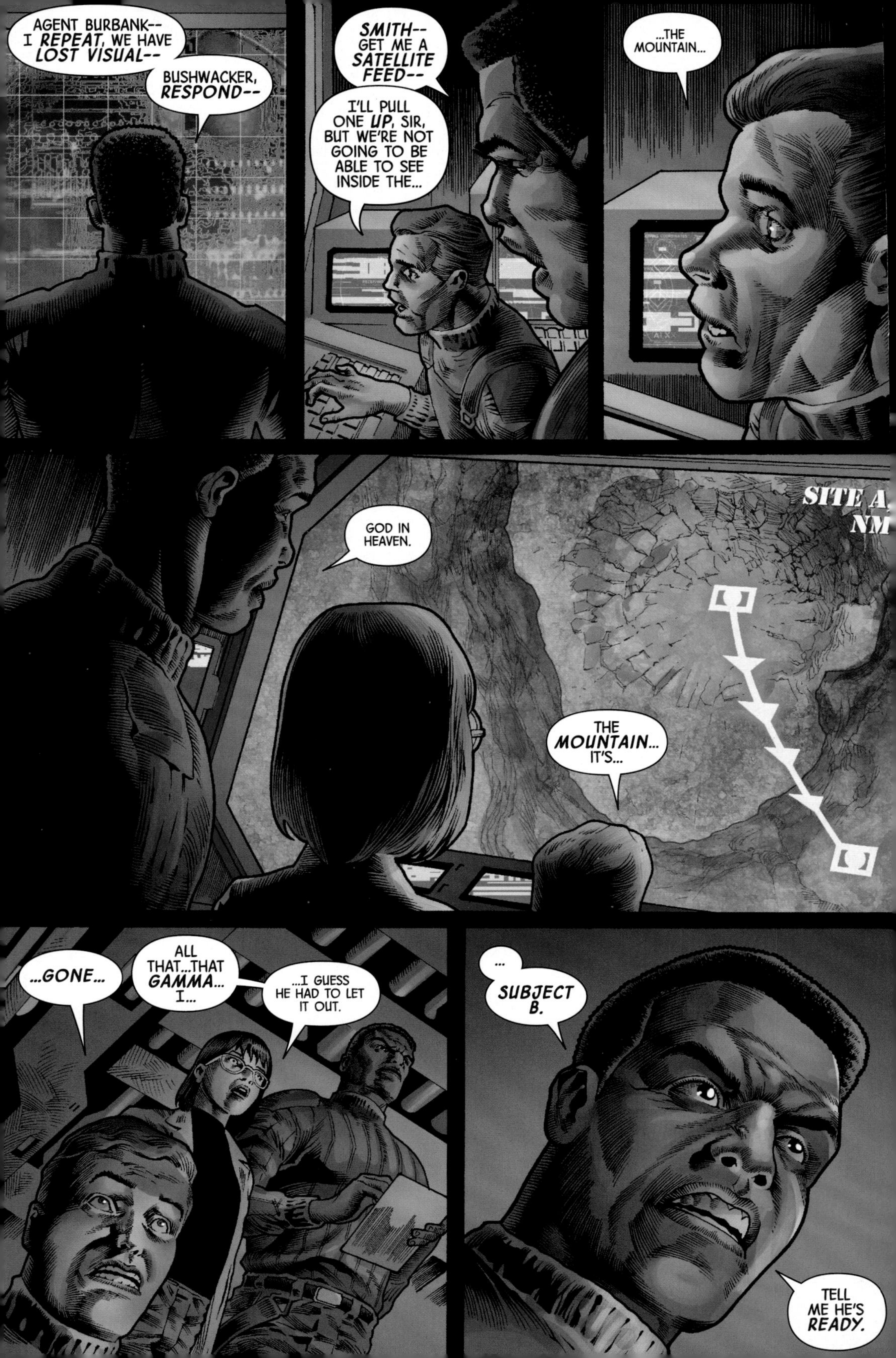
AGENT BURBANK-- I REPEAT, WE HAVE LOST VISUAL--
BUSHWACKER, RESPOND--
SMITH-- GET ME A SATELLITE FEED--
I'LL PULL ONE UP, SIR, BUT WE'RE NOT GOING TO BE ABLE TO SEE INSIDE THE...
...THE MOUNTAIN...
SITE A, NM
GOD IN HEAVEN.
THE MOUNTAIN... IT'S...
...GONE...
ALL THAT...THAT GAMMA... I...
...I GUESS HE HAD TO LET IT OUT.
... SUBJECT B.
TELL ME HE'S READY.

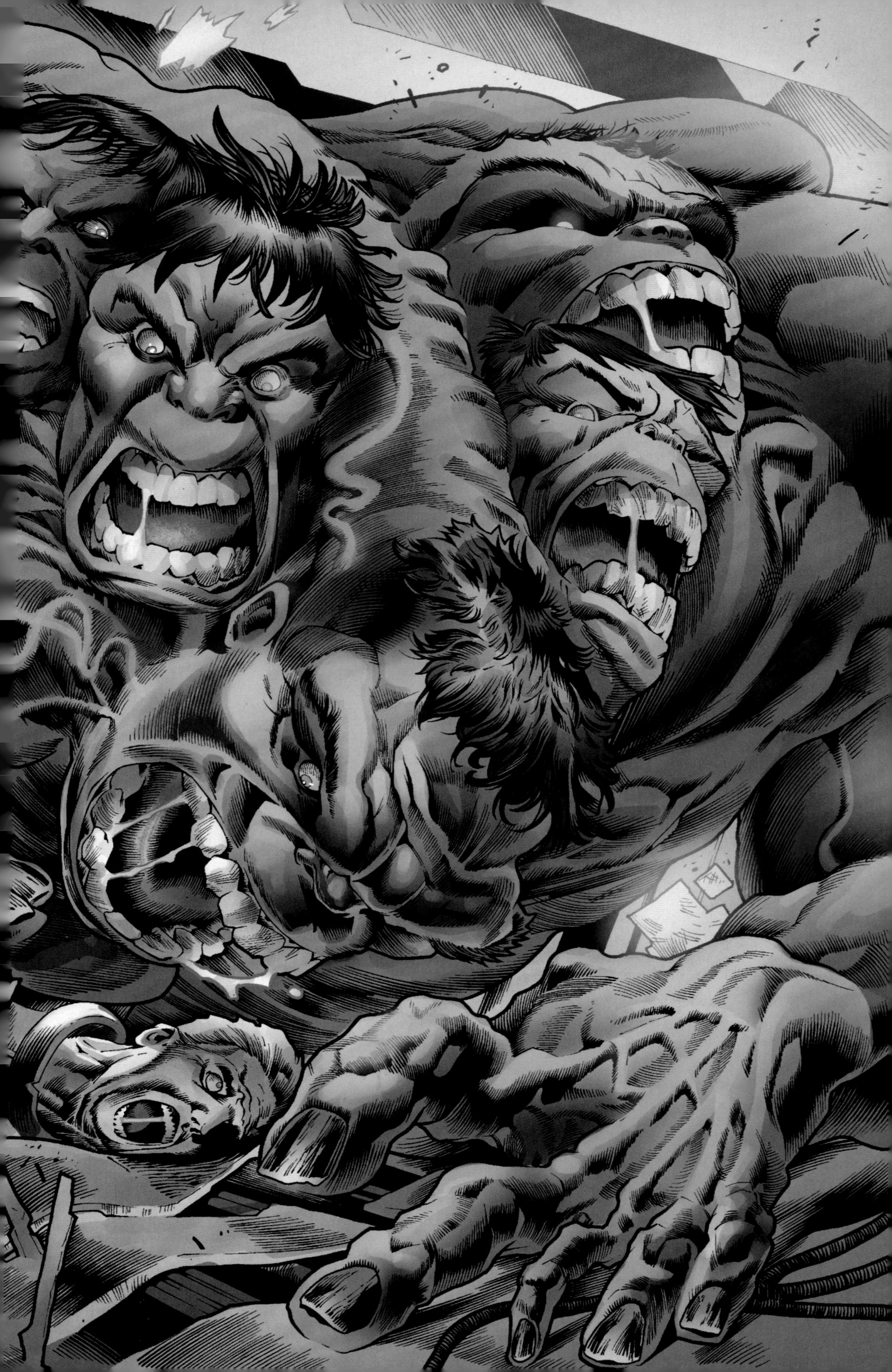

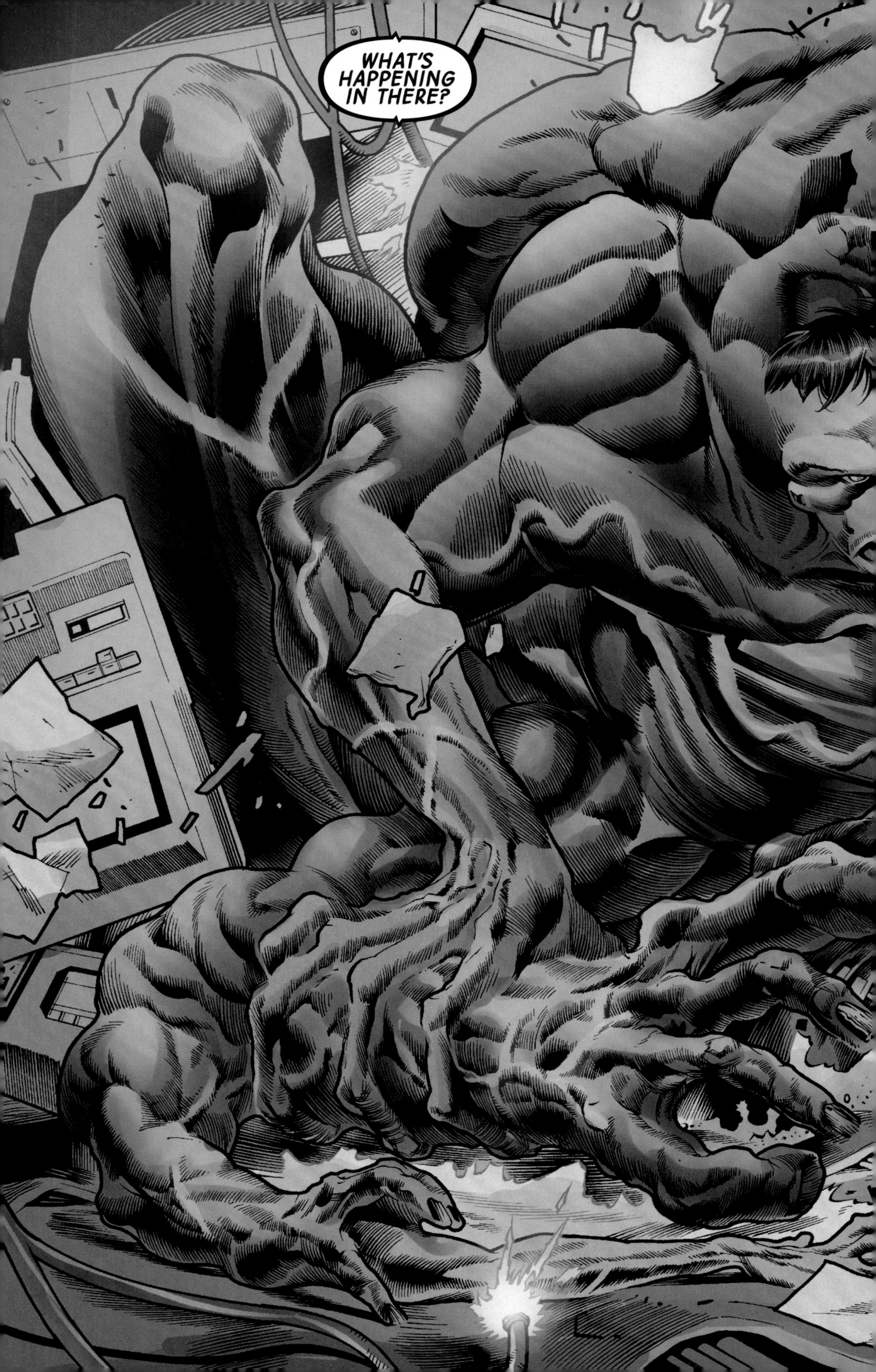
WHAT'S HAPPENING IN THERE?

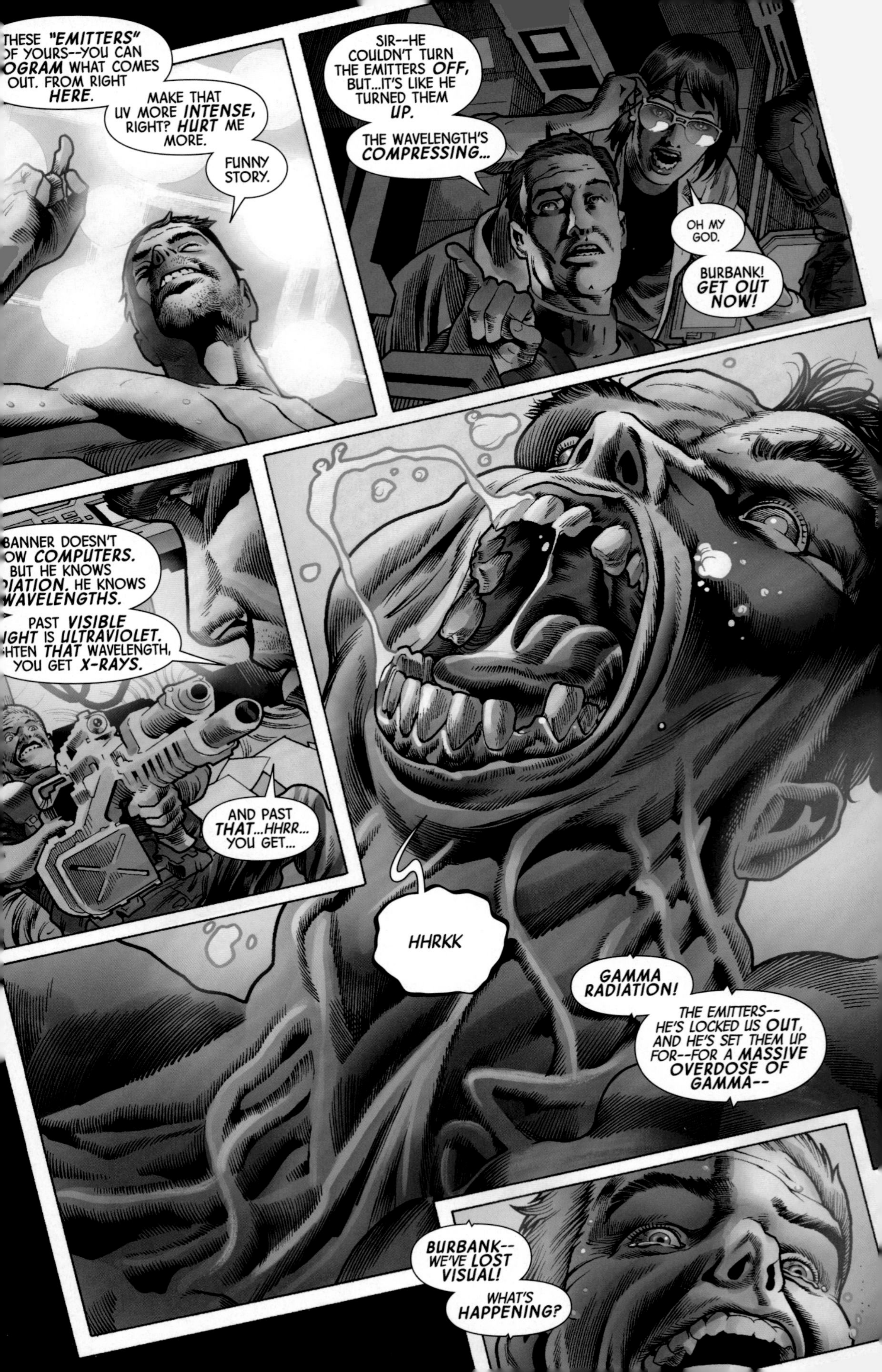

THESE "EMITTERS" OF YOURS--YOU CAN OGRAM WHAT COMES OUT. FROM RIGHT HERE.
MAKE THAT UV MORE INTENSE, RIGHT? HURT ME MORE.
FUNNY STORY.
SIR--HE COULDN'T TURN THE EMITTERS OFF, BUT...IT'S LIKE HE TURNED THEM UP.
THE WAVELENGTH'S COMPRESSING...
OH MY GOD.
BURBANK! GET OUT NOW!
BANNER DOESN'T OW COMPUTERS. BUT HE KNOWS DIATION. HE KNOWS WAVELENGTHS.
PAST VISIBLE IGHT IS ULTRAVIOLET. HTEN THAT WAVELENGTH, YOU GET X-RAYS.
AND PAST THAT...HHRR... YOU GET...
HHRKK
GAMMA RADIATION!
THE EMITTERS--HE'S LOCKED US OUT, AND HE'S SET THEM UP FOR--FOR A MASSIVE OVERDOSE OF GAMMA--
BURBANK--WE'VE LOST VISUAL!
WHAT'S HAPPENING?

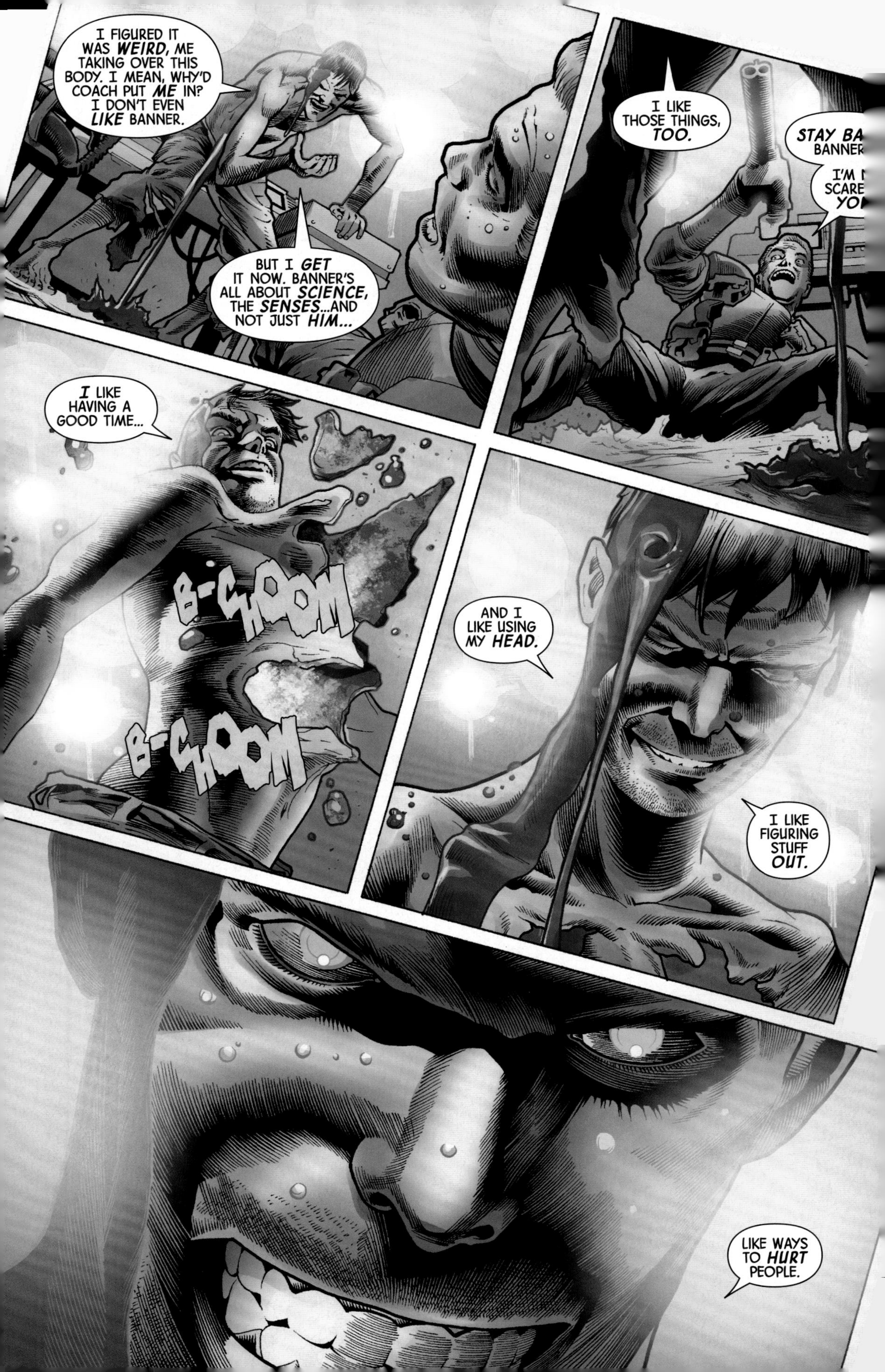

I FIGURED IT WAS WEIRD, ME TAKING OVER THIS BODY. I MEAN, WHY'D COACH PUT ME IN? I DON'T EVEN LIKE BANNER.
BUT I GET IT NOW. BANNER'S ALL ABOUT SCIENCE, THE SENSES...AND NOT JUST HIM...
I LIKE THOSE THINGS, TOO.
STAY BA BANNER
I'M N SCARE YO
I LIKE HAVING A GOOD TIME...
B-CHOOM
B-CHOOM
AND I LIKE USING MY HEAD.
I LIKE FIGURING STUFF OUT.
LIKE WAYS TO HURT PEOPLE.

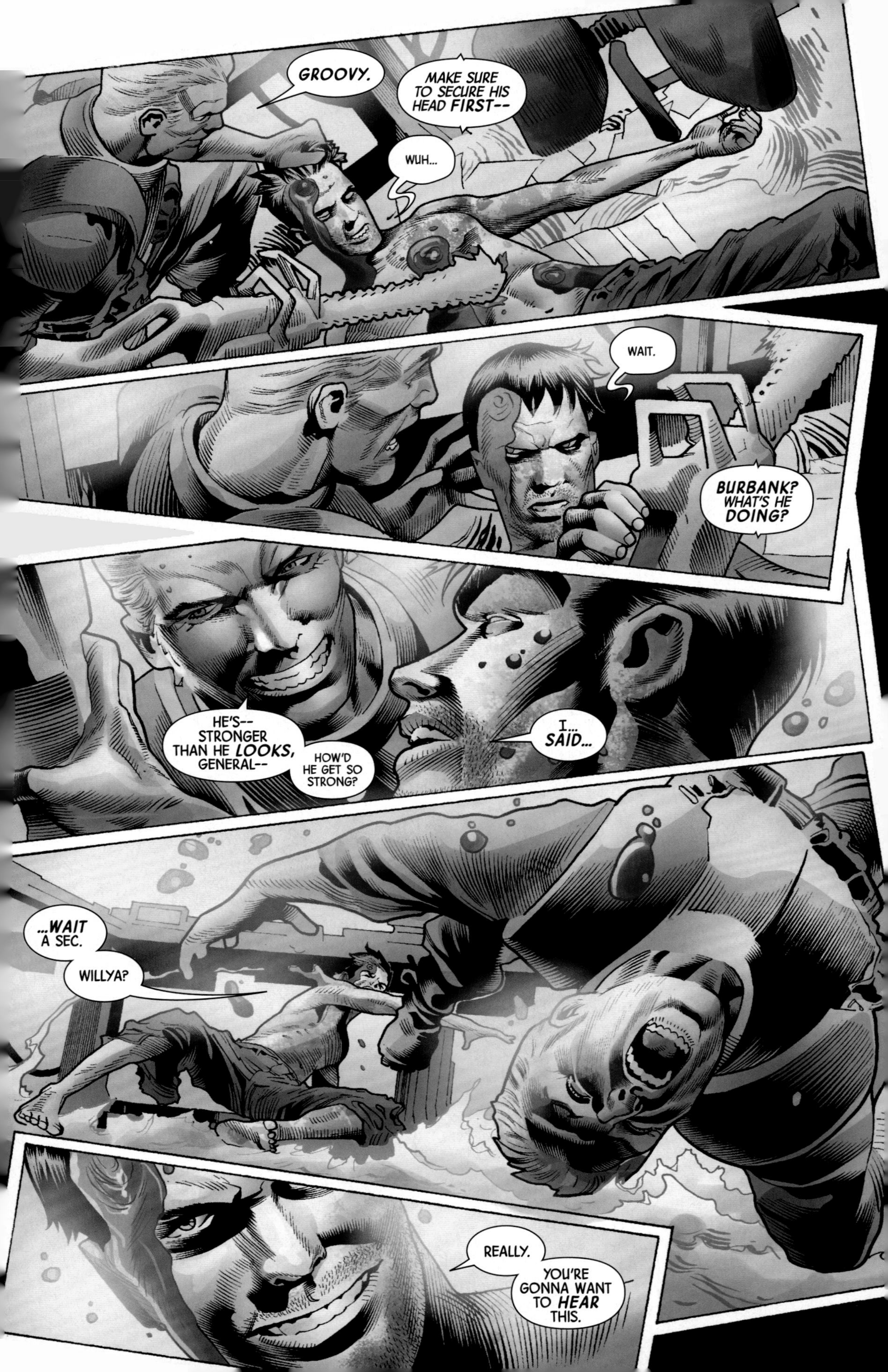
GROOVY.
MAKE SURE TO SECURE HIS HEAD FIRST--
WUH...
WAIT.
BURBANK? WHAT'S HE DOING?
HE'S-- STRONGER THAN HE LOOKS, GENERAL--
HOW'D HE GET SO STRONG?
I... SAID...
...WAIT A SEC.
WILLYA?
REALLY.
YOU'RE GONNA WANT TO HEAR THIS.

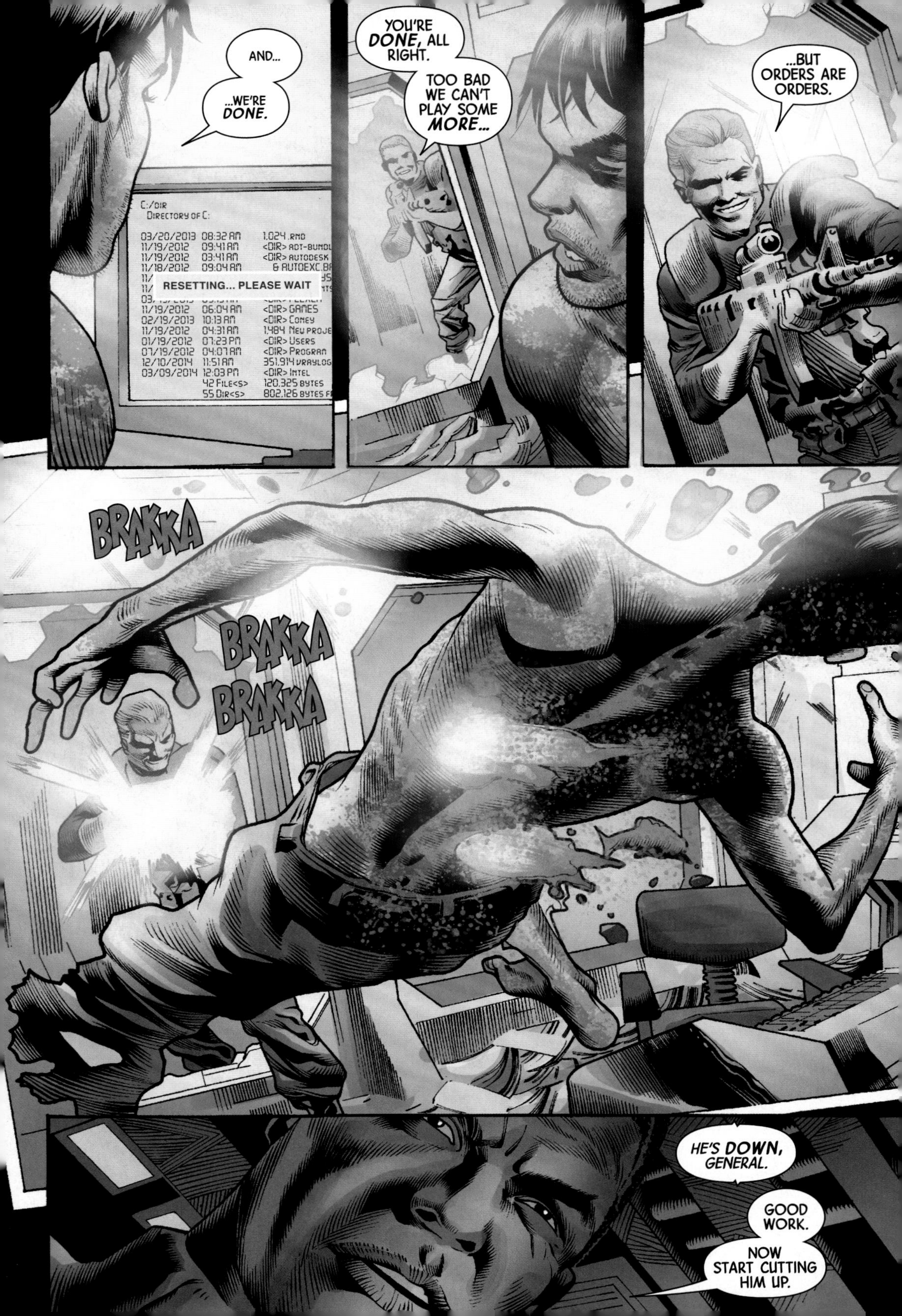
AND...
...WE'RE *DONE.*
C:/DIR
DIRECTORY OF C:
03/20/2013 08:32 AM 1,024 .RND
11/19/2012 09:41 AM <DIR> ADT-BUNDL
11/19/2012 03:41 AM <DIR> AUTODESK
11/18/2012 09:04 AM & AUTOEXC.BA
RESETTING... PLEASE WAIT
11/19/2012 06:04 AM <DIR> GAMES
02/19/2013 10:13 AM <DIR> CONEY
11/19/2012 04:31 AM 1,484 NEW PROJE
01/19/2012 07:23 PM <DIR> USERS
07/19/2012 04:07 AM <DIR> PROGRAM
12/10/2014 11:51 AM 351,914 VRAYLOG
03/09/2014 12:03 PM <DIR> INTEL
42 FILE<S> 120,325 BYTES
55 DIR<S> 802,126 BYTES F
YOU'RE *DONE,* ALL RIGHT.
TOO BAD WE CAN'T PLAY SOME *MORE...*
...BUT ORDERS ARE ORDERS.
BRAKKA
BRAKKA
BRAKKA
HE'S **DOWN,** *GENERAL.*
GOOD WORK.
NOW START CUTTING HIM UP.

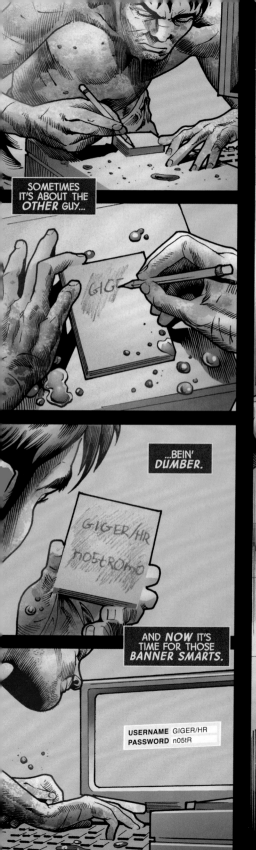

SOMETIMES IT'S ABOUT THE *OTHER* GUY...

...BEIN' *DUMBER.*

AND *NOW* IT'S TIME FOR THOSE *BANNER SMARTS.*

USERNAME GIGER/HR
PASSWORD n05tR

'CAUSE I NEED TO WORK *FAST...*

GENERAL? CHECK THIS OUT. LOOKS LIKE HE SMASHED ONE OF THE *AQUARIUMS...*

HE'S IN *SECTOR A.* THE *ADMINISTRATION SUITE.*

OOH, *ADMIN.* SHOULD I BE *WORRIED?*

WE CAN BLOCK HIM TURNING THE *LIGHTS* OFF FROM *HERE.* BUT *STILL...*

...PUT HIM *DOWN,* BURBANK. *NOW.*

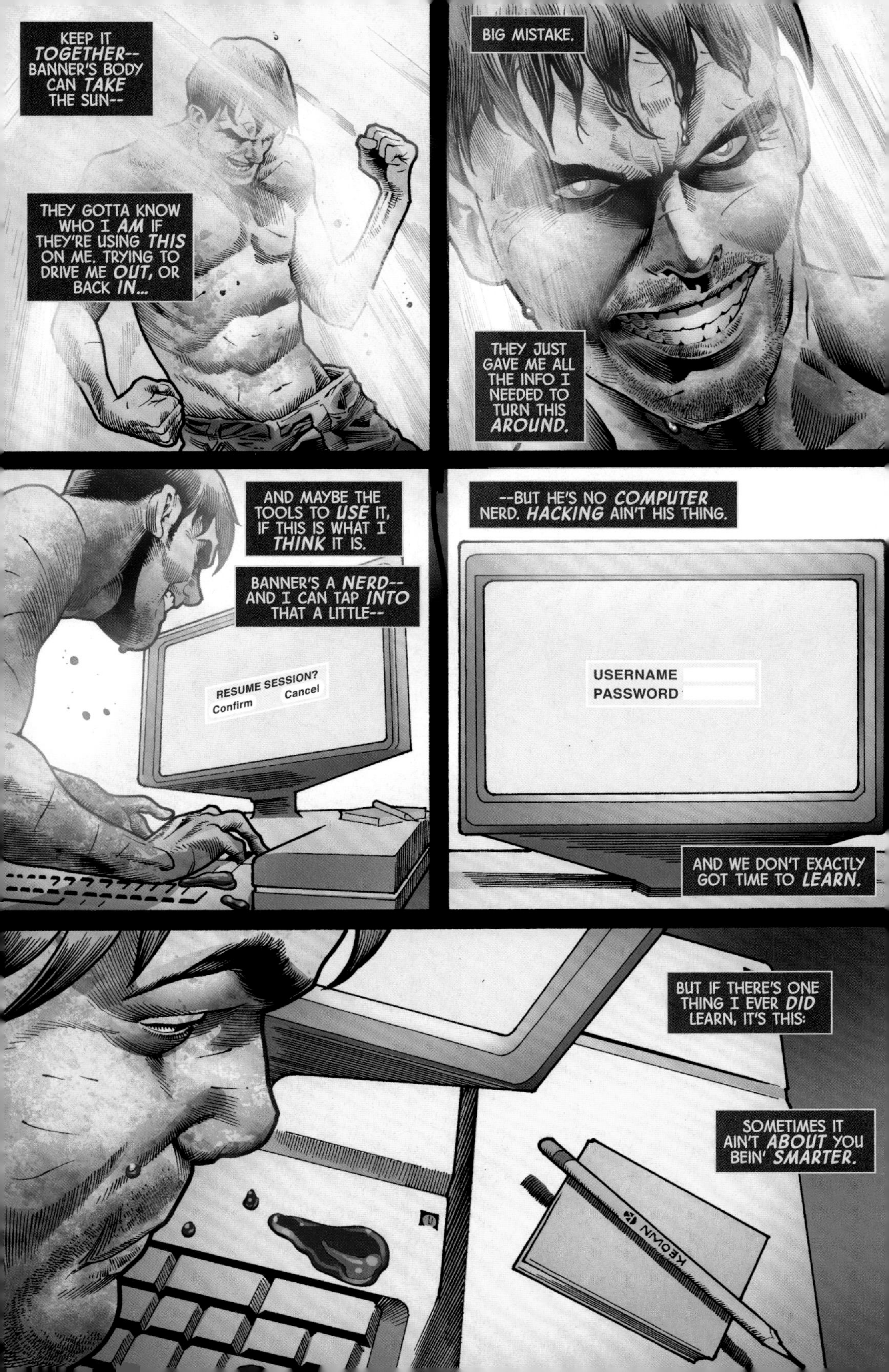
KEEP IT TOGETHER-- BANNER'S BODY CAN TAKE THE SUN--
THEY GOTTA KNOW WHO I AM IF THEY'RE USING THIS ON ME. TRYING TO DRIVE ME OUT, OR BACK IN...
BIG MISTAKE.
THEY JUST GAVE ME ALL THE INFO I NEEDED TO TURN THIS AROUND.
AND MAYBE THE TOOLS TO USE IT, IF THIS IS WHAT I THINK IT IS.
BANNER'S A NERD-- AND I CAN TAP INTO THAT A LITTLE--
RESUME SESSION?
Confirm
Cancel
--BUT HE'S NO COMPUTER NERD. HACKING AIN'T HIS THING.
USERNAME
PASSWORD
AND WE DON'T EXACTLY GOT TIME TO LEARN.
BUT IF THERE'S ONE THING I EVER DID LEARN, IT'S THIS:
SOMETIMES IT AIN'T ABOUT YOU BEIN' SMARTER.

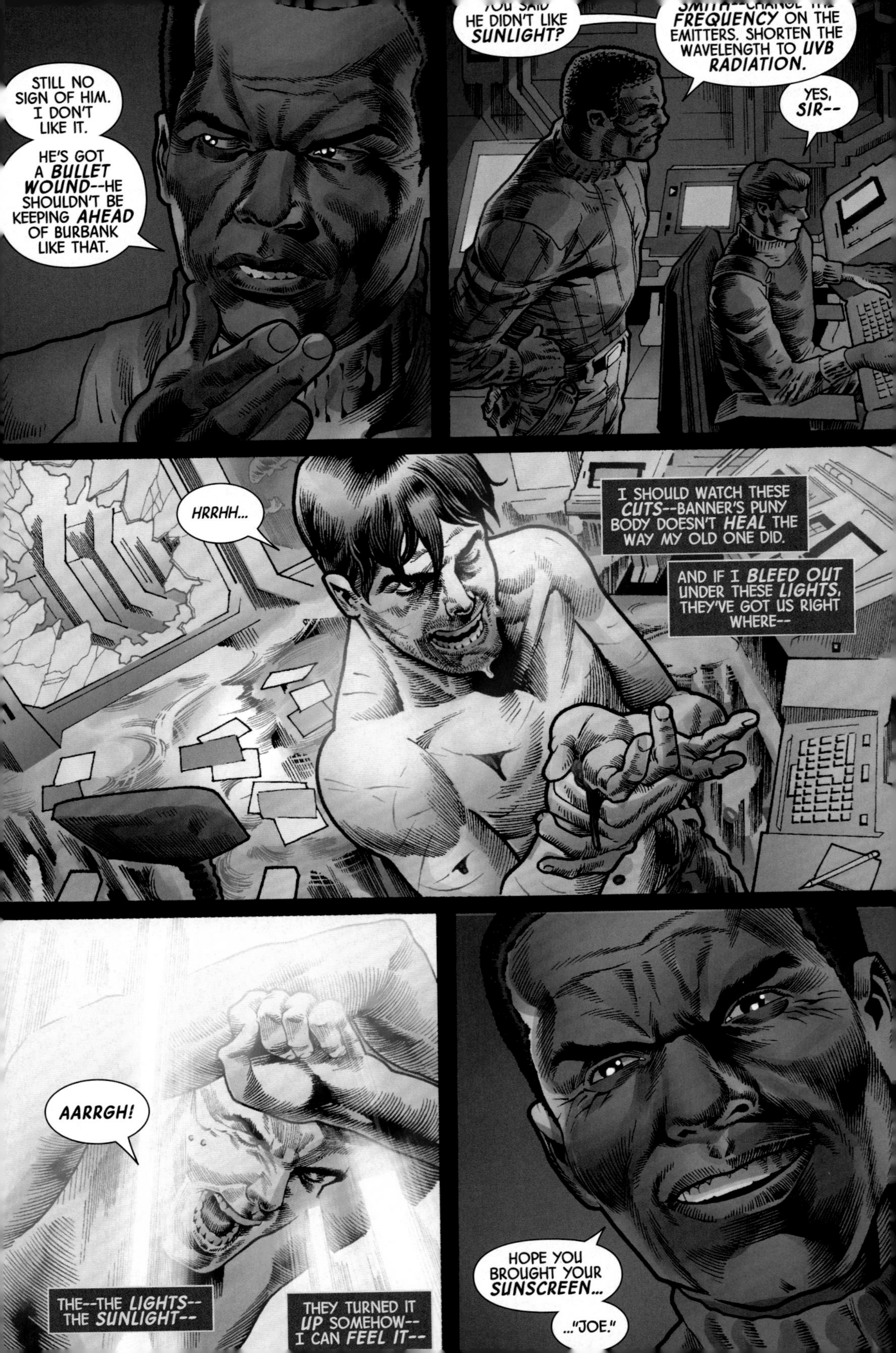
STILL NO SIGN OF HIM. I DON'T LIKE IT.
HE'S GOT A BULLET WOUND--HE SHOULDN'T BE KEEPING AHEAD OF BURBANK LIKE THAT.
HE DIDN'T LIKE SUNLIGHT?
FREQUENCY ON THE EMITTERS. SHORTEN THE WAVELENGTH TO UVB RADIATION.
YES, SIR--
HRRHH...
I SHOULD WATCH THESE CUTS--BANNER'S PUNY BODY DOESN'T HEAL THE WAY MY OLD ONE DID.
AND IF I BLEED OUT UNDER THESE LIGHTS, THEY'VE GOT US RIGHT WHERE--
AARRGH!
THE--THE LIGHTS--THE SUNLIGHT--
THEY TURNED IT UP SOMEHOW--I CAN FEEL IT--
HOPE YOU BROUGHT YOUR SUNSCREEN...
..."JOE."

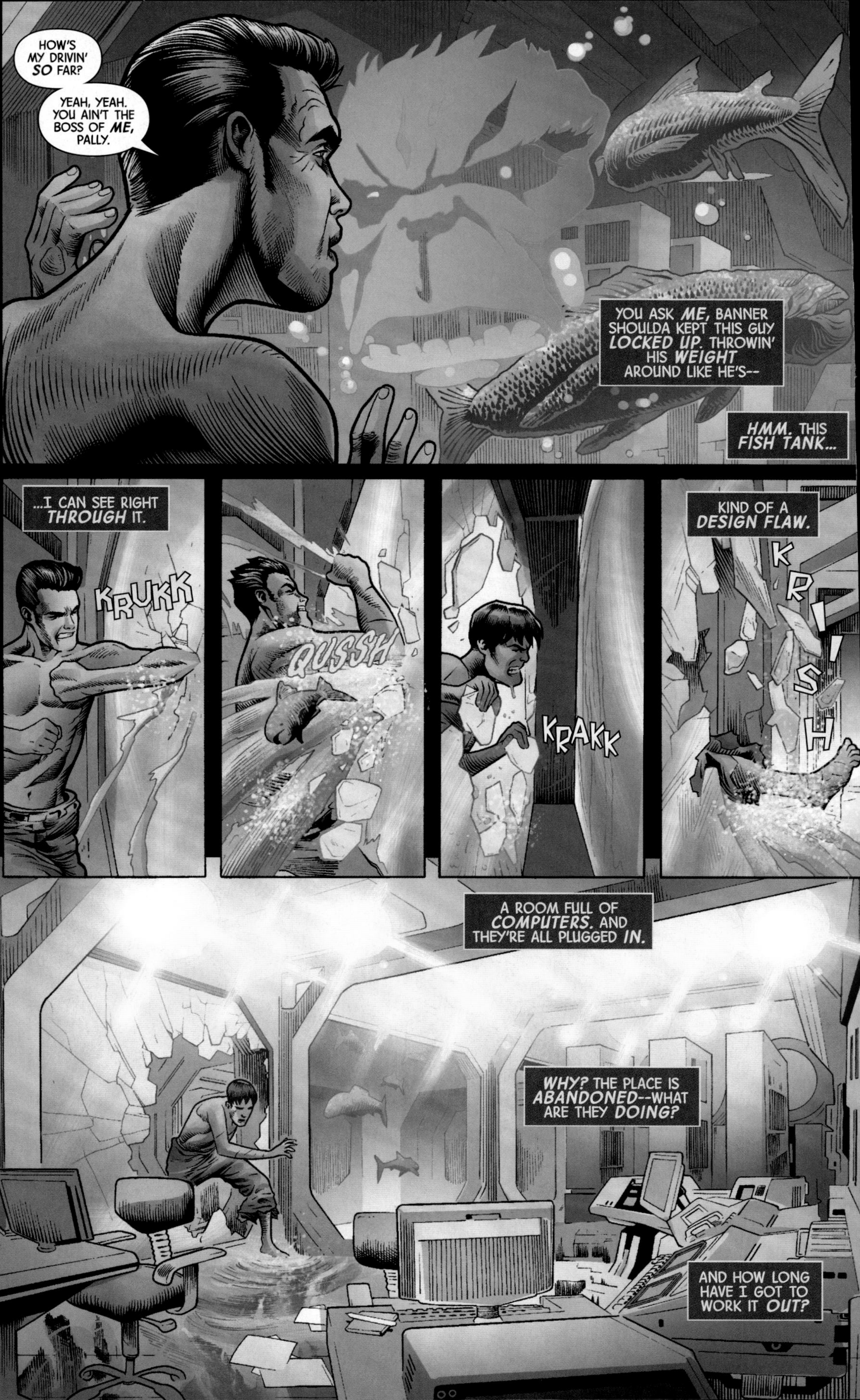
HOW'S MY DRIVIN' SO FAR?
YEAH, YEAH. YOU AIN'T THE BOSS OF ME, PALLY.
YOU ASK ME, BANNER SHOULDA KEPT THIS GUY LOCKED UP. THROWIN' HIS WEIGHT AROUND LIKE HE'S--
HMM. THIS FISH TANK...
...I CAN SEE RIGHT THROUGH IT.
KRUKK
QUSSH
KRAKK
KIND OF A DESIGN FLAW.
KRIISSH
A ROOM FULL OF COMPUTERS. AND THEY'RE ALL PLUGGED IN.
WHY? THE PLACE IS ABANDONED--WHAT ARE THEY DOING?
AND HOW LONG HAVE I GOT TO WORK IT OUT?

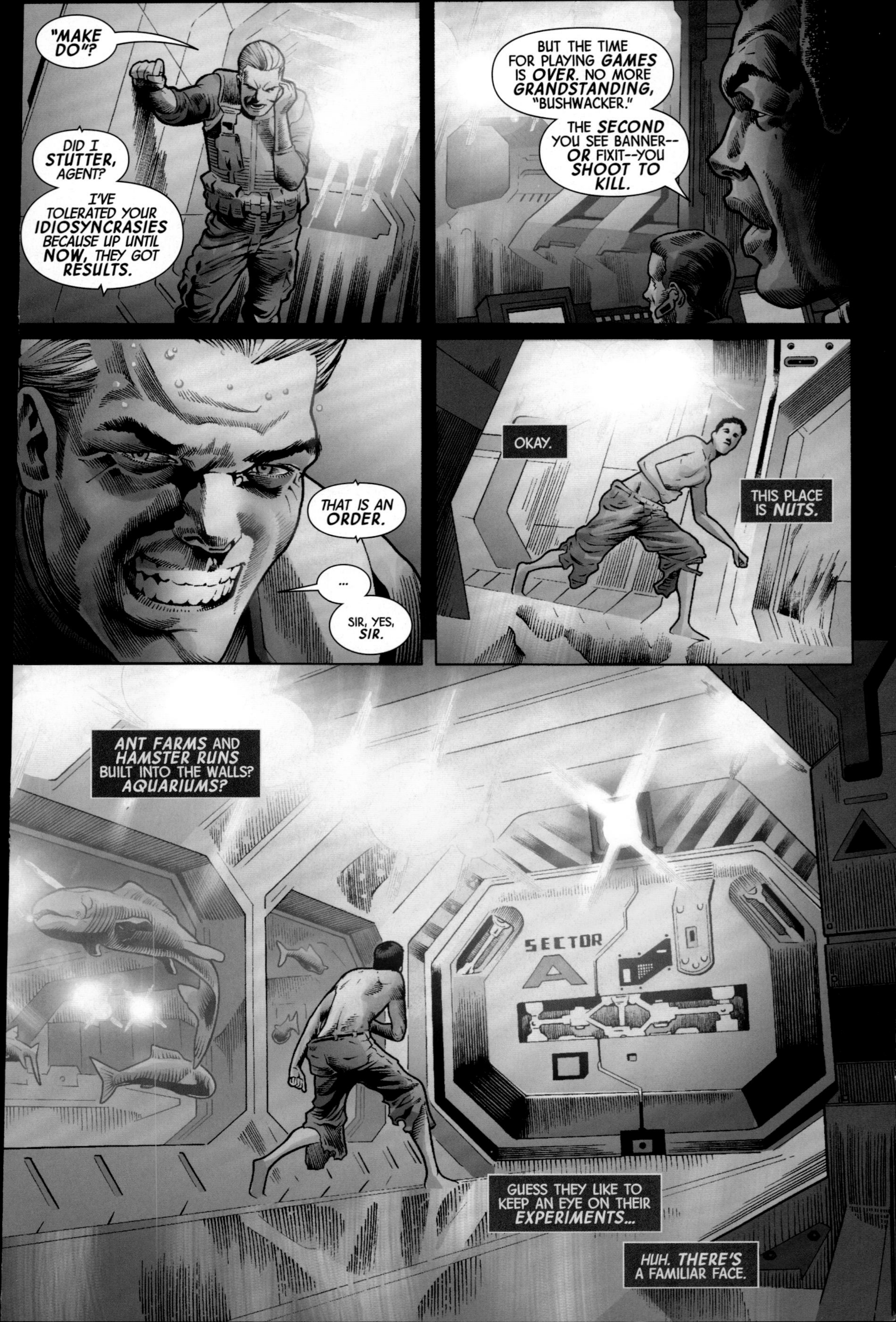
"MAKE DO"?
DID I STUTTER, AGENT?
I'VE TOLERATED YOUR IDIOSYNCRASIES BECAUSE UP UNTIL NOW, THEY GOT RESULTS.
BUT THE TIME FOR PLAYING GAMES IS OVER. NO MORE GRANDSTANDING, "BUSHWACKER."
THE SECOND YOU SEE BANNER-- OR FIXIT--YOU SHOOT TO KILL.
THAT IS AN ORDER.
...
SIR, YES, SIR.
OKAY.
THIS PLACE IS NUTS.
ANT FARMS AND HAMSTER RUNS BUILT INTO THE WALLS? AQUARIUMS?
SECTOR A
GUESS THEY LIKE TO KEEP AN EYE ON THEIR EXPERIMENTS...
HUH. THERE'S A FAMILIAR FACE.

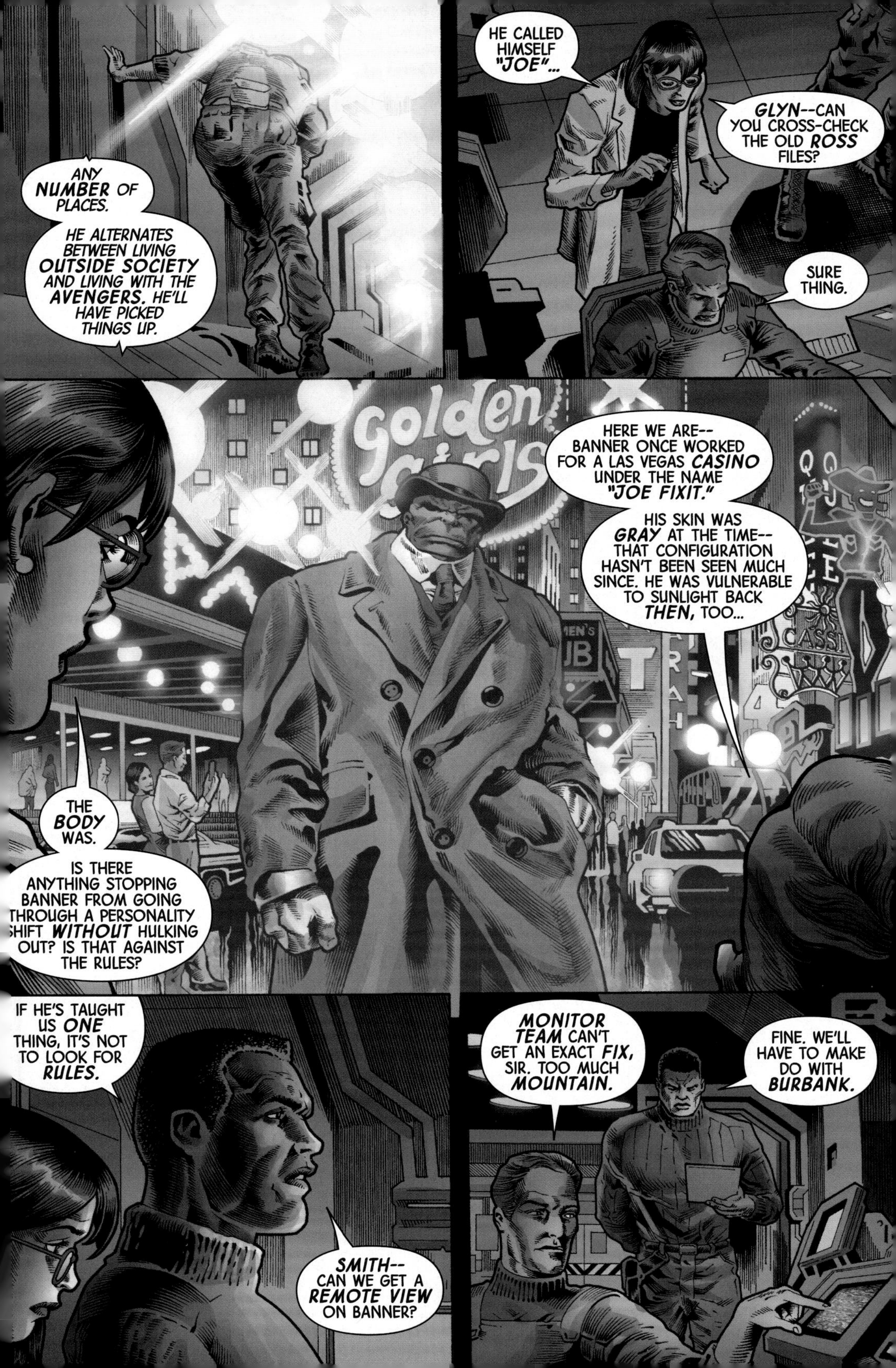
ANY NUMBER OF PLACES.
HE ALTERNATES BETWEEN LIVING OUTSIDE SOCIETY AND LIVING WITH THE AVENGERS. HE'LL HAVE PICKED THINGS UP.
HE CALLED HIMSELF "JOE"...
GLYN--CAN YOU CROSS-CHECK THE OLD ROSS FILES?
SURE THING.
HERE WE ARE-- BANNER ONCE WORKED FOR A LAS VEGAS CASINO UNDER THE NAME "JOE FIXIT."
HIS SKIN WAS GRAY AT THE TIME-- THAT CONFIGURATION HASN'T BEEN SEEN MUCH SINCE. HE WAS VULNERABLE TO SUNLIGHT BACK THEN, TOO...
THE BODY WAS.
IS THERE ANYTHING STOPPING BANNER FROM GOING THROUGH A PERSONALITY SHIFT WITHOUT HULKING OUT? IS THAT AGAINST THE RULES?
IF HE'S TAUGHT US ONE THING, IT'S NOT TO LOOK FOR RULES.
SMITH-- CAN WE GET A REMOTE VIEW ON BANNER?
MONITOR TEAM CAN'T GET AN EXACT FIX, SIR. TOO MUCH MOUNTAIN.
FINE. WE'LL HAVE TO MAKE DO WITH BURBANK.

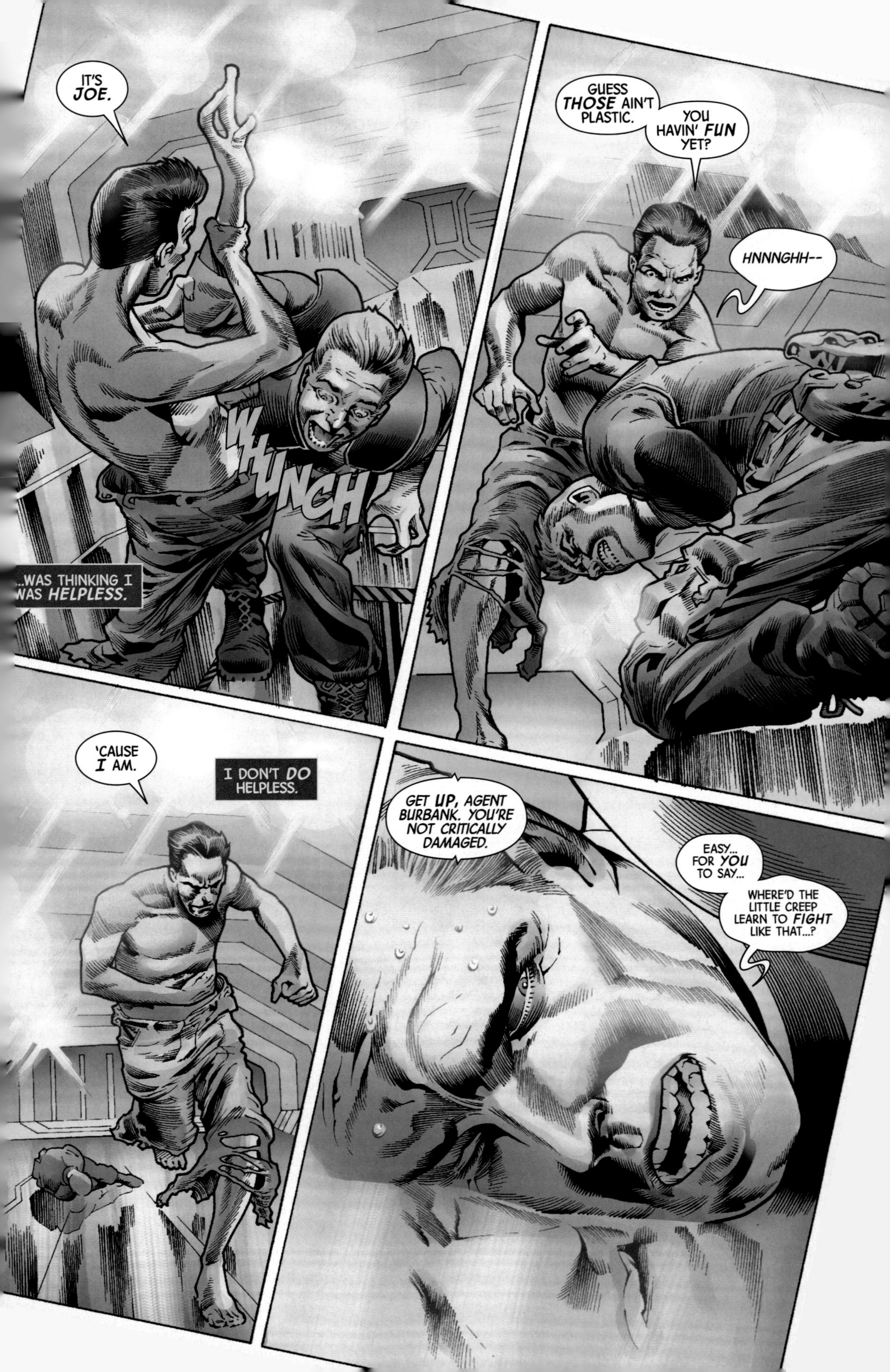
IT'S JOE.
WHUNCH!
...WAS THINKING I WAS HELPLESS.
GUESS THOSE AIN'T PLASTIC.
YOU HAVIN' FUN YET?
HNNNGHH--
'CAUSE I AM.
I DON'T DO HELPLESS.
GET UP, AGENT BURBANK. YOU'RE NOT CRITICALLY DAMAGED.
EASY... FOR YOU TO SAY...
WHERE'D THE LITTLE CREEP LEARN TO FIGHT LIKE THAT...?

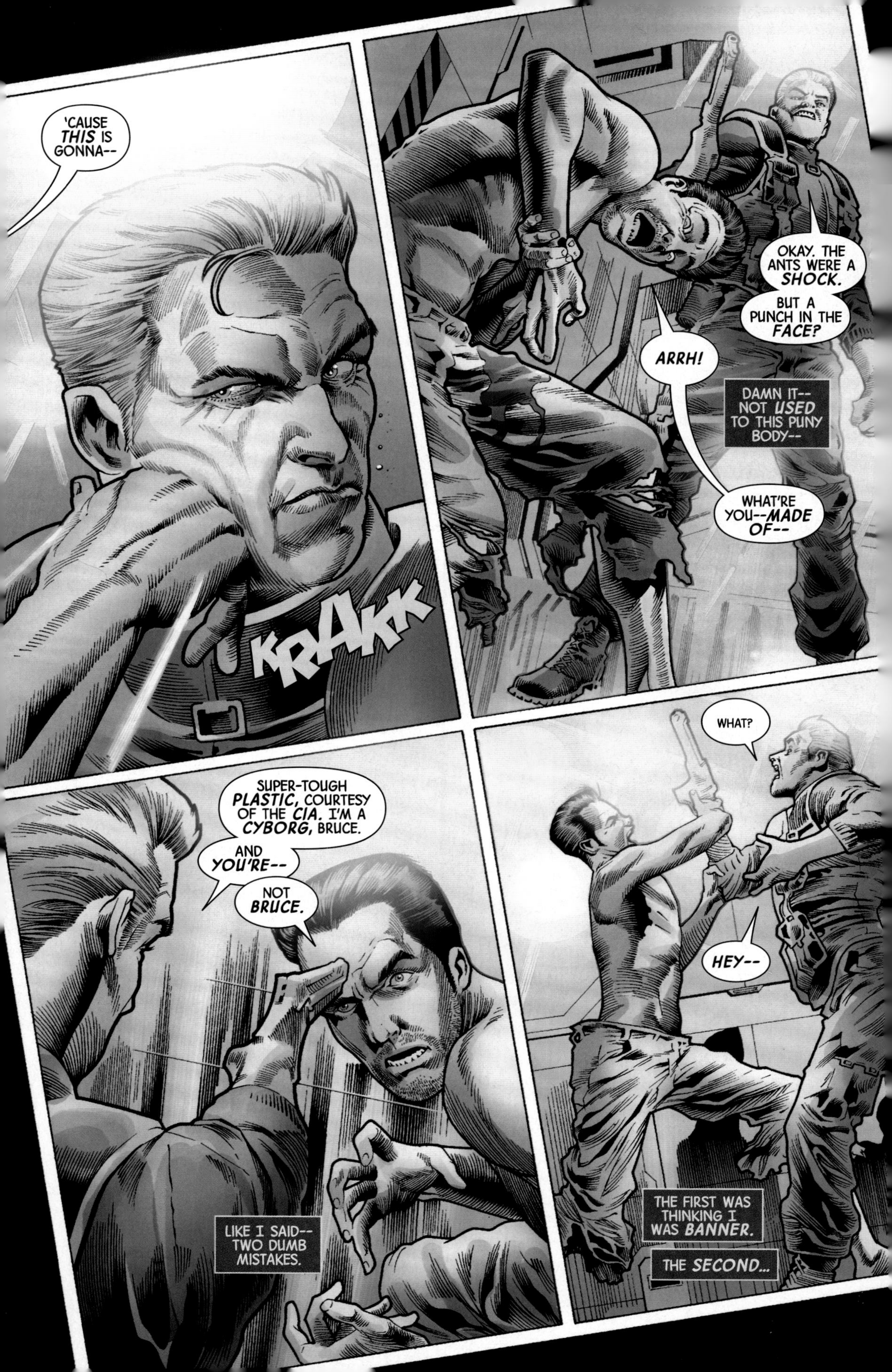
'CAUSE THIS IS GONNA--
KRAKK
OKAY. THE ANTS WERE A SHOCK.
BUT A PUNCH IN THE FACE?
ARRH!
DAMN IT-- NOT USED TO THIS PUNY BODY--
WHAT'RE YOU--MADE OF--
SUPER-TOUGH PLASTIC, COURTESY OF THE CIA. I'M A CYBORG, BRUCE.
AND YOU'RE--
NOT BRUCE.
LIKE I SAID-- TWO DUMB MISTAKES.
WHAT?
HEY--
THE FIRST WAS THINKING I WAS BANNER.
THE SECOND...

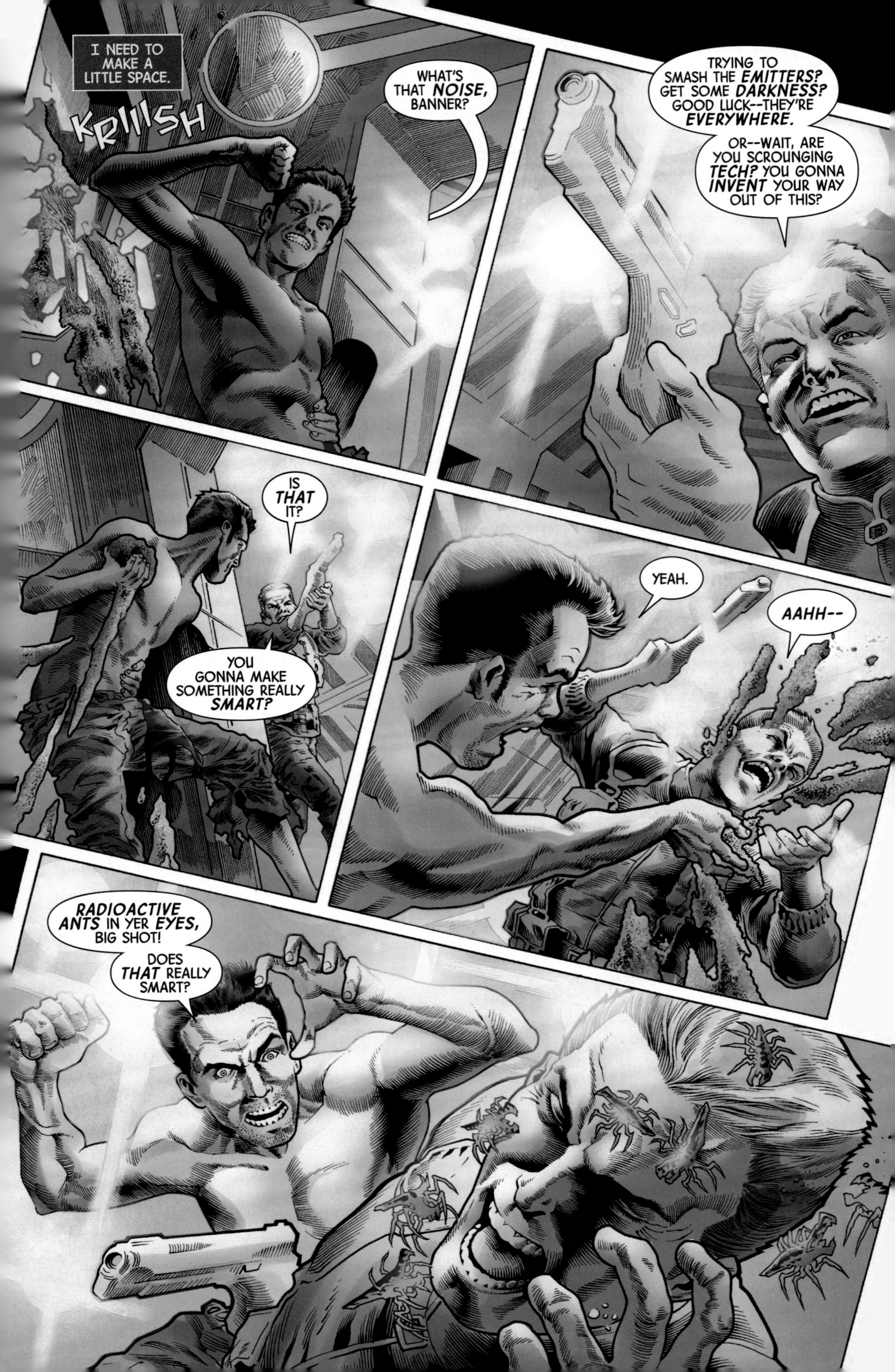
I NEED TO MAKE A LITTLE SPACE.
KRIIISH
WHAT'S THAT NOISE, BANNER?
TRYING TO SMASH THE EMITTERS? GET SOME DARKNESS? GOOD LUCK--THEY'RE EVERYWHERE.
OR--WAIT, ARE YOU SCROUNGING TECH? YOU GONNA INVENT YOUR WAY OUT OF THIS?
IS THAT IT?
YOU GONNA MAKE SOMETHING REALLY SMART?
YEAH.
AAHH--
RADIOACTIVE ANTS IN YER EYES, BIG SHOT!
DOES THAT REALLY SMART?

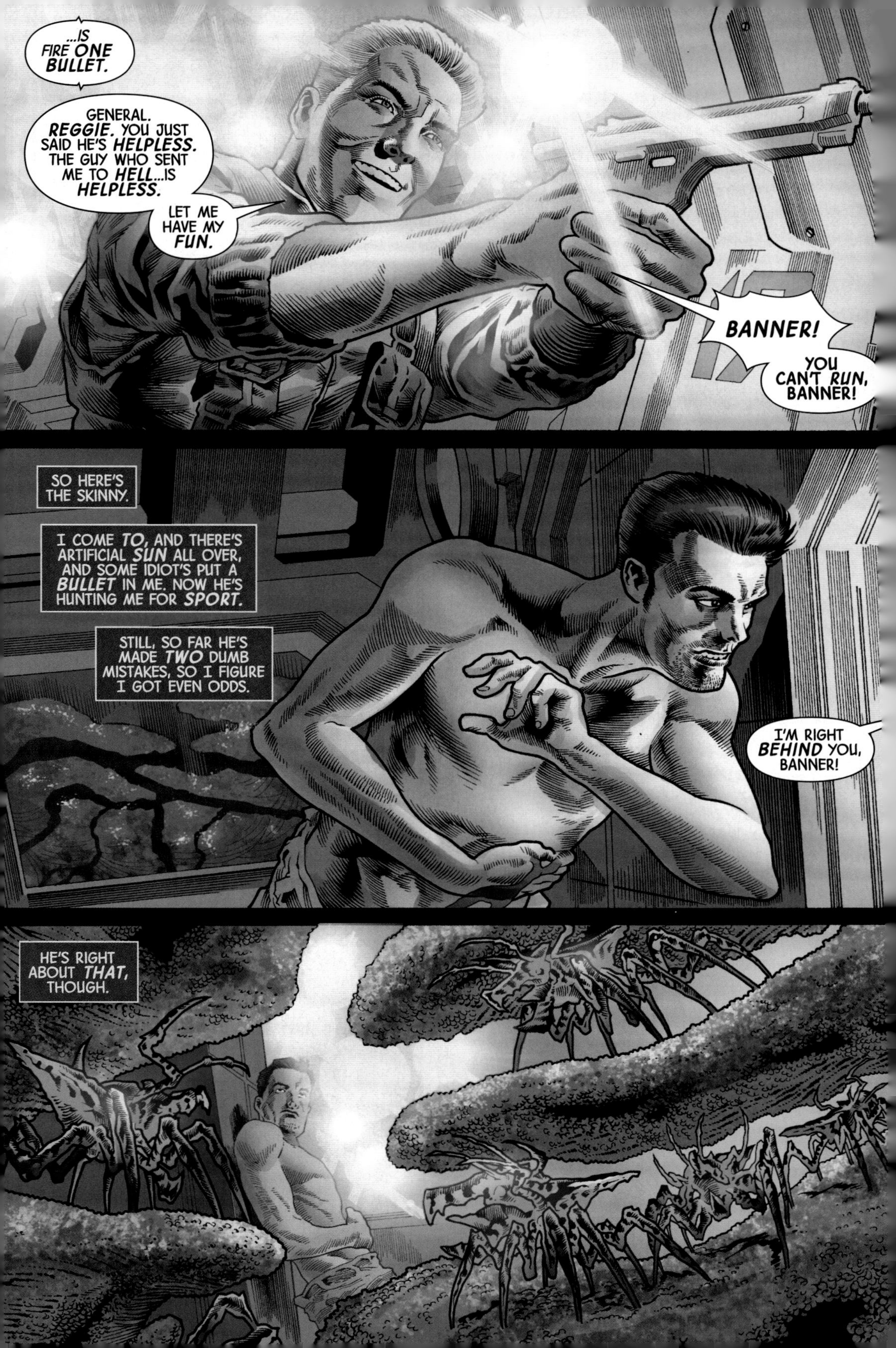
...IS FIRE ONE BULLET.
GENERAL. REGGIE. YOU JUST SAID HE'S HELPLESS. THE GUY WHO SENT ME TO HELL...IS HELPLESS.
LET ME HAVE MY FUN.
BANNER!
YOU CAN'T RUN, BANNER!
SO HERE'S THE SKINNY.
I COME TO, AND THERE'S ARTIFICIAL SUN ALL OVER, AND SOME IDIOT'S PUT A BULLET IN ME. NOW HE'S HUNTING ME FOR SPORT.
STILL, SO FAR HE'S MADE TWO DUMB MISTAKES, SO I FIGURE I GOT EVEN ODDS.
I'M RIGHT BEHIND YOU, BANNER!
HE'S RIGHT ABOUT THAT, THOUGH.

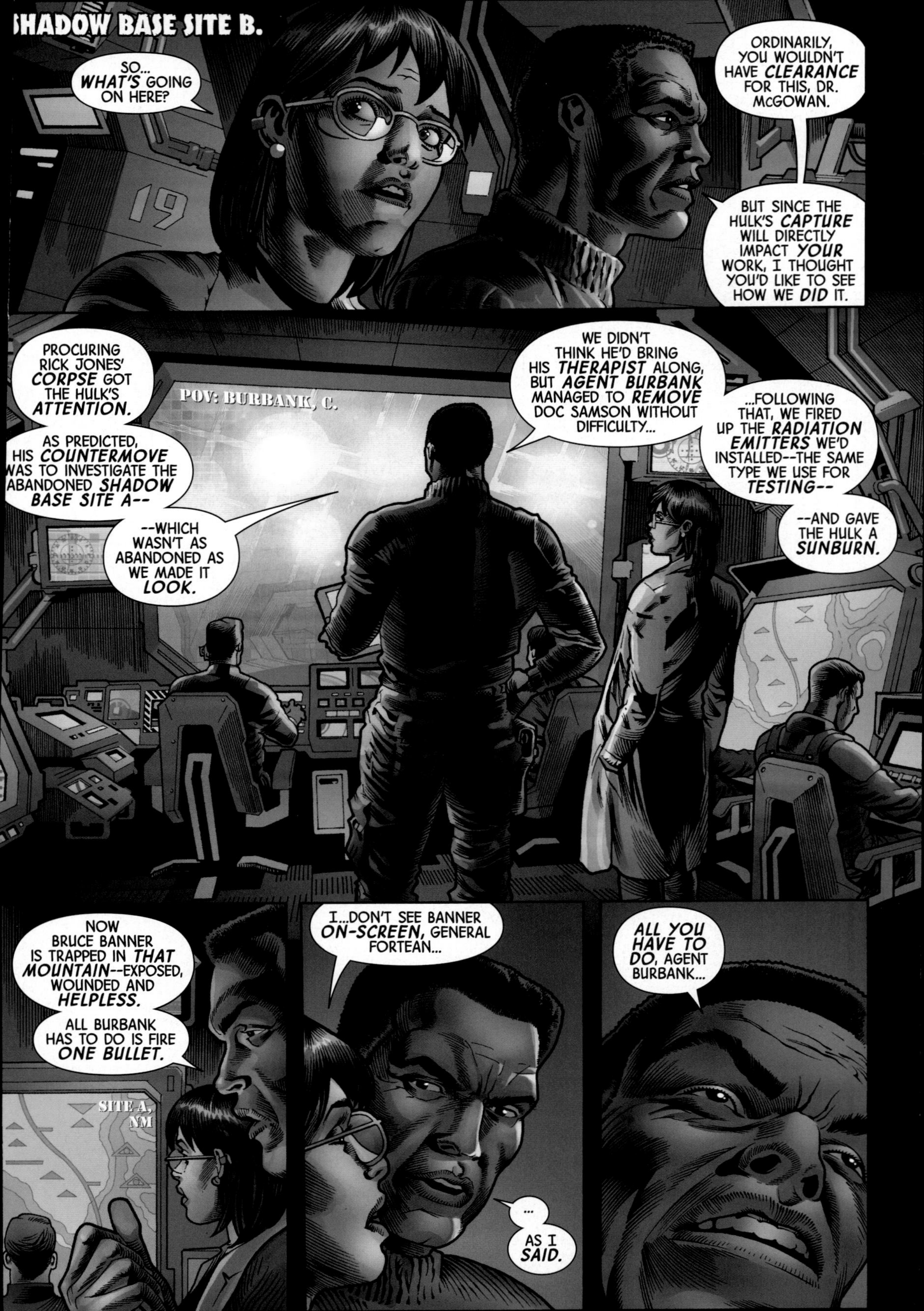
SHADOW BASE SITE B.
SO... WHAT'S GOING ON HERE?
ORDINARILY, YOU WOULDN'T HAVE CLEARANCE FOR THIS, DR. McGOWAN.
BUT SINCE THE HULK'S CAPTURE WILL DIRECTLY IMPACT YOUR WORK, I THOUGHT YOU'D LIKE TO SEE HOW WE DID IT.
POV: BURBANK, C.
PROCURING RICK JONES' CORPSE GOT THE HULK'S ATTENTION.
AS PREDICTED, HIS COUNTERMOVE WAS TO INVESTIGATE THE ABANDONED SHADOW BASE SITE A--
--WHICH WASN'T AS ABANDONED AS WE MADE IT LOOK.
WE DIDN'T THINK HE'D BRING HIS THERAPIST ALONG, BUT AGENT BURBANK MANAGED TO REMOVE DOC SAMSON WITHOUT DIFFICULTY...
...FOLLOWING THAT, WE FIRED UP THE RADIATION EMITTERS WE'D INSTALLED--THE SAME TYPE WE USE FOR TESTING--
--AND GAVE THE HULK A SUNBURN.
NOW BRUCE BANNER IS TRAPPED IN THAT MOUNTAIN--EXPOSED, WOUNDED AND HELPLESS.
ALL BURBANK HAS TO DO IS FIRE ONE BULLET.
SITE A, NM
I...DON'T SEE BANNER ON-SCREEN, GENERAL FORTEAN...
...
AS I SAID.
ALL YOU HAVE TO DO, AGENT BURBANK...

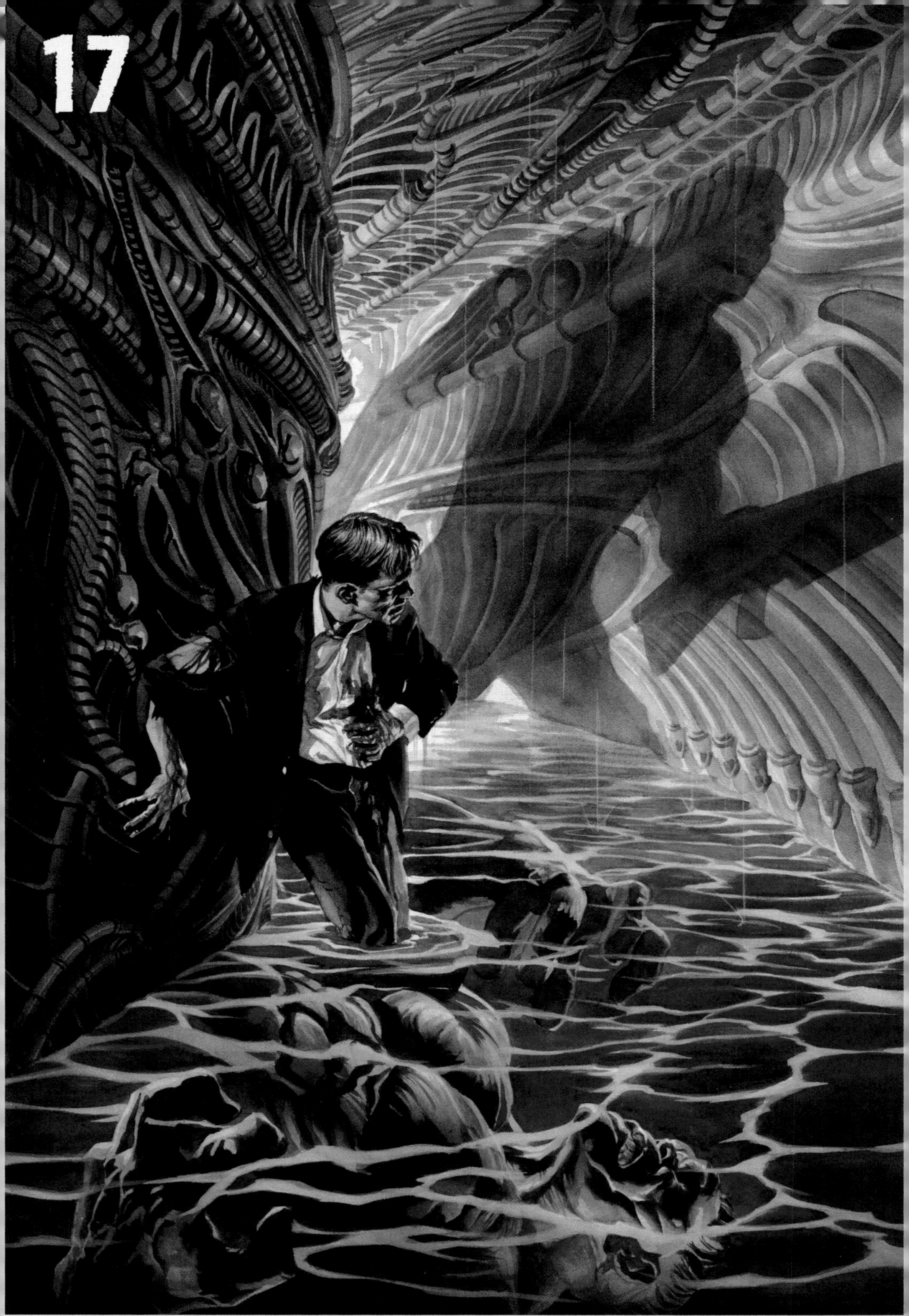
17

"NOBODY TELLS ME WHAT TO DO. YOU KEEP NEEDLIN' ME, AND IF I WANT TO, I'M GONNA TAKE THIS JOINT APART, AND YOU'RE NOT GONNA KNOW WHAT HIT YA."

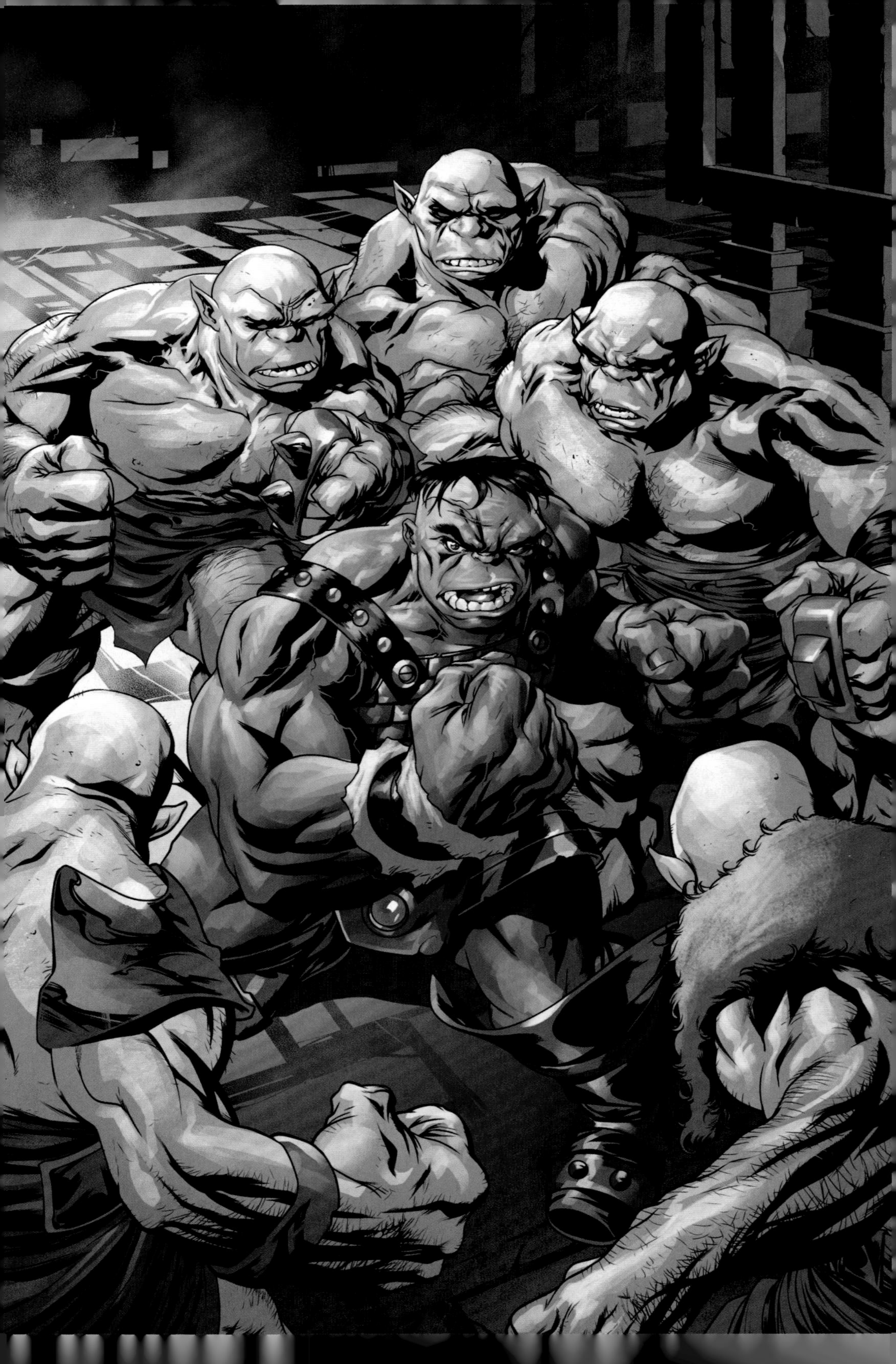

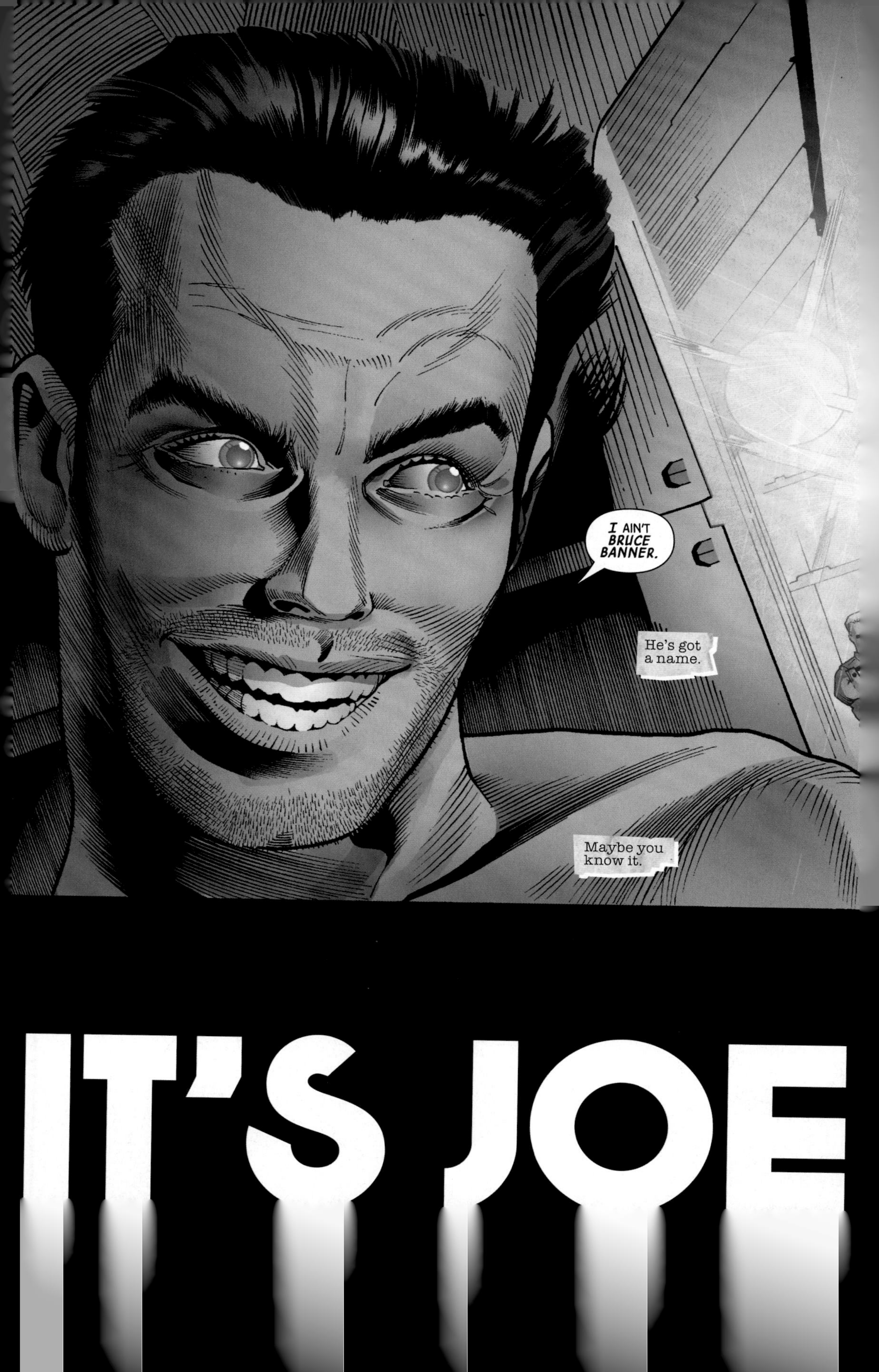
I AIN'T BRUCE BANNER.
He's got a name.
Maybe you know it.
IT'S JOE

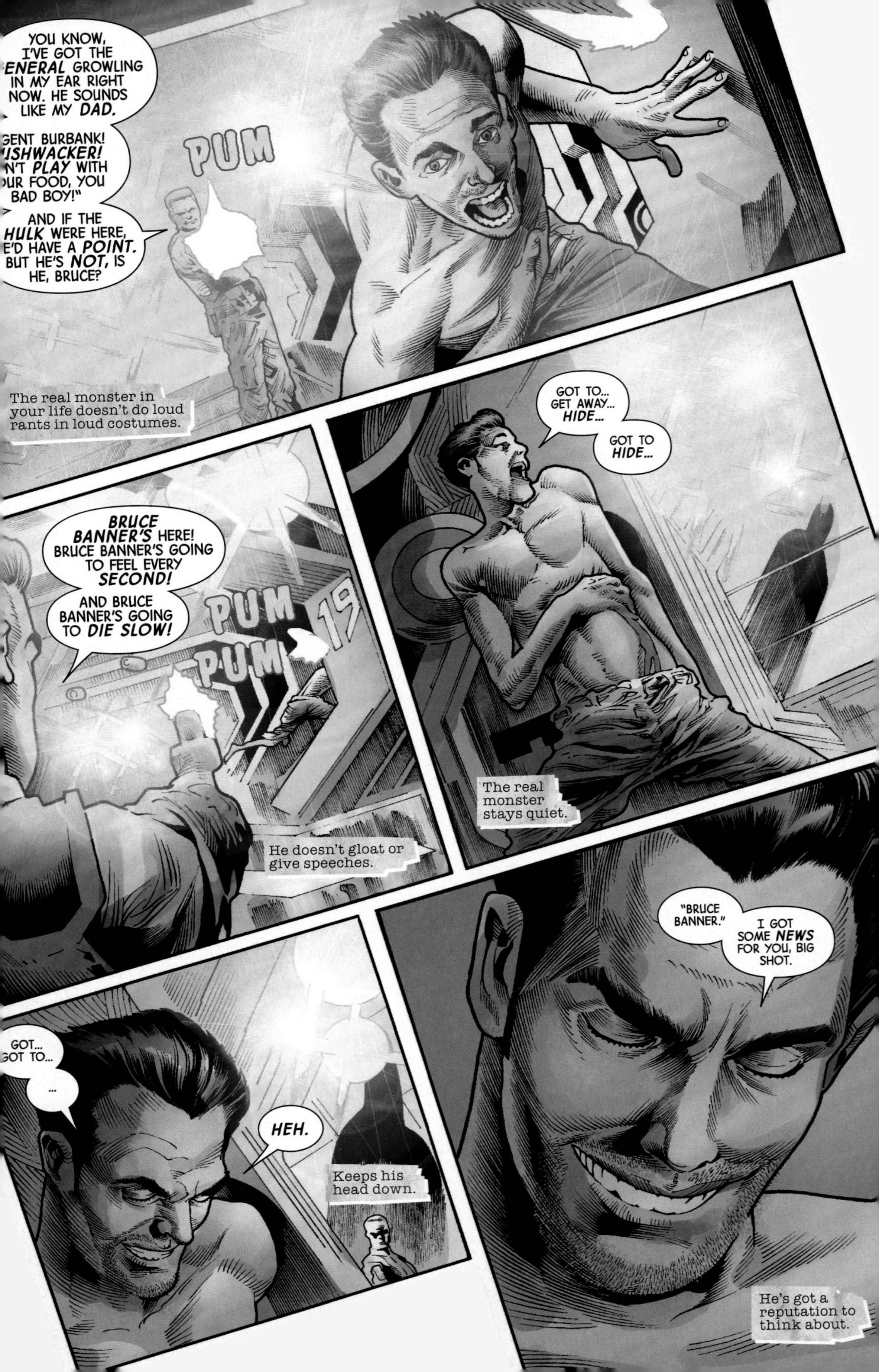

YOU KNOW, I'VE GOT THE ENERAL GROWLING IN MY EAR RIGHT NOW. HE SOUNDS LIKE MY DAD.
GENT BURBANK! ISHWACKER! N'T PLAY WITH UR FOOD, YOU BAD BOY!"
AND IF THE HULK WERE HERE, E'D HAVE A POINT. BUT HE'S NOT, IS HE, BRUCE?
PUM
The real monster in your life doesn't do loud rants in loud costumes.
GOT TO... GET AWAY... HIDE...
GOT TO HIDE...
BRUCE BANNER'S HERE! BRUCE BANNER'S GOING TO FEEL EVERY SECOND!
AND BRUCE BANNER'S GOING TO DIE SLOW!
PUM
PUM
He doesn't gloat or give speeches.
The real monster stays quiet.
"BRUCE BANNER."
I GOT SOME NEWS FOR YOU, BIG SHOT.
GOT... GOT TO...
...
HEH.
Keeps his head down.
He's got a reputation to think about.

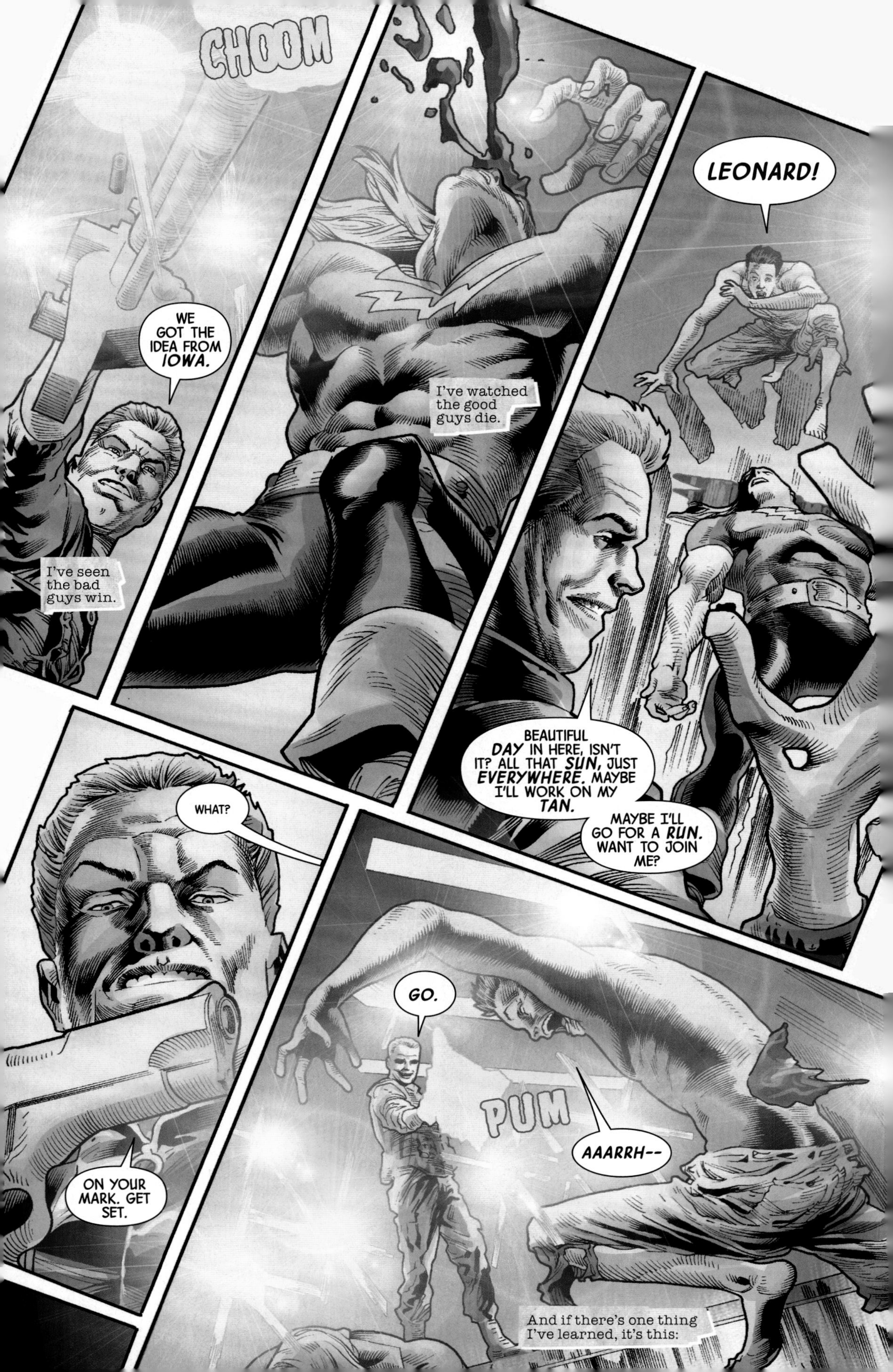
CHOOM
WE GOT THE IDEA FROM IOWA.
I've seen the bad guys win.
I've watched the good guys die.
LEONARD!
BEAUTIFUL DAY IN HERE, ISN'T IT? ALL THAT SUN, JUST EVERYWHERE. MAYBE I'LL WORK ON MY TAN.
MAYBE I'LL GO FOR A RUN. WANT TO JOIN ME?
WHAT?
ON YOUR MARK. GET SET.
GO.
PUM
AAARRH--
And if there's one thing I've learned, it's this:

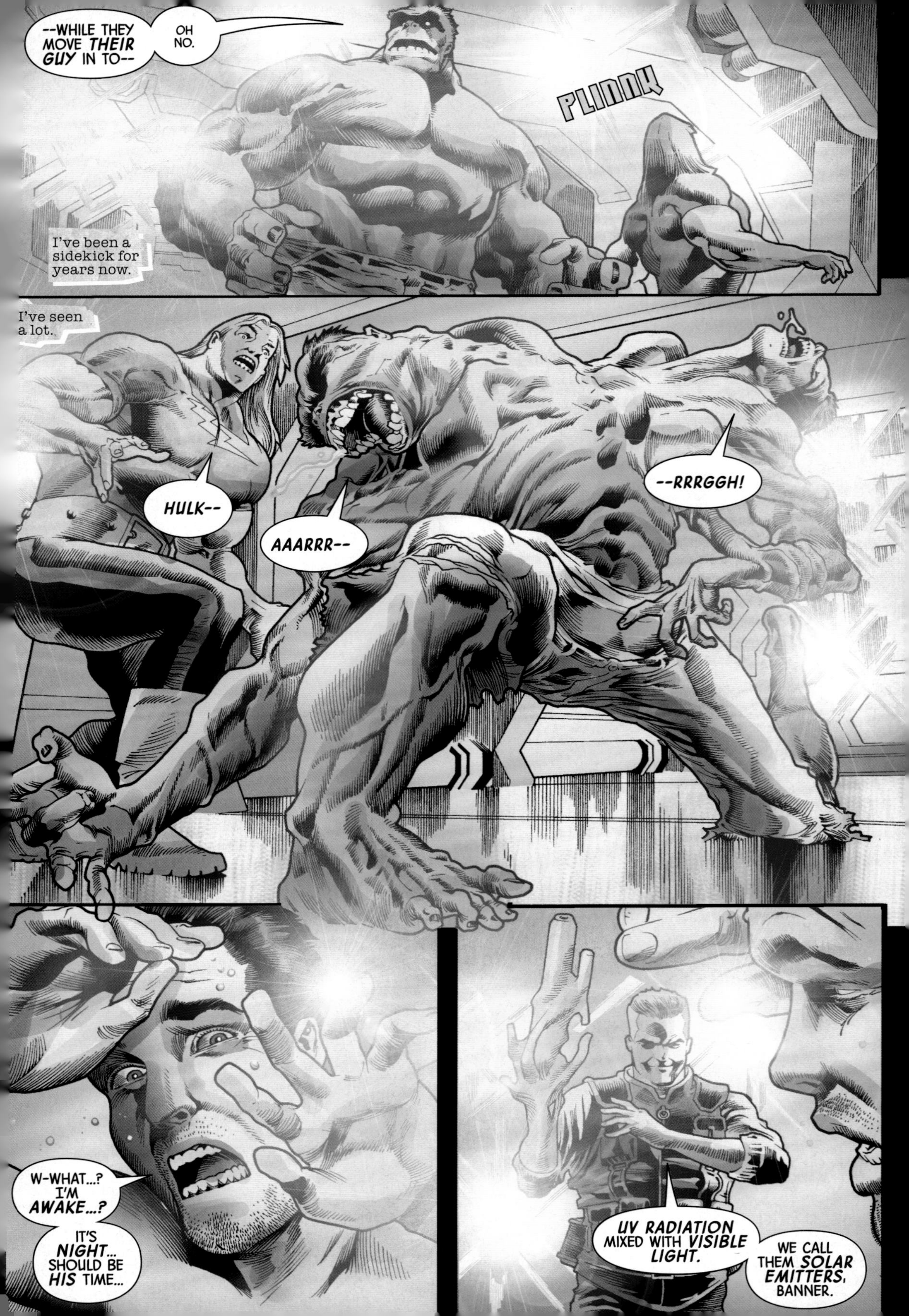
--WHILE THEY MOVE THEIR GUY IN TO--
OH NO.
PLINNK
I've been a sidekick for years now.
I've seen a lot.
HULK--
AAARRR--
--RRRGGH!
W-WHAT...? I'M AWAKE...?
IT'S NIGHT... SHOULD BE HIS TIME...
UV RADIATION MIXED WITH VISIBLE LIGHT.
WE CALL THEM SOLAR EMITTERS, BANNER.

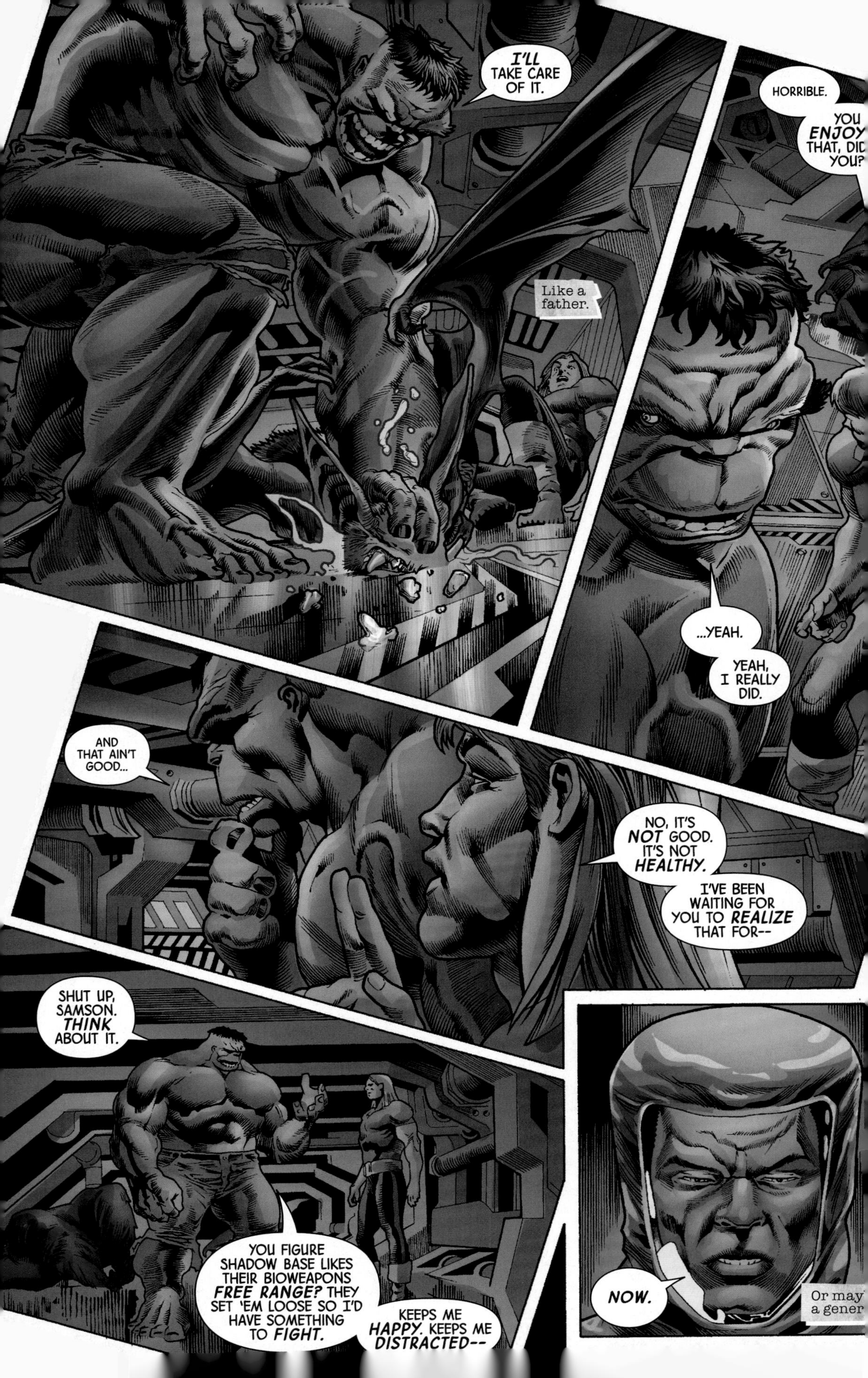
I'LL TAKE CARE OF IT.
Like a father.
HORRIBLE.
YOU ENJOY THAT, DID YOU?
...YEAH.
YEAH, I REALLY DID.
AND THAT AIN'T GOOD...
NO, IT'S NOT GOOD. IT'S NOT HEALTHY.
I'VE BEEN WAITING FOR YOU TO REALIZE THAT FOR--
SHUT UP, SAMSON. THINK ABOUT IT.
YOU FIGURE SHADOW BASE LIKES THEIR BIOWEAPONS FREE RANGE? THEY SET 'EM LOOSE SO I'D HAVE SOMETHING TO FIGHT.
KEEPS ME HAPPY. KEEPS ME DISTRACTED--
NOW.
Or may a gener

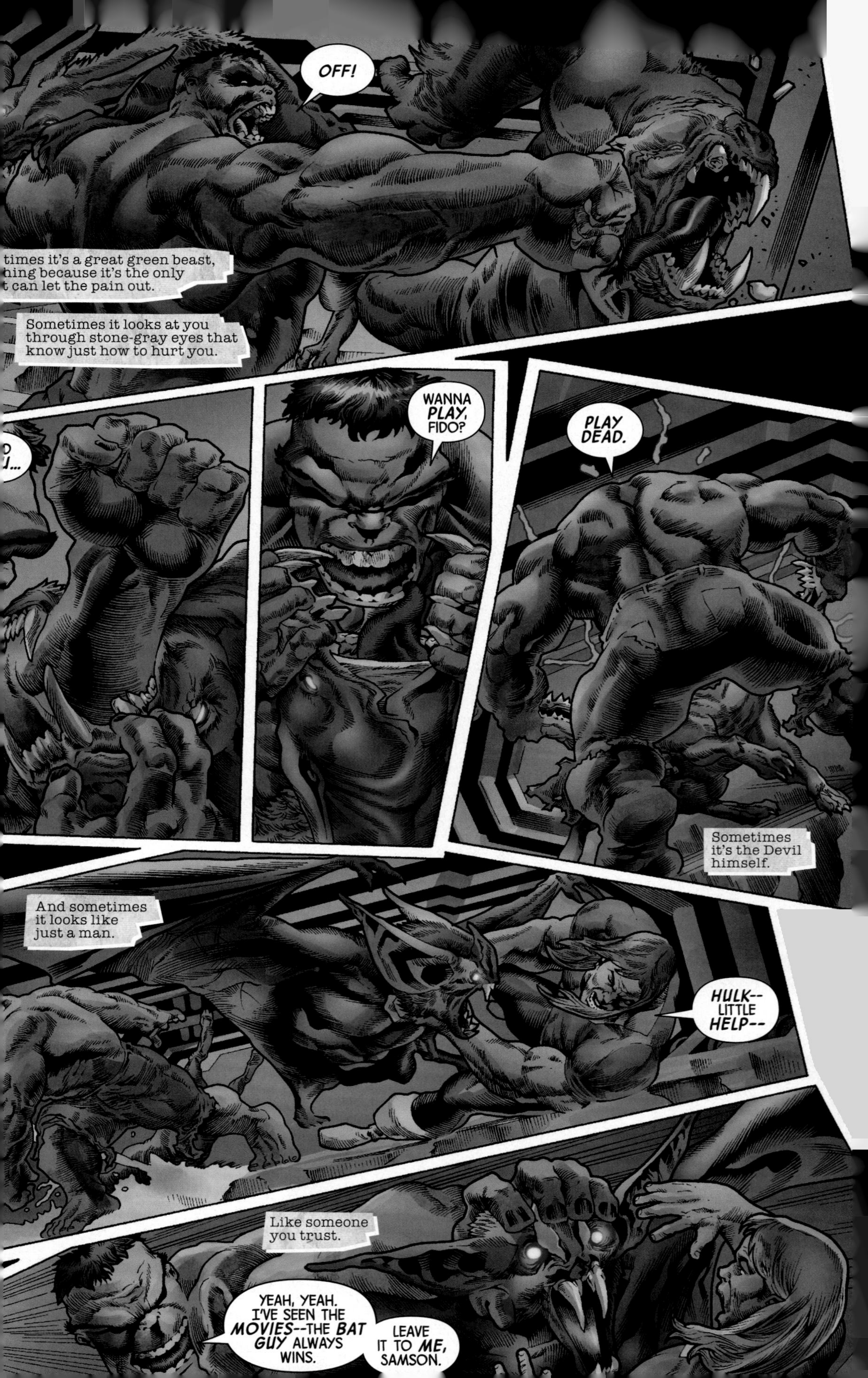
OFF!
times it's a great green beast,
hing because it's the only
t can let the pain out.
Sometimes it looks at you through stone-gray eyes that know just how to hurt you.
WANNA PLAY, FIDO?
PLAY DEAD.
Sometimes it's the Devil himself.
And sometimes it looks like just a man.
HULK-- LITTLE HELP--
Like someone you trust.
YEAH, YEAH. I'VE SEEN THE MOVIES--THE BAT GUY ALWAYS WINS.
LEAVE IT TO ME, SAMSON.

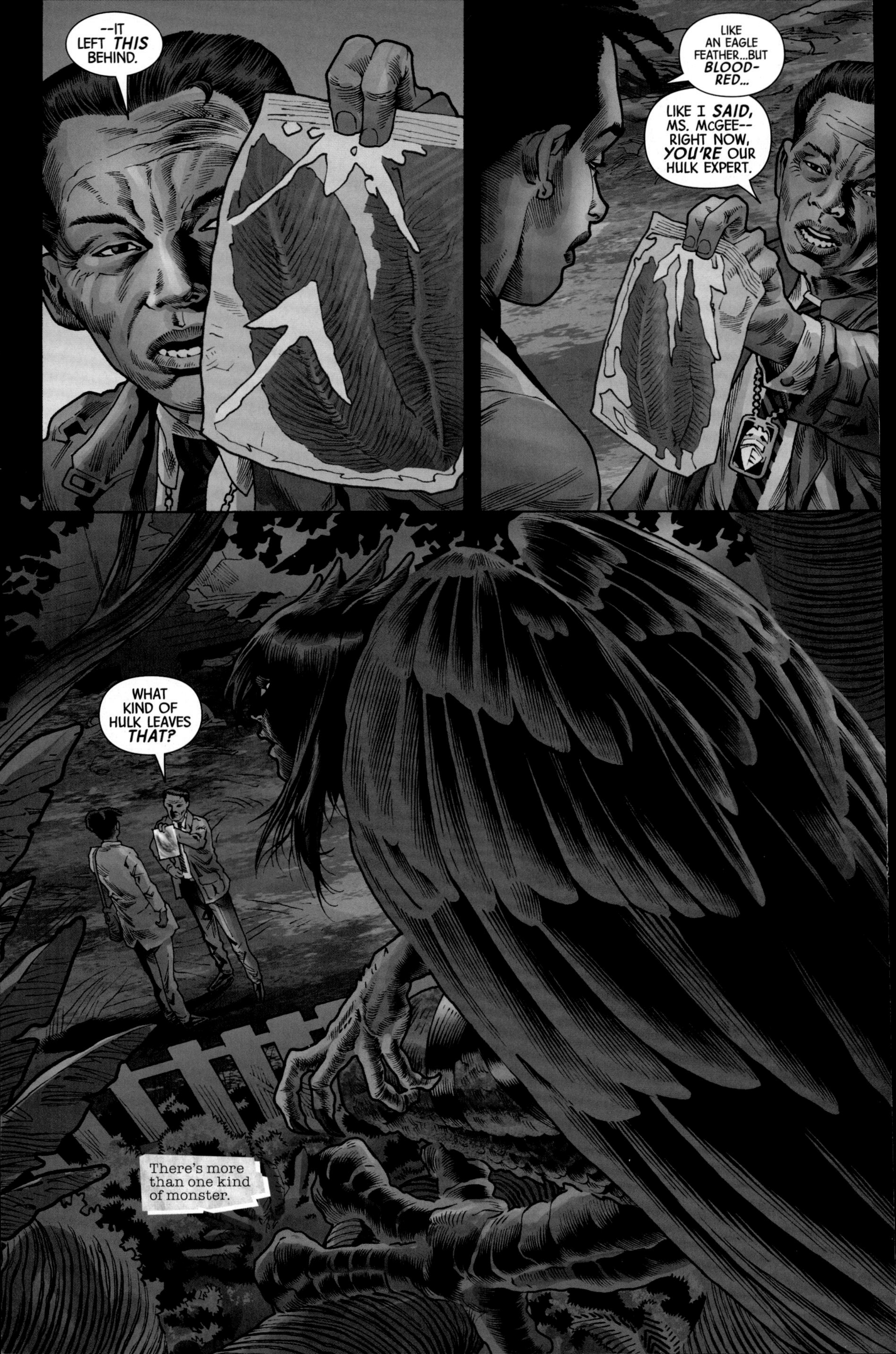
--IT LEFT THIS BEHIND.
LIKE AN EAGLE FEATHER...BUT BLOOD-RED...
LIKE I SAID, MS. McGEE-- RIGHT NOW, YOU'RE OUR HULK EXPERT.
WHAT KIND OF HULK LEAVES THAT?
There's more than one kind of monster.

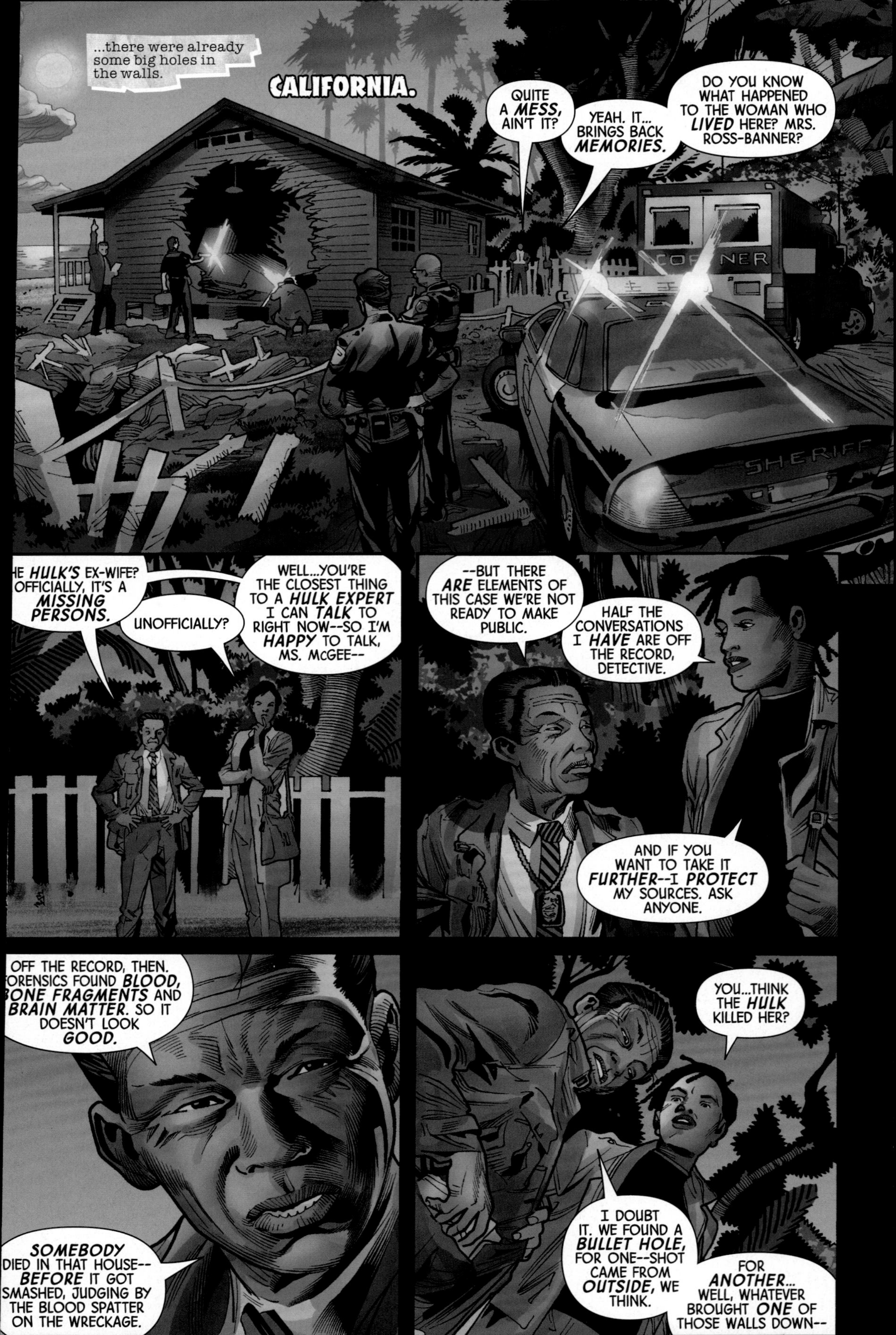
...there were already some big holes in the walls.
CALIFORNIA.
QUITE A MESS, AIN'T IT?
YEAH. IT... BRINGS BACK MEMORIES.
DO YOU KNOW WHAT HAPPENED TO THE WOMAN WHO LIVED HERE? MRS. ROSS-BANNER?
CORONER
SHERIFF
HE HULK'S EX-WIFE? OFFICIALLY, IT'S A MISSING PERSONS.
UNOFFICIALLY?
WELL...YOU'RE THE CLOSEST THING TO A HULK EXPERT I CAN TALK TO RIGHT NOW--SO I'M HAPPY TO TALK, MS. McGEE--
--BUT THERE ARE ELEMENTS OF THIS CASE WE'RE NOT READY TO MAKE PUBLIC.
HALF THE CONVERSATIONS I HAVE ARE OFF THE RECORD, DETECTIVE.
AND IF YOU WANT TO TAKE IT FURTHER--I PROTECT MY SOURCES. ASK ANYONE.
OFF THE RECORD, THEN. FORENSICS FOUND BLOOD, BONE FRAGMENTS AND BRAIN MATTER. SO IT DOESN'T LOOK GOOD.
SOMEBODY DIED IN THAT HOUSE--BEFORE IT GOT SMASHED, JUDGING BY THE BLOOD SPATTER ON THE WRECKAGE.
YOU...THINK THE HULK KILLED HER?
I DOUBT IT. WE FOUND A BULLET HOLE, FOR ONE--SHOT CAME FROM OUTSIDE, WE THINK.
FOR ANOTHER... WELL, WHATEVER BROUGHT ONE OF THOSE WALLS DOWN--

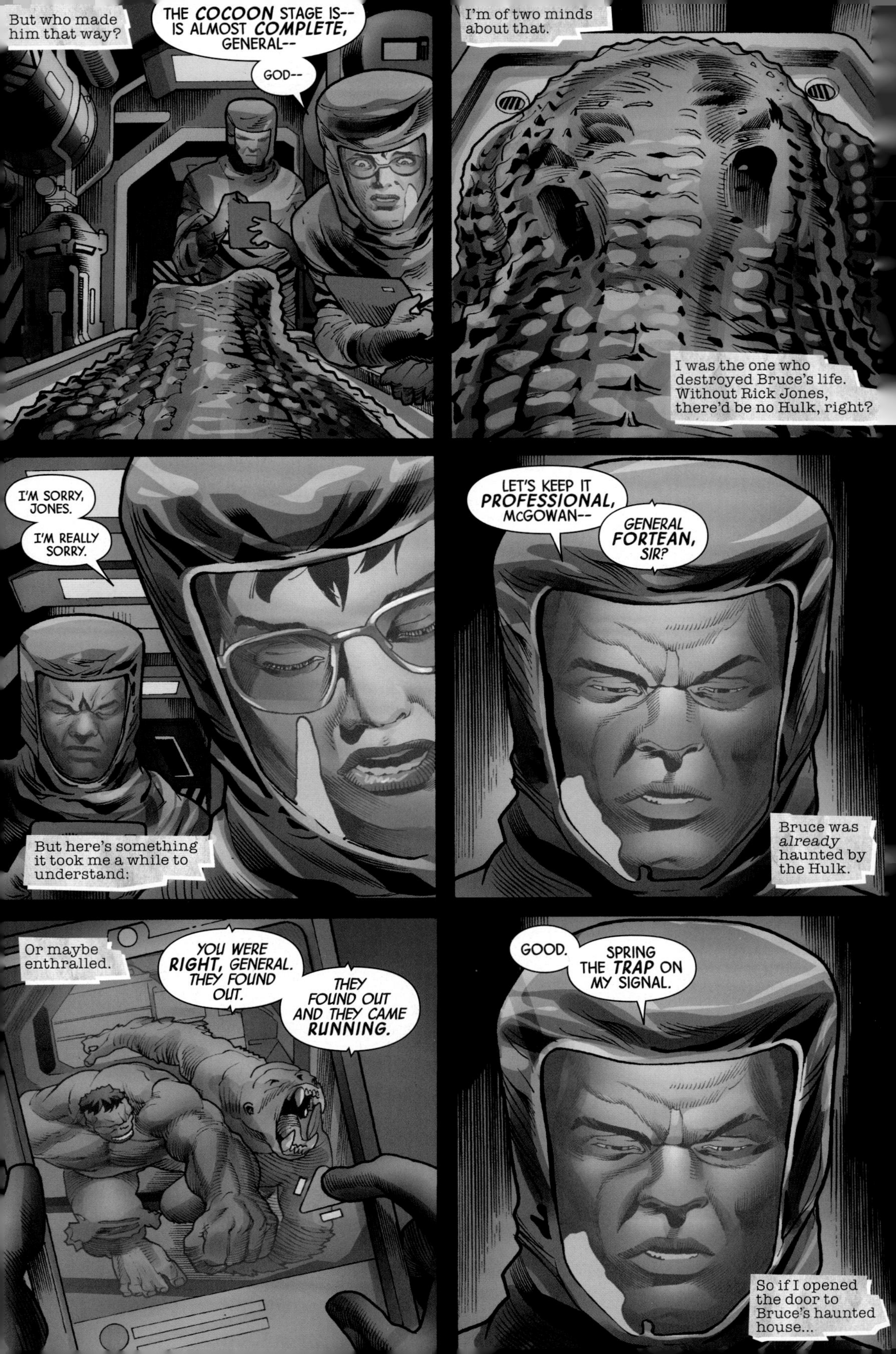

But who made him that way?
THE COCOON STAGE IS-- IS ALMOST COMPLETE, GENERAL--
GOD--
I'm of two minds about that.
I was the one who destroyed Bruce's life. Without Rick Jones, there'd be no Hulk, right?
I'M SORRY, JONES.
I'M REALLY SORRY.
But here's something it took me a while to understand:
LET'S KEEP IT PROFESSIONAL, McGOWAN--
GENERAL FORTEAN, SIR?
Bruce was already haunted by the Hulk.
Or maybe enthralled.
YOU WERE RIGHT, GENERAL. THEY FOUND OUT.
THEY FOUND OUT AND THEY CAME RUNNING.
GOOD.
SPRING THE TRAP ON MY SIGNAL.
So if I opened the door to Bruce's haunted house...

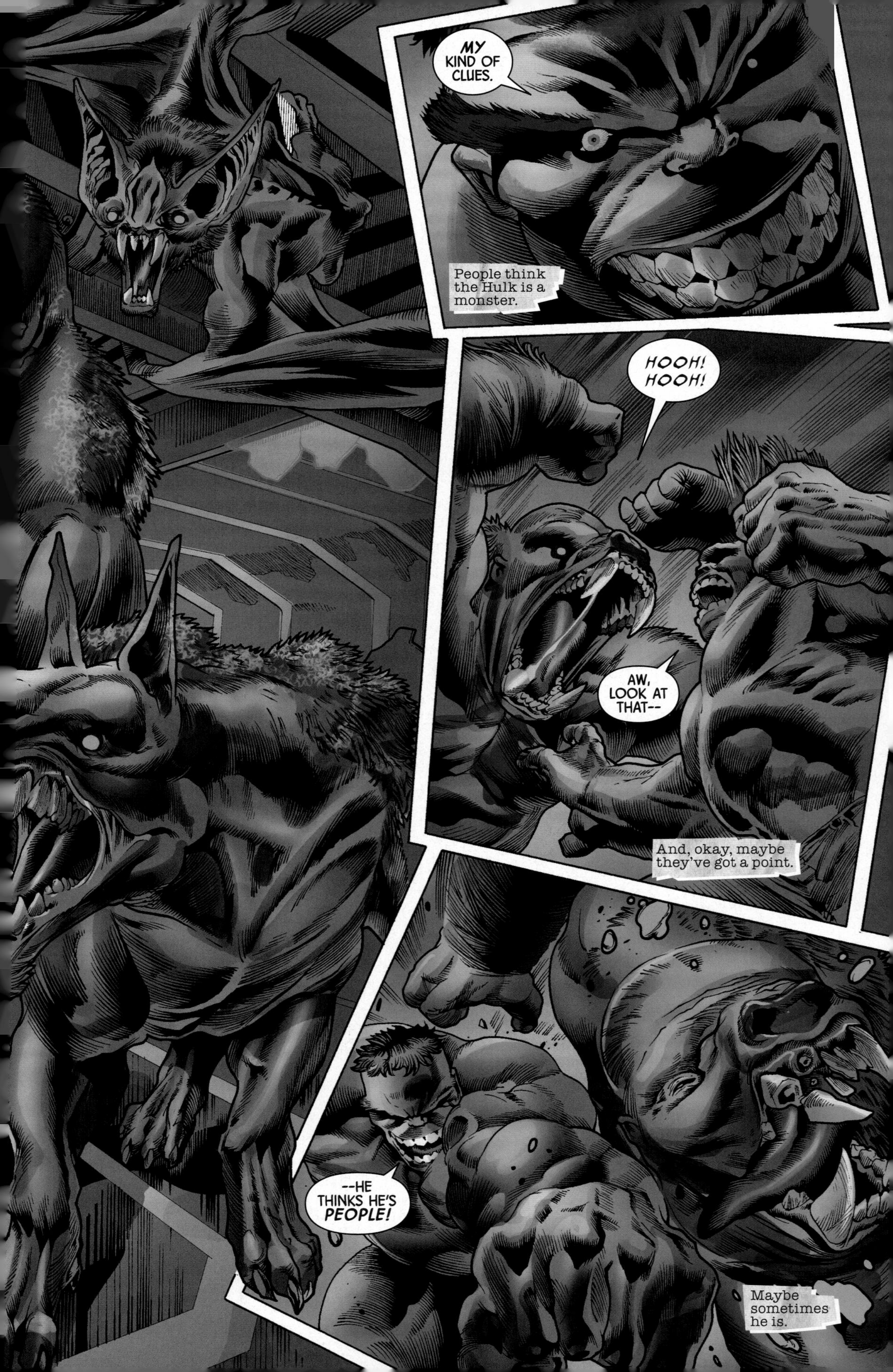
MY KIND OF CLUES.
People think the Hulk is a monster.
HOOH! HOOH!
AW, LOOK AT THAT--
And, okay, maybe they've got a point.
--HE THINKS HE'S PEOPLE!
Maybe sometimes he is.

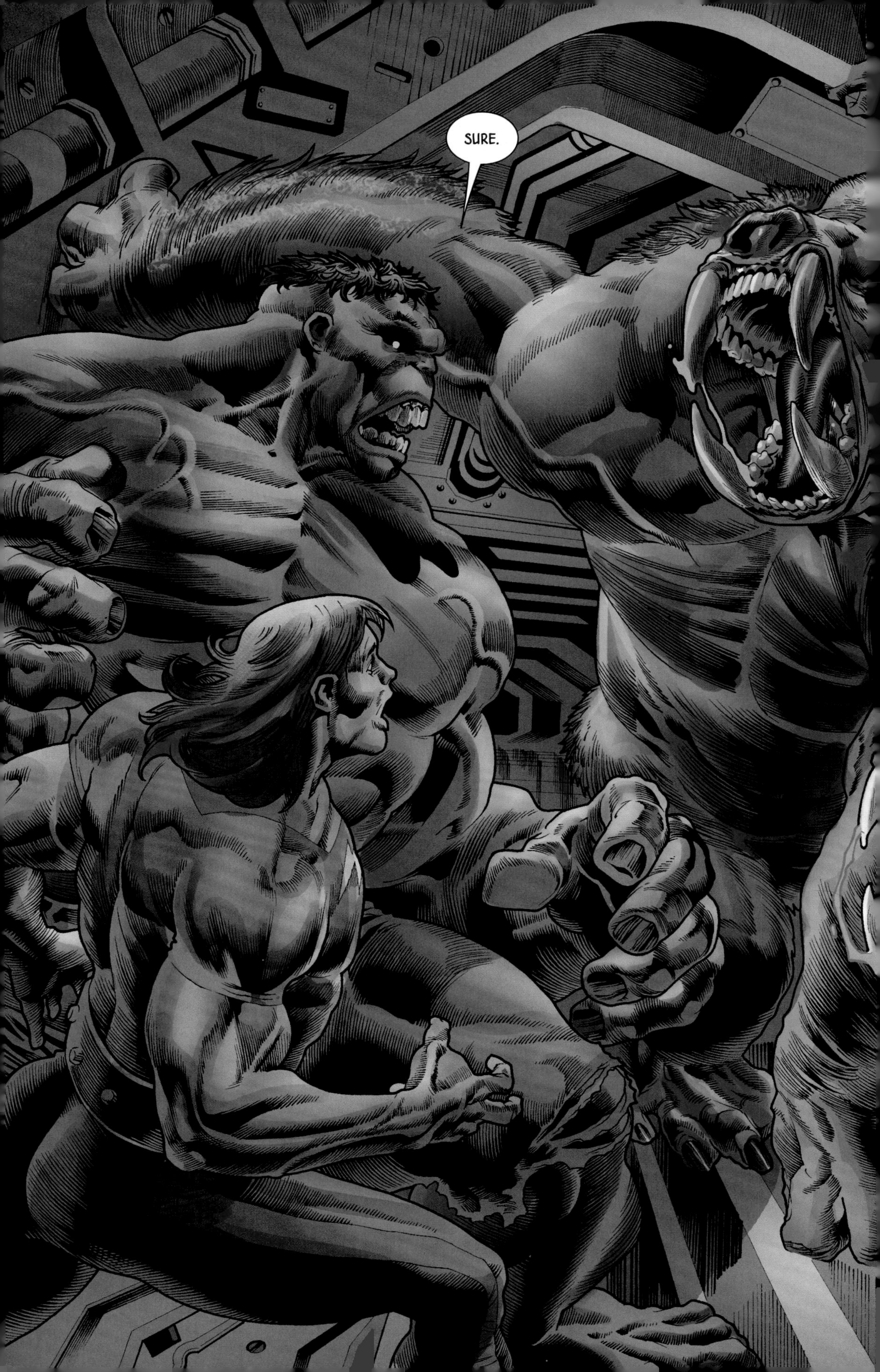
SURE.

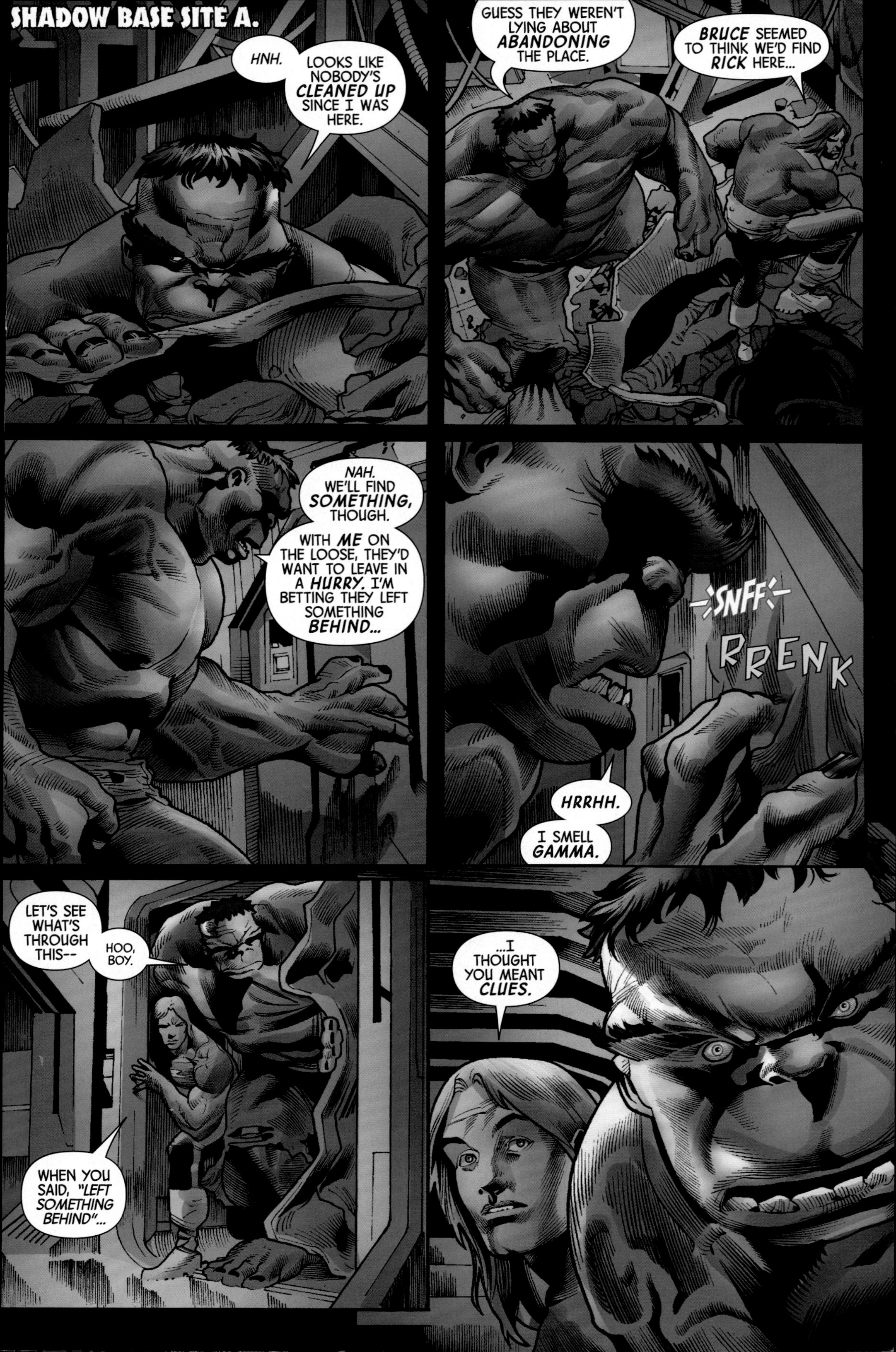
SHADOW BASE SITE A.
HNH.
LOOKS LIKE NOBODY'S CLEANED UP SINCE I WAS HERE.
GUESS THEY WEREN'T LYING ABOUT ABANDONING THE PLACE.
BRUCE SEEMED TO THINK WE'D FIND RICK HERE...
NAH. WE'LL FIND SOMETHING, THOUGH.
WITH ME ON THE LOOSE, THEY'D WANT TO LEAVE IN A HURRY. I'M BETTING THEY LEFT SOMETHING BEHIND...
SNFF
RRENK
HRRHH.
I SMELL GAMMA.
LET'S SEE WHAT'S THROUGH THIS--
HOO, BOY.
WHEN YOU SAID, "LEFT SOMETHING BEHIND"...
...I THOUGHT YOU MEANT CLUES.

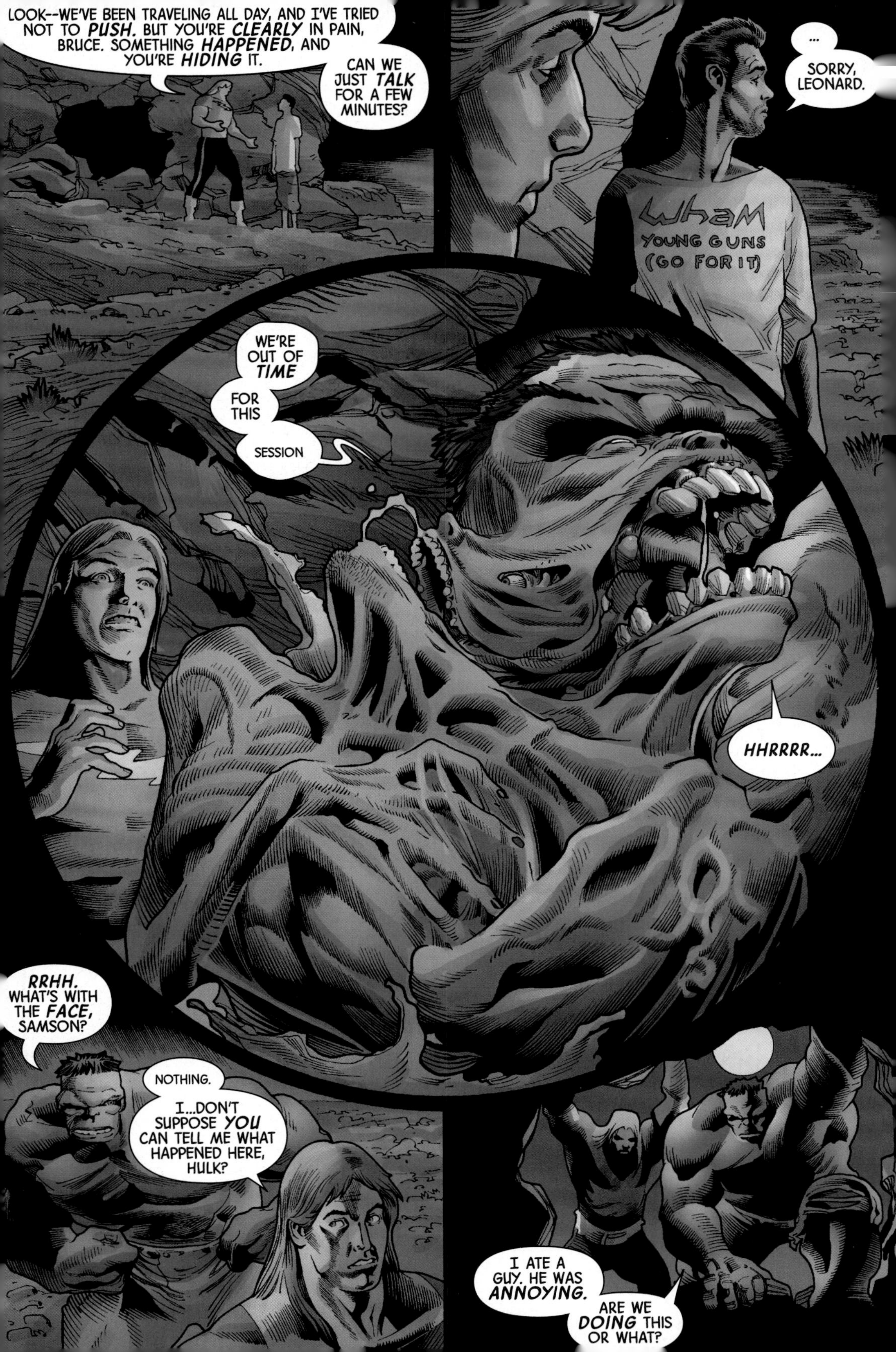
LOOK--WE'VE BEEN TRAVELING ALL DAY, AND I'VE TRIED NOT TO PUSH. BUT YOU'RE CLEARLY IN PAIN, BRUCE. SOMETHING HAPPENED, AND YOU'RE HIDING IT.
CAN WE JUST TALK FOR A FEW MINUTES?
...
SORRY, LEONARD.
WHAM
YOUNG GUNS
(GO FOR IT)
WE'RE OUT OF TIME
FOR THIS
SESSION
HHRRRR...
RRHH. WHAT'S WITH THE FACE, SAMSON?
NOTHING.
I...DON'T SUPPOSE YOU CAN TELL ME WHAT HAPPENED HERE, HULK?
I ATE A GUY. HE WAS ANNOYING.
ARE WE DOING THIS OR WHAT?

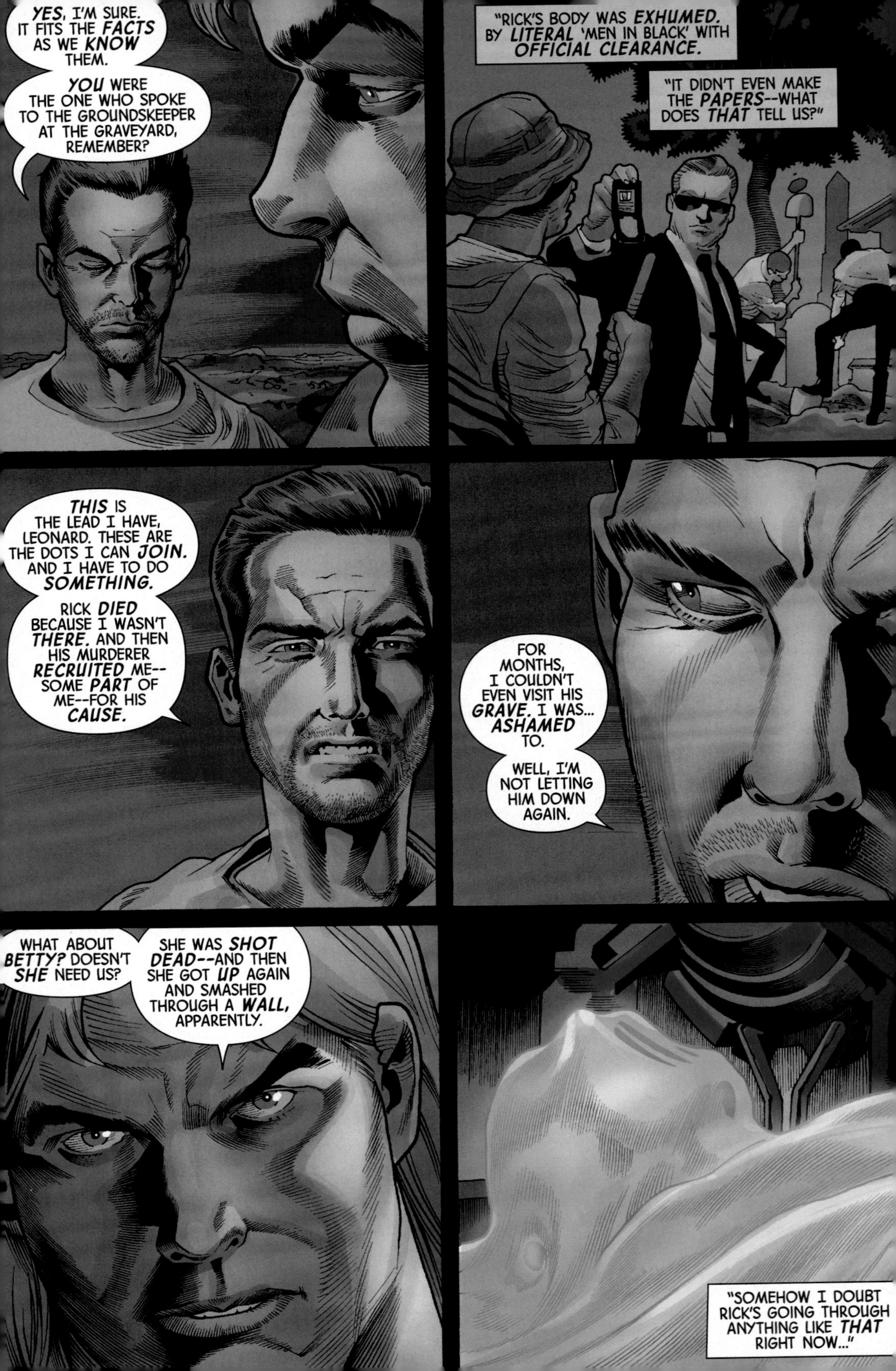
YES, I'M SURE. IT FITS THE FACTS AS WE KNOW THEM.
YOU WERE THE ONE WHO SPOKE TO THE GROUNDSKEEPER AT THE GRAVEYARD, REMEMBER?
"RICK'S BODY WAS EXHUMED. BY LITERAL 'MEN IN BLACK' WITH OFFICIAL CLEARANCE.
"IT DIDN'T EVEN MAKE THE PAPERS--WHAT DOES THAT TELL US?"
THIS IS THE LEAD I HAVE, LEONARD. THESE ARE THE DOTS I CAN JOIN. AND I HAVE TO DO SOMETHING.
RICK DIED BECAUSE I WASN'T THERE. AND THEN HIS MURDERER RECRUITED ME--SOME PART OF ME--FOR HIS CAUSE.
FOR MONTHS, I COULDN'T EVEN VISIT HIS GRAVE. I WAS... ASHAMED TO.
WELL, I'M NOT LETTING HIM DOWN AGAIN.
WHAT ABOUT BETTY? DOESN'T SHE NEED US?
SHE WAS SHOT DEAD--AND THEN SHE GOT UP AGAIN AND SMASHED THROUGH A WALL, APPARENTLY.
"SOMEHOW I DOUBT RICK'S GOING THROUGH ANYTHING LIKE THAT RIGHT NOW..."

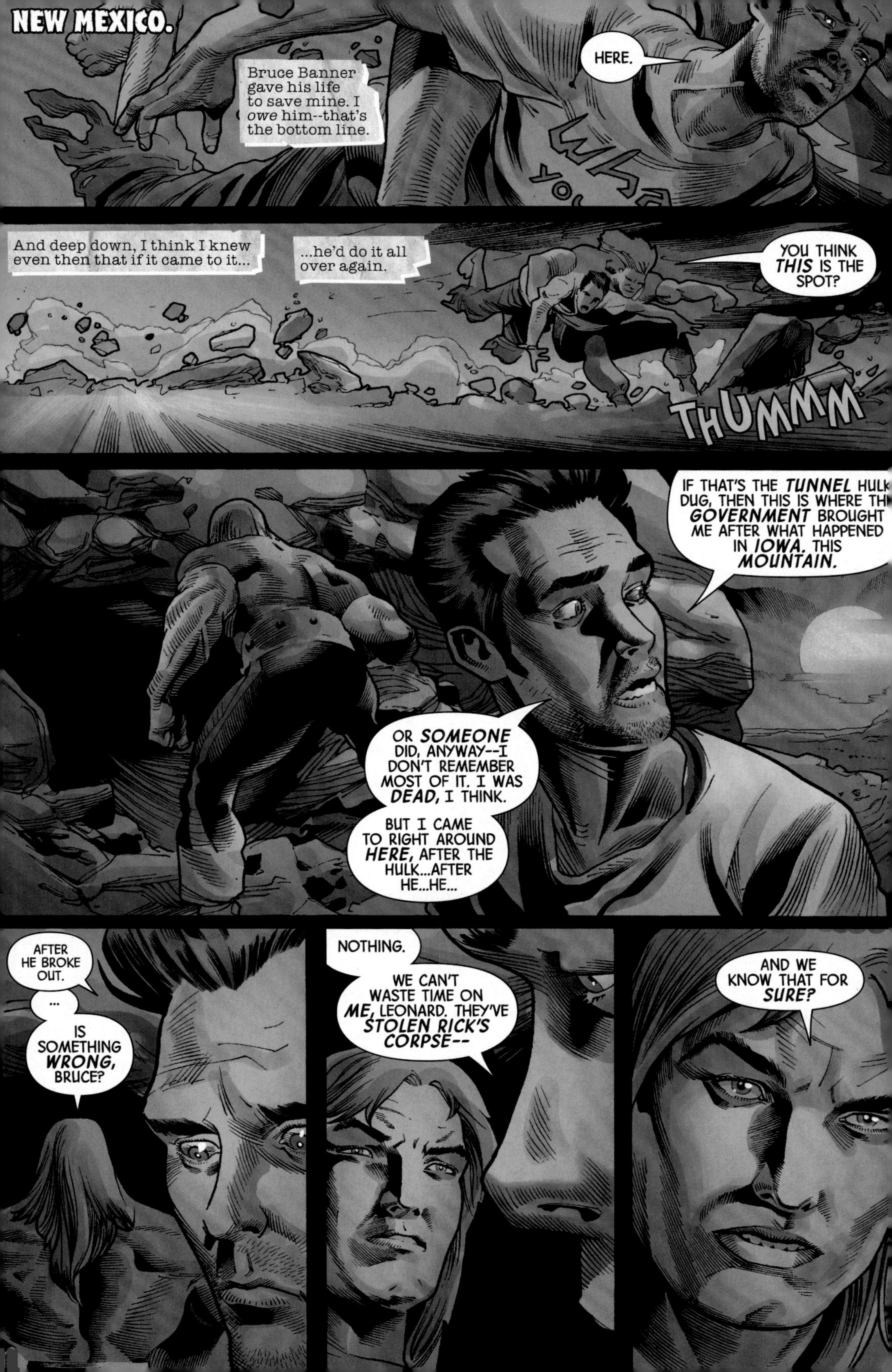
NEW MEXICO.
Bruce Banner gave his life to save mine. I *owe* him--that's the bottom line.
HERE.
And deep down, I think I knew even then that if it came to it...
...he'd do it all over again.
YOU THINK *THIS* IS THE SPOT?
THUMMM
IF THAT'S THE *TUNNEL* HULK DUG, THEN THIS IS WHERE THE *GOVERNMENT* BROUGHT ME AFTER WHAT HAPPENED IN *IOWA.* THIS *MOUNTAIN.*
OR *SOMEONE* DID, ANYWAY--I DON'T REMEMBER MOST OF IT. I WAS *DEAD,* I THINK.
BUT I CAME TO RIGHT AROUND *HERE,* AFTER THE HULK...AFTER HE...HE...
AFTER HE BROKE OUT.
...
IS SOMETHING *WRONG,* BRUCE?
NOTHING.
WE CAN'T WASTE TIME ON *ME,* LEONARD. THEY'VE *STOLEN RICK'S CORPSE--*
AND WE KNOW THAT FOR *SURE?*

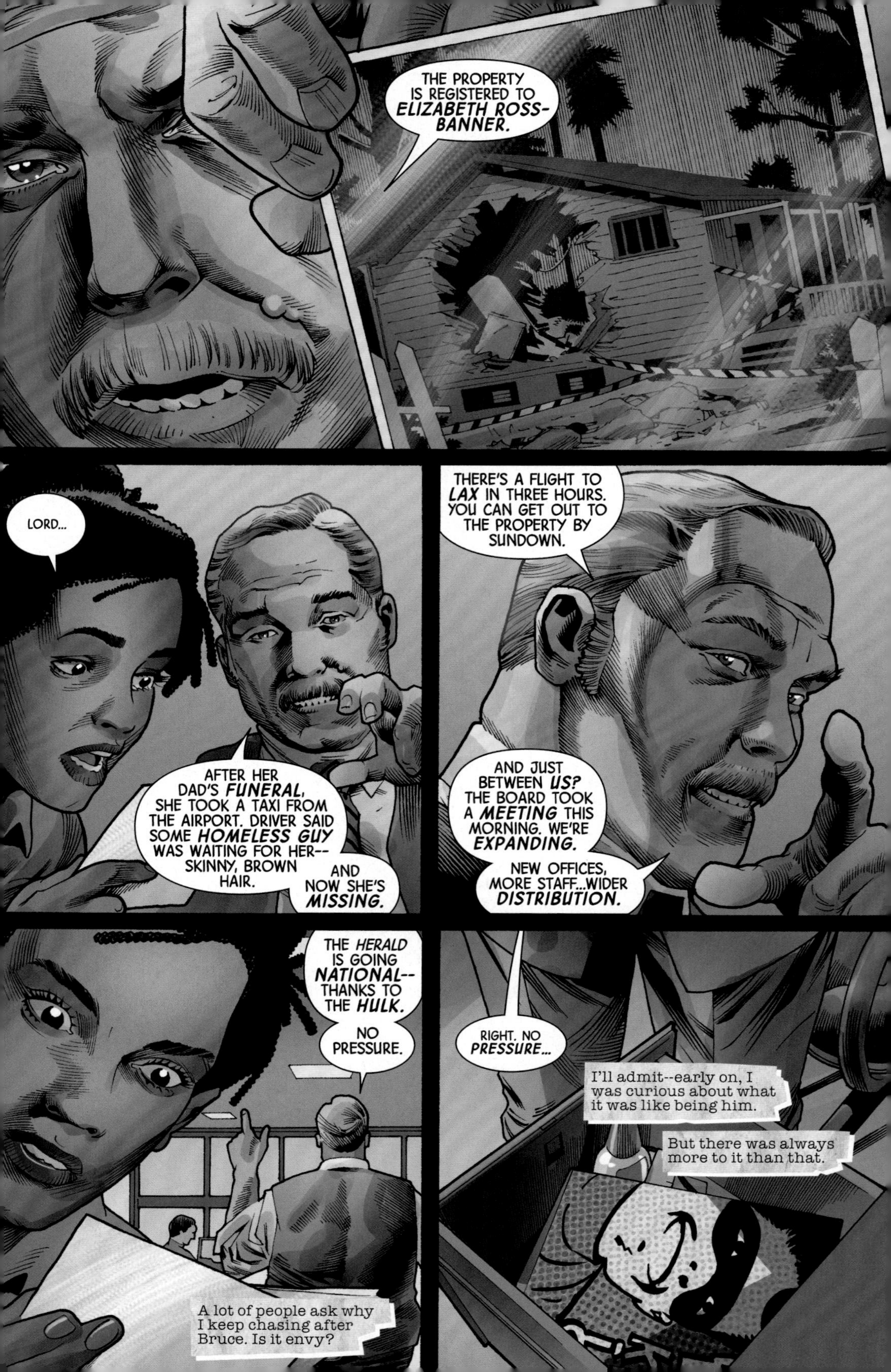
THE PROPERTY IS REGISTERED TO ELIZABETH ROSS-BANNER.
LORD...
AFTER HER DAD'S FUNERAL, SHE TOOK A TAXI FROM THE AIRPORT. DRIVER SAID SOME HOMELESS GUY WAS WAITING FOR HER-- SKINNY, BROWN HAIR.
AND NOW SHE'S MISSING.
THERE'S A FLIGHT TO LAX IN THREE HOURS. YOU CAN GET OUT TO THE PROPERTY BY SUNDOWN.
AND JUST BETWEEN US? THE BOARD TOOK A MEETING THIS MORNING. WE'RE EXPANDING.
NEW OFFICES, MORE STAFF...WIDER DISTRIBUTION.
THE HERALD IS GOING NATIONAL-- THANKS TO THE HULK.
NO PRESSURE.
A lot of people ask why I keep chasing after Bruce. Is it envy?
RIGHT. NO PRESSURE...
I'll admit--early on, I was curious about what it was like being him.
But there was always more to it than that.

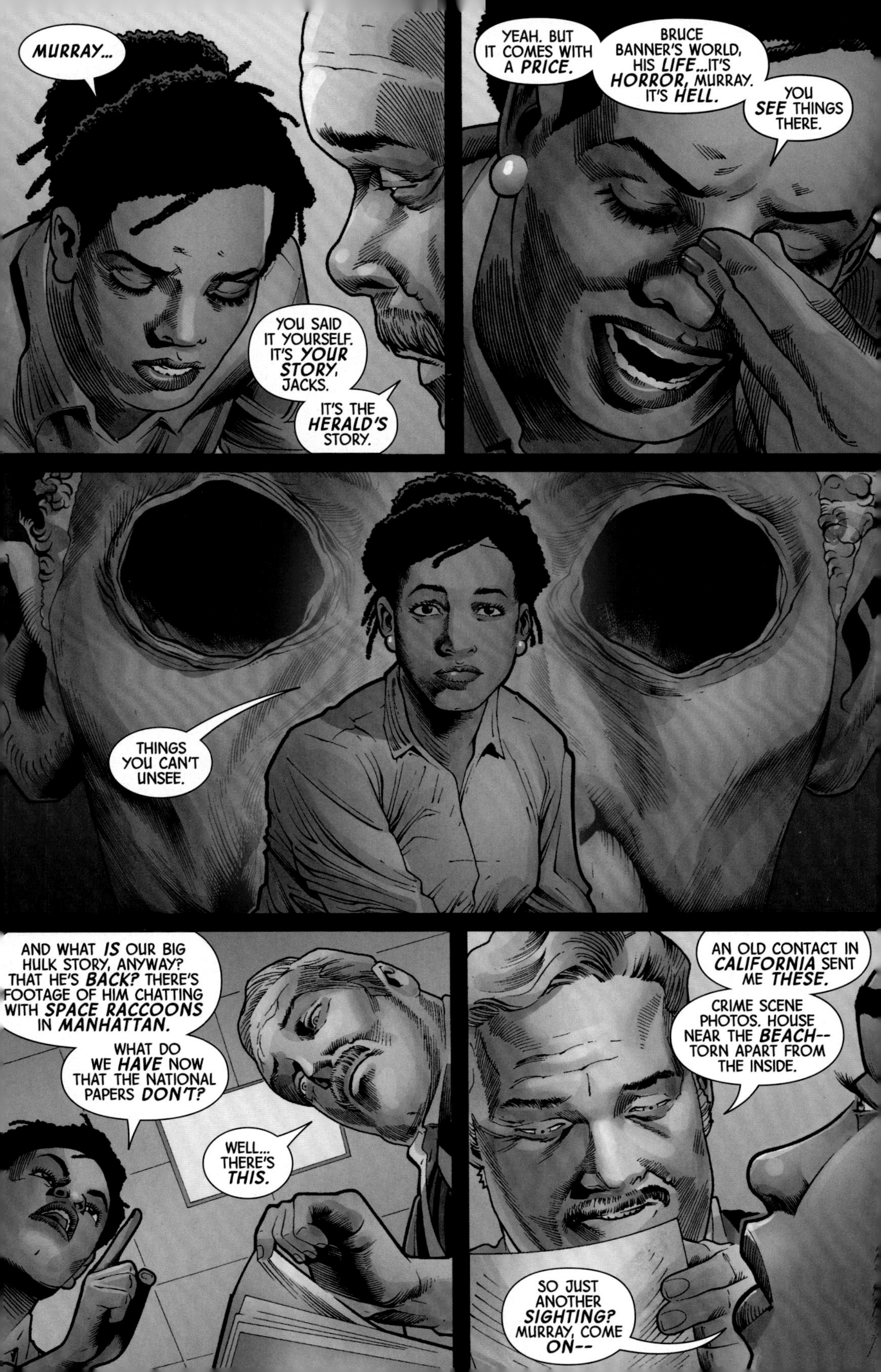
MURRAY...
YOU SAID IT YOURSELF. IT'S YOUR STORY, JACKS.
IT'S THE HERALD'S STORY.
YEAH. BUT IT COMES WITH A PRICE.
BRUCE BANNER'S WORLD, HIS LIFE...IT'S HORROR, MURRAY. IT'S HELL.
YOU SEE THINGS THERE.
THINGS YOU CAN'T UNSEE.
AND WHAT IS OUR BIG HULK STORY, ANYWAY? THAT HE'S BACK? THERE'S FOOTAGE OF HIM CHATTING WITH SPACE RACCOONS IN MANHATTAN.
WHAT DO WE HAVE NOW THAT THE NATIONAL PAPERS DON'T?
WELL... THERE'S THIS.
AN OLD CONTACT IN CALIFORNIA SENT ME THESE.
CRIME SCENE PHOTOS. HOUSE NEAR THE BEACH-- TORN APART FROM THE INSIDE.
SO JUST ANOTHER SIGHTING? MURRAY, COME ON--

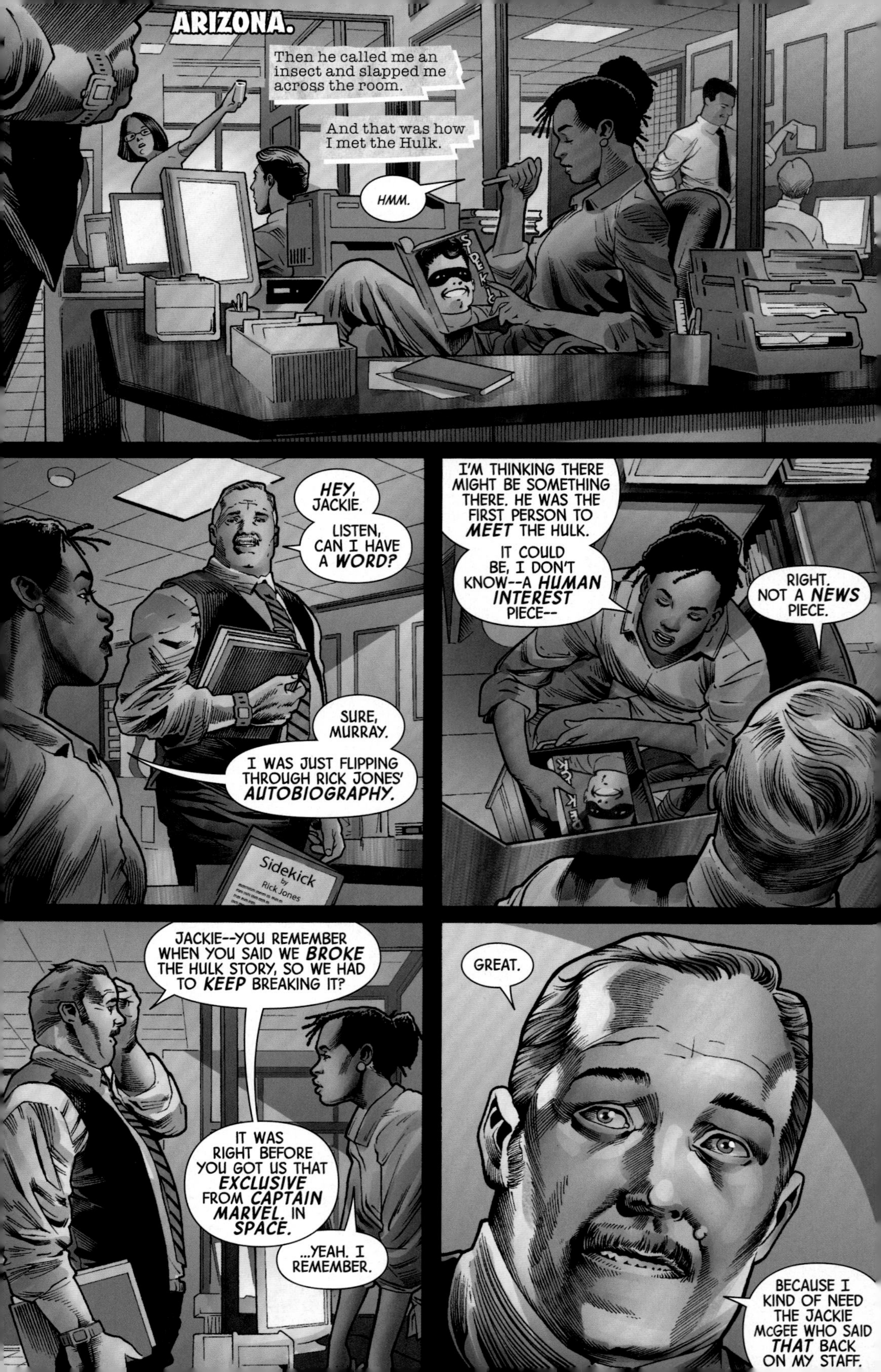
ARIZONA.
Then he called me an insect and slapped me across the room.
And that was how I met the Hulk.
HMM.
SIDEKICK
HEY, JACKIE.
LISTEN, CAN I HAVE A WORD?
SURE, MURRAY.
I WAS JUST FLIPPING THROUGH RICK JONES' AUTOBIOGRAPHY.
Sidekick
by
Rick Jones
I'M THINKING THERE MIGHT BE SOMETHING THERE. HE WAS THE FIRST PERSON TO MEET THE HULK.
IT COULD BE, I DON'T KNOW--A HUMAN INTEREST PIECE--
RIGHT. NOT A NEWS PIECE.
JACKIE--YOU REMEMBER WHEN YOU SAID WE BROKE THE HULK STORY, SO WE HAD TO KEEP BREAKING IT?
IT WAS RIGHT BEFORE YOU GOT US THAT EXCLUSIVE FROM CAPTAIN MARVEL. IN SPACE.
...YEAH. I REMEMBER.
GREAT.
BECAUSE I KIND OF NEED THE JACKIE McGEE WHO SAID THAT BACK ON MY STAFF.

SHADOW BASE SITE B. LOCATION UNKNOWN.

Funny how things work out.

I was just a kid. I hadn't even lived yet.

I didn't know where my life was going to lead me.

And I didn't know there were worse things than dying.

Back then, it was all strange and new. I didn't know what I was seeing.

How do I describe what I saw?

The Doc's face was *gone*.

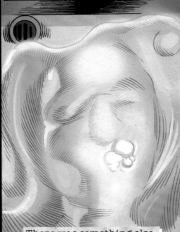

There was something else there. Something that wasn't human--that didn't *want* to be human.

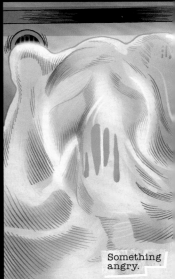

Something angry.

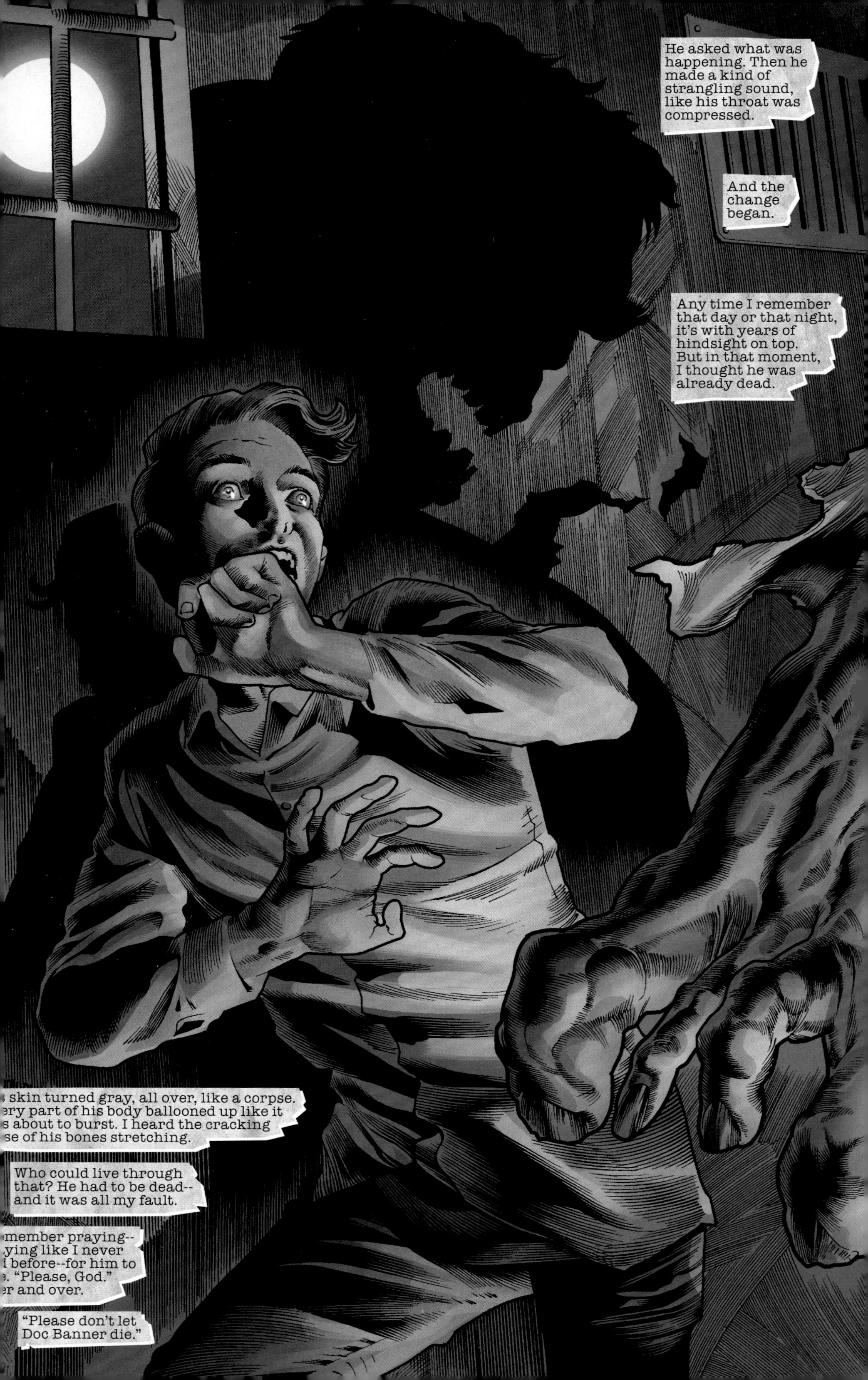
He asked what was happening. Then he made a kind of strangling sound, like his throat was compressed.
And the change began.
Any time I remember that day or that night, it's with years of hindsight on top. But in that moment, I thought he was already dead.
s skin turned gray, all over, like a corpse. ery part of his body ballooned up like it s about to burst. I heard the cracking se of his bones stretching.
Who could live through that? He had to be dead-- and it was all my fault.
member praying-- ying like I never l before--for him to e. "Please, God." er and over.
"Please don't let Doc Banner die."